ANEMONE IN A DESERT LANDSCAPE

HARRY D. STERN

Anemone in a Desert Landscape

Copyright © 2016 by Harry D. Stern

All rights reserved. No part of this book may be reproduced or transmitted in any form or by any means without written permission of the author.

ISBN 978-0-9978573-0-6

Library of Congress Control Number: 2016950967

Published by:

REJA PRESS
Marietta, Georgia, USA

The deep imprint of my parents, Margaret and Paul Stern, is woven throughout this memoir.

My Wonderful Family, Lora and Jason, Ayal, and Ilan and Marsha continue to add meaning and happiness to my life.

My Marvelous Grandchildren, Rachel, Evan, Jake and Aiden, while questioning whether I really grew up with no cell phone, are my newest stepping stones to the future.

Aviva, My Loving Wife, has from the day we met added more than I can describe to my life's journey.

After a rare spring rain,
the barren Negev Desert
is transformed into a carpet
of red anemones.

Chapter One

AS IF GROWING up in New York City in the 1940s and 50s wasn't tough enough. The acrimonious American reception awaiting my family, and most European-Jewry, fleeing the German onslaught, only added to that challenge. My pre-teen mind was like a dysfunctionally calibrated instrument: simultaneously proud and embarrassed by my parents; angry and resentful about so many things that managed to evade my understanding; joyful of my Jewish heritage and feeling victimized by its invisible and apparent burdens.

My working-class, Manhattan neighborhood was comprised of block-by-block ethnic enclaves. Our block, while seemingly adding European-Jewish refugees weekly, consisted mainly of Italian, Irish or Polish families. Many of these families were already second-generation arrivals to the shores of America. My mother's heavy, Viennese accent seemed never more pronounced than when she called from our third floor window: "Haaarreee, kom vor dinner." My neighborhood's American-born Italian and Irish playmates, mimicked her six o'clock oration.

My father seemed to get better looking, and in better physical shape, as he aged. Perhaps the external scars of the Holocaust faded with the passing years. His receding hairline and non-athletic build, made him appear older than his years-a sharp, but deceptive, contrast to the more virile appearing fathers of my street friends.

In contrast to my friends' "Americanized" families, my parents' limited, English and heavy Viennese accent, was frustrating to me in my early years. How could my parents, whom I loved dearly, cause me such discomfit? Their harrowing journey, evading the most sinister of Holocaust outcomes, required extraordinary resourcefulness. Despite their very meager financial resources, they were generous to a fault. In spite of their multi-year escape to Ellis Island and the New World anti-Semitism that they encountered, they were loving and considerate. They were also reluctant to share, or refer to, their Holocaust-related experiences. In retrospect, it must have been too brutal a subject for discussion with their children. The suppression of their experiences was confusing to me. I felt excluded from so seminal a family experience.

As I wade through the labyrinth of my earliest memories into young adulthood, I am intrigued by the outcome. What shaped my pervasive anti-authority behavior over the first two decades of my life? Was it solely my parents' brave and fortunate escape to America that fed my lifetime dedication to confronting anti-Semitism? What contributed to my infatuation with Israel, despite its myriad challenges? What propelled me into the Jewish service arena and a significant commitment to Jewish causes? Were it not for the seemingly serendipitous influences of several people at various milestones, how would my life, and those around me, have been affected?

So many events in my life, like flowering dandelions in a steady breeze, seem randomly dispersed. My early recollections are of me as a petulant individual with little regard for conventional limits, and even less use for authority figures who oversaw those limits. It is not unusual for parents to endure their children's quirky and confrontational teenage years. My rebellious adolescence lasted for two decades.

What appears as recalcitrance at one stage may morph at a later time into personal and professional conviction. Throughout the course of my life, I often called upon a residual toughness, inherited from my parents, and honed to a degree that served me well in my professional and personal life. Few events, in the fifty years of my professional career, were met with fear or ambivalence. My decisions were many times faulty, but my dedication to play fair, but firm, and my commitment to serving people in need, never wavered. Similarly, the centrality of Jewish continuity, and my disdain for those who blindly and unjustifiably castigate Israel, intensified as I aged. There was, and is, however, plenty to criticize about our Jewish homeland. Perhaps it was the multitude of imperfections that attracted me to Israel in such an inexorable way.

The title of this document alludes to the sprouting of vast beds of multi-colored flowers that are hidden beneath the Israeli desert's dry and crusty terrain. The bright flora are released in abundance from their dark and dreary imprisonment, by a rare spring, desert rainfall. In so many ways, I began allowing myself to emerge from a magnetic pull toward counter authority. A vortex of confrontation and feelings of inadequacy, ensured that I was conforming to a life of frustration and unhappiness. Key events influenced the redirection of the course of my life: my figurative rainfall, and emergence.

The successful rechanneling of my directionless early years, and the personal, academic and professional outcomes of my life, is gratifying. My dedication to serving persons in need, irrespective of my personal circumstances, was guided by my family's overarching credo: "someone has less than we do, that's why we must always help others."

Chapter Two

SAVED BY AN Arab Sheikh. A Moroccan Sheikh, to be precise. Paul and Margaret, my parents, and Josephine, my then two year old sister, had miraculously arrived at the safe harbor of Casablanca, after almost two years of narrowly eluding Nazi encounters in three countries. Casablanca: crossroad for spies, Nazis, French resistance fighters, renegades and traitors of so many descriptions, paradoxically provided a respite from their treacherous escape route. They had evaded the escalating waves of European anti-Semitism. It was Sheikh Hassan who was to help open their door to freedom.

Paul had anticipated the cataclysmic events soon to unfold. My father mobilized his fiery wife and infant daughter, advised remaining cousins that they would, hopefully, meet in Casablanca, and left all behind in Vienna. Two months before the 1938 *Anschluss*, the German invasion and annexation of Austria, they were on the move. Belgium, still independent, offered several months of ephemeral security for Jews fleeing the Austrian complicity.

My father had carefully studied reasonable escape routes with his preliminary destination marked as Toulon, France. As Belgium's resistance to the Nazis began to crumble, they left their short-term lodgings in Brussels, and headed south.

Josephine remembers (or maybe, she thinks she does) the cold, February rain that greeted them after their two-week journey to Paris. "We were cold and hungry, with no place to live," she recalls. "We lived in a dank, moldy, Paris metro station for over a week. Mostly, we ate carrots and raw potatoes that we bought from a nearby stall. We had to speak in whispers, as our German language aroused great suspicion. To this day," she recalls, "we don't know why our father felt France was not secure. Everyone around us argued that the Germans wouldn't dare attack France." France surrendered to the Germans four months after my parents fled south toward Toulon.

Toulon, a naval port in Southern France, was the launching site to Morocco, some thousand miles to the south west. The city, and its port, offered a begrudging welcome to the flood of Jews heading for the safety of Morocco. North Africa, home to about four hundred thousand Jews, was considered welcoming and protective. Morocco was thought to be the gateway to a refugee's path to America. Their almost two year trek would now take the three of them to Casablanca, Morocco.

Freight ships were leaving infrequently and were increasingly oversubscribed. My father, whose assessment was, that France was growing fragile, bargained heavily to secure spaces on a steamer headed to Casablanca. Despite Morocco's status as a French protectorate, the prevailing thought among those refugees still able to think rationally, was that Sultan Muhammad V, ruler of Morocco, was a friend to the Jews and would treat them with dignity and fairness.

My father was offered the three remaining spaces on the next outgoing freighter, in the ship's hold. He accepted. "I counted sixty of us in that airless space," my father shared. A rare commentary from him, as I believe my mother swore him to a joint reluctance to share any of the trauma that so engulfed her soul. "At first, it seemed bearable. We got to know one another; we were relieved about this next phase of our escape. There was more space than we originally feared, and there were two bathrooms."

The thousand-mile journey was to take four days. The Balearic and Alboran Seas, separating Toulon from Casablanca, were increasingly restless during their March crossing. The heaving sea took its toll. Sanitation became an afterthought, the bathrooms reeked of vomit; clean drinking water, at a premium at the outset of the voyage, became virtually non-existent. "Your mother arrived at Casablanca laid low with dysentery," my father recalled, "which somehow, Josephine and I avoided. Within a few days, she had recovered." My father, in describing risk, was an absolute minimalist.

It was in Casablanca where my parents were reunited with several cousins who had preceded their arrival. "Within days after your parent's arrival," Aunt Elsa, who had been in Casablanca for three weeks, recounted, "they met Sheikh Hassan." Aunt Elsa was now living just across the hallway, in the same Washington Heights tenement that was home to all of us for over twenty years.

"Sheikh Hassan, I know he had additional names, but I can't remember them, was very handsome, with a beautiful, black beard and shiny, black hair." Aunt Elsa held her hand to her breast and looked skyward to emphasize his good looks. "He came to visit new Jewish arrivals in the medical clinic that was treating your mother. Your father and Josephine never left her bedside. They welcomed Hassan's visit and warmth. They also accepted his invitation to visit the community services building upon your mother's recovery. Even in bed with dysentery, your mother was beautiful. Her good looks caused the formation of many friendships. No wonder Paul was always jealous."

The relationship with Hassan proved invaluable. A generous sprinkling of luck helped. Toulon, the French port from where they had just departed, was soon to be occupied by the Germans, with all French ships in port scuttled. Sultan Muhammad V, nominal ruler of Morocco, received orders restricting Jewish emigration imposed by the increasingly hostile Vichy government. The edicts were reluctantly implemented, soon after my family's escape from Morocco.

My father's extraordinary prescience had guided the family through towns and cities that were described as too risky by advisers who, themselves, were never again seen or heard from. On numerous occasions, my mother, on the rarest of lapses, would share with me that they often looked back on their improvised escape routes, only to see the towns they had just exited, being bombed by the Luftwaffe. "How did he know?" she would ask.

The war clouds were darkening in 1941. Hassan invited my father to coffee at his community services building. Unusual, in the words of Aunt Elsa, because he was much more interested in my mother. The meeting proved to be indispensible. My father described the meeting. "In English and French, Hassan told me that we must leave Casablanca, as soon as we can. He told me that the "Magallanes," a Spanish freighter, was to leave for America within weeks. It would probably be the last ship to leave carrying Jews to safety. We had to be on it, he said."

My father had a stash of American dollars and some diamonds, which he kept taped, around his ankles. He had only sufficient funds for the fare. He also had the foresight to have secured a sponsor letter from an American entrepreneur. The letter was required both to exit Casablanca and to enter America.

Hassan had done his homework. He informed my father that the safest transportation by sea was via a Spanish vessel. Spain was officially, a non-belligerent state in World War Two. Germany was prepared to honor Spain's status, Hassan explained, at least for now. "Spain has many laws regulating Jewish migration," Hassan continued, "but like our Sultan, they ignore most of them. It appears that the route that the "Magallanes" will take is: Casablanca to Cadiz, Spain then to Havana, Cuba, and finally, up the eastern coast of America to Ellis Island. I have secured a guarantee, that you and all of your family members in Casablanca, can be on that ship; you must be on that ship."

My parents had grown fond of Casablanca and its endless intrigues. They regarded it as a brief, and friendly, oasis as they sailed out of its port on the steamship "Magallanes." Their three-week journey, on the route outlined by Hassan, was accurate and uneventful. They were finally headed toward America. Hassan had been an extraordinary friend and had played a significant role in their survival.

Their long awaited arrival at Ellis Island had more of a wait than they had anticipated. Josephine, then three years old, arrived with whooping cough, and was required to spend one week in a quarantine clinic on the Island. She had company. So many of the children, of the two hundred families crammed on to the "Magallanes," joined her, with an endless array of maladies. The health of their child was a family's foremost concern, but, so many feared deportation, should the child's condition not improve sufficiently. Thankfully, Josephine's condition cooperated, and on June of 1941, a healthy Josephine, Margaret, six month's into her pregnancy with me, and Paul Stern arrived in New York City. The only casualty upon their arrival, had been the Ellis Island immigration clerk's "strongly suggested" change of my father's name, from Pesach to Paul.

It was only six months later that they learned that the steamship "Magallanes" had been attacked by the Japanese in the Philippines and scuttled and sunk. It was unclear if there were passengers aboard.

My parents had all the credentials of assimilated immigrants. That is, almost all. They were Holocaust survivors, they were cultured, my mother was an attractive and vital brunette and my intelligent father spoke nine languages. He had achieved legendary status among family and friends, for guiding his wife and two year old daughter through the side roads and backwoods of Austria, Belgium, France and Morocco. Josephine, my sister who preceded me by three and a half years, was cute, with long, blonde, interlocking curls and, until my arrival, well-behaved.

They had just passed through the rapidly closing welcome gates of Ellis Island, only months before the attack on Pearl Harbor, in December of 1941. My parents were then unaware of their good fortune (and mine) of their timely arrival. America was soon to declare war on Japan and Germany, reducing immigration to a trickle. My mother entered her new, American home while in the sixth month of her difficult pregnancy. She spoke English haltingly, and was in a tumultuous psychological state, having recently lost many members of her close-knit family to the Nazi onslaught in Europe.

My father searched for employment in an environment that had become increasingly hostile to Jewish immigrants. He looked older than his thirty-eight years, with a balding pate with prematurely grey remnants of wispy hair surrounding his shiny crown.

My mother approached her due date with yours truly, about to make The Beth Israel Hospital in lower Manhattan, the site of the first, American born member of our family. Simultaneously, my father was signing a rental agreement for an apartment in Washington Heights, in north Manhattan. The move from their tiny, Lower East Side apartment, could not have come at a better time.

Washington Heights was, for German, Jewish immigrants, where they could recreate their beloved Rhine community. For Viennese Jews, the neighborhood was the embodiment of their fabled Danube community. The grey waters of the Hudson River, several miles westward, seemed to adequately represent both utopian and nostalgic ideals.

By no means a homogeneous neighborhood, it was nonetheless common, to hear German spoken on Broadway. The conservative synagogue on 166th Street, featured long and monochromatic sermons in German. There was a generous comingling of Irish and Italian working class families, with a sharp demarcation separating the Hispanic and African-American, Harlem community.

My parents, Josephine and me, their newborn son, moved into apartment thirty-four of 602 west 165th Street. And very soon thereafter, it became clear, that I might be the cause of the credential that was missing from my parents' successful assimilation.

My father's brother Lazo, and a number of my mother's cousins, lived within a twenty minute subway ride. From an early age, I was the anomaly from the family norm: getting ahead by working hard and studying harder. I resisted structure and developed behavior patterns that had my parents and our relatives scratching their heads. My cousins were continually held up as the Platonic ideal for me to strive towards. The more often, and the more strident, the comparisons were hurled my way, the less likely I was to aspire to academic greatness...or in my case, adequacy.

Mrs. O'Brien, my kindergarten teacher in a ground floor, private school, some five blocks from my home, was, by my mother's account, quite nice. What was not so nice, was having my ear pulled upon coming to class late, or when I misbehaved. Upon arriving at school late one morning, I apparently decided to leave the class and, at just short of five years old, walked five, busy, city blocks to my aunt's apartment in our building. I told my surprised aunt, "no one is going to pull my ear again."

Upon leaving the conservative synagogue on Broadway, my parents stopped to talk with an acquaintance. I walked a bit further and hesitated in front of the forbidden Cuban, Carioca Casino, a rowdy bar, on our street corner, with dancing women on small stages. At four years old, I was forbidden to even look in its direction. I approached the public fire alarm box. Fire emergency posts were placed on every third city block. Casually, I pulled the emergency call lever. As the fire engines came roaring and clanging up Broadway, I stood on the corner shouting, "I did it." I was proud of my achievement and was developing a talent at angering those close to me. My mother quickly wrapped her hand across my mouth and dragged me, with strength that I had heretofore been unaware of, across the avenue to our apartment. My father was left to sort things out.

My parents deserved better. They had been through hell. They were in a not-so-brave new world, and their first-born son, seemed to have recalcitrance stamped into his DNA.

Things got worse, before they got better. How dismayed they must have been when six members of a local, African-American and Hispanic gang, came to visit me close to my fifteenth birthday, as I was recuperating from aggravated appendix surgery, in a mid Manhattan hospital. Did they have to choose the same time that my parents were visiting me?

I was pleased that my parents never found out that Russian, security agents fired upon Joe Finger and me, as we drove through the open gates of the Killenworth Estate in Glen Cove, Long Island. The estate was a retreat where Soviet Union visitors to the United Nations and their staff relaxed, while the U.N. was in session.

Despite warm and loving parents as my dependent variables, it seemed that much of the trajectory of my life would be determined by external, or independent variables: The influences of Eddie, my football coach and mentor; Norman, my cantankerous, but artistic friend; and Aviva, my wife of forty-eight years. Each of them helped weave a concatenated thread that shaped the arc of my life.

The extraordinary generosity of spirit and material resources of my parents and their universal credo of: "someone has less than we do," certainly influenced my dedication to serving persons in need. Coach Eddie, in his laconic way, piqued my irrevocable interest and involvement in higher education. My zany compatriot Norman, influenced my zest and yearning for learning and stepping out of the mode of conventionality. Aviva simply helped me put the pieces of the puzzle of my life together in a manner that I find too all encompassing to describe.

The professional and personal path along which my life hurtled, displayed not the slightest trace of preplanning or organized thought. Rather, I careened along, from one life event to another, resembling a runaway bumper car, bouncing off one fixed or moving obstacle, and simply allowing myself to be involuntarily redirected.

Inexplicably, seemingly serendipitous events were, however tenuously, intertwined. The high wire balancing act of my life might have evolved into a miasma of despair, had I turned left instead of right, or the reverse.

As the perennial underachiever in our family, I was generally comforted by unusually modest expectations from our extended family. They often heralded me as "the Jewish athlete," a search for synonyms in any Jewish thesaurus, would yield: "bound for nowhere," "academically hopeless."

The models of appropriate academic and social performance were, to name a few family members: Henry, who severed contact with the family, and refused to care for his family's cemetery plots; David, a brilliant cousin, whose grades were consistently in the ionosphere, who committed suicide at age thirty, and Sammy, also, gifted academically, who still resides in a mental institution, the name of which eludes me. How and why did I escape?

What follows is an accounting of aspects of my life that blend elements of the unusual generosity of my parents, the indomitable will of my father, my unshakable resistance to conventionality, my father's chutzpah that was unconsciously cultivated in me, and the randomness of events that shape our destiny in so many inexplicable ways.

Chapter Three

THERE WAS NO way that I was going to get this job. Mr. Lee stared at me with a relentless, searing and inscrutable gaze. He leaned on his unevenly varnished office desk, his right elbow partially obscured by a gaudy, brass, name plate announcing, to those who might be even remotely interested, that he was a vice president. Shit, if he's a VP, then why is he interviewing my lazy ass and the seven or eight equally bedraggled candidates, for the one entry level position available?

1960 was a year that was highlighted by my great achievement: a high school diploma from Washington Irving night school. The year was also marked by my parent's admonitions, that I was an eighteen year old underachiever and needed to find a job…and quickly. Armed with my meritorious academic award, I applied for a clerical position at Textile Manufacturing, a misnomer, as no textiles were manufactured within miles. The company was simply the centralized accounting venue for a variety of textile firms in the New York area.

And Mr. Lee wasn't having any of me. He proceeded to give me numerous reasons why I was the wrong person for this highly desirable job, paying eighty five dollars a week. I wasn't really listening. I had heard it all before…no work experience, did I really have an aptitude for bookkeeping, was I the kind of person who would be happy performing repetitive tasks? etc., etc.

The rankness of his office, the cheap reproductions of Chinese, calligraphy hanging askew on the walls of his tiny space, may have had some ancestral meaning to him, but it spoke of a low level bureaucrat, despite his title. My constitutional inability to take no for an answer and my belief that he wanted no part of this uptown Jew, motivated me to ask, "Mr. Lee, who are you responsible to in this company?" His deeply furrowed brow could have presaged him asking me to vacate his territorial burrow immediately. Instead, however, he responded, with no small tinge of incredulity and indignation.

"Mr. Adderly is the Executive Vice President, and is my immediate superior…why?"

"Well, Mr.Lee, I intend to try to convince him why you should hire me."

He rose noisily from his scratched and squeaking, vinyl office chair with as much menace as his five foot five inch frame could muster, glaring at me all the while. But I'd grown up in Manhattan's Washington Heights, and I wasn't scared easily. When he looked right at me and announced that Mr. Adderly's office was just next door, it was as if he was assuring me, that I would last about two minutes before being escorted to the blustery, New York wintry street below. He left his office with short, officious steps and returned with Mr. Adderly about four or five minutes later.

"How can I help you, young man?" The young man part seemed to be a nice way to defuse a potentially unpleasant scene. He seemed sincere and pleasant enough. I estimated that he was Irish, about fifty, slightly paunchy at the belt with gray, thinning hair and horn-rimmed spectacles. He had obviously doused himself generously, with Old Spice after shave lotion.

"Mr. Adderly," I mustered up my patented chutzpah, "I wonder if I could meet with you privately for a moment? I would like to share my thoughts about how important it is for me to be working with you," I emphasized the "you." In nasalized diction that could never really be adequately replicated, and spoke of a double barreled deviated septum with perennial blockage, he responded, "Come into my office, it's next door." I had no idea what I would say, but I wasn't worried.

It was now eighteen years after my parent's arrival on the shores of Ellis Island. My father's navigation around endless Nazi death traps set for Europe's Jews, both inspired and amazed me.

When my father, an immensely clever and hard-working man, searched for work, he found what so many before and after him were to discover: that Jewish refugees were not welcomed in the New York workplace. And so, after numerous rejections, he made an offer to the owner of a small, tailor shop on 18th street and Third Avenue. "I will work for no wages, until you feel that my labor is worthy of a salary." Out of the goodness of his heart, the new employer had my father work for seven weeks, before he decided that his labor was "worth a wage."

I was now prepared to offer Mr. Adderly the same deal. I had been so taken by my father's sharing the ordeal of rejection in the land of salvation, and was motivated to emulate his tenacity.

Frankly, I had never heard of this company before, and just happened to catch a "help wanted" ad in The Daily News that morning. But, here I was, insisting that my life's ambition was to work for Textile Manufacturing Company.

"So, young man, what can I do for you?"

"Mr. Adderly," I mustered some conviction, "I feel this company is a perfect fit for me, and I am prepared to work for as long as you like, for no salary... until you feel me worthy of being paid."

As he slowly rose from his newer than Mr. Lee's office chair and desk, he looked straight at me, through thick-lensed glasses that were lodged astride his bountiful nose, and said with no shortage of incredulity, "You really mean that don't you, son?"

"Yes sir, I mean it." My Israeli friend had recently told me, in the nicest way one could say it, that I talked too much. "When you have made a sale, shut up." And that's what I did, when I made the sale to Mr. Adderly.

He guided me back to Mr. Lee's office, where he was about to conduct another interview. Mr. Adderly politely asked the young interviewee to step outside the office.

"Mr. Lee," Mr. Adderly opened...not on a first name basis, "I sincerely wish that all of the candidates seeking employment with us had the same level of dedication to our company, and frankly, the same guts to push for a job. So, unless you are terribly opposed, I would like to hire Mr. Stern."

I focused on a blue fountain pen on Mr. Lee's desk. I thought that it might be too confrontational to make eye contact with him and so, I averted what must have been a searing glare. It felt as though I had just vanquished my opponent in a fencing duel. Rejecting rejection came with many penalties, but when it worked, it was glorious. He answered in a rather subservient tone, "Of course, Mr. Adderly, I will expedite the process."

Mr. Adderly shook my hand, welcomed me to the firm, and made sure to ask Mr. Lee what my starting salary would be, a clear message to me that my generous, but insincere, offer had been unnecessary. I thanked both Mr. Adderly and Mr. Lee, and informed them, that I would soon be an exemplary employee. What proved even more certain was that, as long as I was employed there, Mr. Lee would hate me and look for any reason to prove Mr. Adderly had made a grave mistake. His opportunity to criticize and reprimand me lasted for the entire two year period of my stay in that inhospitable surrounding.

Mr. Lee did not hold the international patent on anger towards me. Opportunities, mostly quite justified, were abundant and began very early in my life. My bottomless reservoir of irascibility and my rejection of authority, was wrapped in a veneer of self-righteousness.

My well-intentioned parents sent me to a Yeshiva, a private day school, to ensure that I would maintain my Jewish identity. The parochial Yeshiva would keep me from mingling with "those others"...a euphemism for the gentiles in NYC's public schools.

For eight years, I studied the bible, in Hebrew, four hours a day, wherein I questioned just about every interpretation and conclusion, trying desperately to stay awake during those torpid morning sessions. "Rabbi Danziger, exactly how many drops of liquid are we allowed to drink on Yom Kippur? And is it a sin if that number is exceeded?" It meant little to me, other than to try to elicit responses that generally bordered on the ridiculous. In contrast, the four afternoon hours of mathematics, literature and other subjects in English, were a blissful departure from the inflexible, strict constructionist, iron-clad truths of my morning classes.

I believe that the rabbis and lay teachers of that institute met weekly, to reaffirm that I was a misfit in that school, incapable of dedicated study and bound to end up in one of Dante's seven stages of Purgatory. I often envisioned their conversations concerning me: "About Stern, is it sloth, avarice, wrath, just what is it about him?" My parents were summoned to the principal's office so often to bail me out, and endure a torrent of familiar reprimands, that I was surprised that we didn't move closer to school to cut down on their travel time.

Very few of their uptown sojourns to school, were the result of academic inadequacies, although my rejection of the formulaic Hebrew bible studies was becoming legendary. Most of the reprimands that my folks absorbed continually, focused on the charge that I was about as incorrigible a behavioral anomaly as the school had experienced in years. I would call out answers to questions posed by teachers without being recognized; I organized my fourth grade class to wear green in honor of St. Patrick's Day, and I was perennially late returning to class from our mid-morning and afternoon recesses.

One late, winter Sunday morning (we only had half a day of school on Sunday), several rabbinic administrators and our Hebrew school principal visited our eighth grade class. While public junior high schools ended in ninth grade, the Yeshiva concluded its bonsai-like nurturing at the conclusion of the eighth grade. The visitors were cordial enough as they greeted our teacher, Rabbi Danziger.

The visiting entourage had come to "market" the Yeshiva High School, which actually had a somewhat less confining reputation, had a good academic standing and was a stepping stone to a good college. The administrators asked Shelly, an academically strong, and well-behaved student, "So, Shlomo (always the Hebrew name), why Bronx High School of Science, why not Yeshiva High?" Constance was next, "Chaya, Stuyvesant High, what's wrong with Yeshiva High?" It was all very chummy and cordial. Each student in the class was systematically asked where they intended to apply to high school; the better schools were not compelled to accept an incoming student with less than stellar grades. Every student in the class was asked for their selection, except me.

There were no excuses made, no comments about the clear exclusion of their favorite rebel. The self-important group left the classroom some twenty minutes later. I wanted to scream out: "What about me, you pompous fools?" Instead, I buried my reddened face in the thankfully, oversized, Talmud book that we were studying. And so, it was clear to me, that my high school address was to be the neighborhood public school.

Not long thereafter, on an unusually cool summer, Sunday morning in early June, Yeshiva held its annual graduation. This event was conducted with a minimum of pomp and circumstance in the small, poorly lit auditorium on the school's main floor. Three dusty, chandeliers of arcane origin, dangled precariously overhead. I counted three unlit bulbs in two of those fixtures. Rabbi Weinberg, the Hebrew school principal and Mr. Lichtenberg, the English school equivalent, stood on the creaky stage, no more than ten feet deep, and greeted the fifty or sixty family members present.

Rabbi Weinberg stared out across the auditorium, as if he could see each one of us individually. Once, after having come across me eating an ice cream sandwich at Jimmy's luncheonette on Broadway, during our eight day Passover break, he said nothing. Not a word. But, yet he had seen me methodically licking the vanilla ice cream, generously packed between two wafers. Jewish tradition is quite restrictive about what foods may and may not be consumed during that holiday. An ice cream sandwich was nowhere to be found on the permitted list. I expected to be excoriated upon my return to school; yet another glaring example of my misalignment with school and Judaic principles.

Instead, he waited for my Bar Mitzvah, which was celebrated in the orthodox synagogue, over which he officiated. After my fairly good chanting of the appropriate bible portion, it was customary for the Rabbi to give a brief congratulatory message and offer some words of encouragement to the Bar Mitzvah candidate. How hypocritical it would be for his most reviled student to receive even tepid praise on the bimah. Rabbi Weinberg must have had a sleepless night, combing his conscience for anything remotely positive about me to share with his congregation. To my alarm, he looked directly at me and with uncharacteristic verve in his voice, he concluded his cool comments: "I know that you will grow to be a fine young man and…..will not eat ice cream sandwiches on Passover, like some children."

It was like a thunderclap that only I heard and felt. Beads of untimely perspiration were forming around every exposed orifice, as I somehow persevered to conclude my portion of the remaining prayers. As I joined my father after the service, my mother sat in the segregated women's section, he asked me what that "ice cream sandwich" comment was about. I felt relieved when he muttered that he thought that Rabbi Weinberg was "losing it." "Where on Earth could a comment like that come from?" "Dad," I whispered, "he really is strange."

Mr. Lichtenberg, the English school principal, sat patiently on the stage at the center of a row of eighth grade teachers, preparing to welcome the graduates on that Sunday morning. With his thick, eye glasses perched precariously on his reddened nose, and white tufts of hair protruding from under his quilted, multi-colored, yarmulke, which partially hid both of his over-sized ears, he looked rather benign, maybe even fatherly, but it was an illusion. He was an authority freak dedicated, it appeared, to discovering a daily antidote to my rule-testing behavior.

On numerous occasions, he would enter my fourth or fifth grade classroom, ask me to step out into the hallway, and solicit the class to vote whether they wanted me to remain in the class. I believe that he was dedicated to exploring creative ways to humiliate me and to prove to my teachers and parents that I was a deviant worthy of isolation. I believe that both he and Rabbi Weinberg were chief architects in the early development of what was to result in the anti-Jewishness of my youth.

My two chief detractors: Rabbi Weinberg and Mr. Lichtenberg, were now standing side-by-side on the bleak, weather-beaten, stage that early summer morning, preparing to bestow those hallowed diplomas on eighteen graduating and deserving students. Well, I managed to receive a diploma in English studies, and only a certificate of attendance in Hebrew studies. I wish I could say that my parents were mortified...they really expected anything. So, this wasn't so bad, they concluded. Nonetheless, my mother got teary-eyed.

"What will become of you in a public high school, Harry?" She was morose.

"Wait and see mom," I answered with all of the sincerity that I could rally, "this will be a new beginning." I wanted so to believe it. It really hurt me deeply when I saw her upset. Although, I suffered from a dearth of self-awareness, when my supportive and vulnerable mother was upset, it pained me. "Remember mom, the school yearbook predicted that I would someday play shortstop for the New York Yankees." It was probably the only positive prediction that the editors of that publication could think of. And now, I would leave this small, private school and head to a massive, public high school, George Washington High.

Chapter Four

IT DIDN'T TAKE me long to get the prevailing joke at G. Dub, as George Washington High was referred to by many of its three thousand students. The physical education locker rooms often smelled of reefer, which helped neutralize the mildew and sweat odors that blanketed those cavernous and noisy, underground dungeons. The clanging of metal lockers could be deafening, as some students were hurrying to class, while others milling around, were already boarding an express train to oblivion. "Even George Washington would have gotten high," the kids boarding that train joked, "at George Washington High." A new, and not-so-traditional, world opened up before my very curious eyes.

In those first weeks at G. Dub, I was intimidated by the sheer size, tumult in the hallways between classes, and by the navigation of long and winding hallways from class to class. However, like a smoldering, seismic implosion heading toward its new terrestrial environment, I emerged from my early weeks of somnolence. I made friends easily: I was athletic, nice looking, fast talking and disrespectful of authority.

Not surprisingly, few first year teachers were overly impressed. My failure to ingratiate myself to my battery of teachers was all the more contradictory, since I repeatedly tested at a second year high school level, a year ahead of my fellow students academically. I had learned, and pretty well mastered, in my eighth and last year at the Yeshiva, what we were now learning in a public high school. The chemistry of my boredom and confrontational persona proved to be a volatile mix.

Most teachers tolerated my antics and developed an attitude of benign neglect toward me. After all, it was a tough school with big classes, with a sizable percentage of the student population coming from nearby Harlem and other tough neighborhoods. My athletic ability and fast-talking, wise guy stuff, helped shape a cross-section of friends from many different neighborhoods. On the positive side of belonging to this strange admixture of cronies, was the minimal amount of fights that I was involved in.

Charles O'brien, a big Irish kid, bound for some underworld life style, and a moribund future before his twenty first birthday, waited until the end of the Spanish class that we occasionally frequented, and said, with a degree of unnecessary bravado: "I'm not afraid of you!" "No need to be," I muttered spontaneously. He was already down the hallway. My response was meant literally, I was close to six foot tall and probably weighed one hundred forty five pounds. He was several inches taller than me and had muscles in places where I wasn't sure I ever would. But it made me a bit more aware of how I must be perceived, with a large network of tough friends. How far I had come from the Yeshiva…in some ways.

If Miss Curtain, my first year, home room teacher, had visited me at the Yeshiva, she would have had an answer to her perennial question to me: "where did you get your basic training for such deviant behavior?" Mid-fiftyish, probably never been married- or laid for that matter- and probably anti-Semitic to boot, she constituted my most unfortunate encounter at G. Dub. Perhaps it was paranoia, but I always sensed that she treated Jewish students with a dismissive air.

Sending me to Mr. Kalinski, the dean of first and second year students, became her obsession. I guess that I made it easy for her as I came in late to class repeatedly. One day I came to class early, ten minutes earlier than the bell. The bell rang with its usual interminable and abrasive clanging. My nemesis looked at me and said, "Stern, you are late."

"Miss Curtain," I confidently responded, "the bell just rang, and here I am." Just then, the classroom door opened, and in sauntered Sherman Garnes, the base singer for the wildly, popular rock and roll singing group, The Teenagers. We often played basketball together at a Harlem court. Not to be distracted for too long, and ignoring Sherman's leisurely stroll into the classroom after the bell, she stared at me with her usual disdain, and with a contorted smile said, "today the bell is late."

Back to Mr. Kalinski I went, with a late-to-class notice crumpled in my right front, pants pocket.

Kalinski was basically a good guy. I think he even liked me and subliminally hinted, sometimes with a grimace or with a sigh of resignation, that Miss Curtain was a bitch. My poor mother had been summoned to school so often concerning my absences, class cutting and uncooperative classroom behavior, that if her English had been a bit more fluent, they might have offered her an office job. Kalinski may have been a good guy, but no such luck, with the third and fourth year dean of students, Mr. Kenny. I often tried to picture him having sex with Miss Curtain. What a totally, revolting image.

Mr. Kenny was a wiry, grey haired rodent in a suit. I did have to give him credit for being a snazzy dresser. But, what an officious and mean-spirited prick. I believe that this saurian was waiting for me to enter my third year at glorious G.Dub, so that he could exercise the New York State law, allowing expulsion of recalcitrant students as soon as they hit sixteen years of age. He probably had a calendar, with a large circle around October twenty-sixth, my birthday. My faith in Mr. Kenny's vindictiveness and his dislike of yours truly, was only partially earned. He waited until after the New Year, January third, to be exact, to oversee my permanent departure from that bastion of higher learning, G.Dub….a full twelve weeks later than I had anticipated.

While I hardly considered it a stimulating environment, some good things did emerge there: most notably, Yolanda's incredible body, the highlight of my third period, American History class. I had never seen such beautiful, soft breasts that seemed to be struggling to be exhibited in public view. I couldn't take my eyes off them, which made both Yolanda and me uncomfortable. Yolanda, I would imagine, was ill at ease, because not many third year high schoolers were as obvious as I was about my enchantment with her bounty. For me, the embarrassment extended to the end of each class when I had to stand up. I made sure that I always had books handy as camouflage. I was convinced that the most beautiful girls rarely get approached by guys their age, simply because they appear to be way beyond us, and have so many imagined guys chasing them.

The number three St. Nicholas Avenue public bus heading uptown to G. Dub, was my daily transportation to school. It was that twenty five minute ride that seemed to be the arena in which my daily struggle with puberty would take place in earnest. It was my good and bad luck that Yolanda rode that same bus, and chatted with her girlfriends all wearing, as if to torment me, short skirts and tight tops. So, it wasn't just Yolanda who had great boobs. They all did. And so, began my restless battle with my emerging puberty, which made it difficult to stand up to get off the bus.

Girls at the Yeshiva, it seemed, were not allowed to have breasts. They were all flat-chested, with only occasional little bumps, where nipples struggled to make a surreptitious, adolescent appearance.

Pauline, Evelyn and Constance of the Yeshiva, had mothers who went to great lengths to dress their daughters in drab, loose fitting blouses and plaid sweaters that would seek to hide whatever puberty had brought on. But, at G.Dub, girls had breasts, and seemed to enjoy exhibiting them, and I was in heaven. Until Mr. Kenny, and the top brass at G. Dub, brought my voyeuristic career to an abrupt end. All that I could think of, was the many girls that I would miss, and those who were my constant libidinal images during my school days.

Chapter Five

SO, HERE I was sixteen years old, aimless and puzzling to my parents who, while not formally college educated themselves, placed a high value on learning, diplomas and their purported path to success. My mother, was a perambulating contradiction in so many spheres. "Harry, I never had much use for the rigid Viennese high schools. But, I could quote Schiller and Goethe better than most of my instructors." My father had built a successful women's wear manufacturing business in Vienna, but abandoned it, as he led his family to safety, through Europe and ultimately to America. "You are squandering your chances to become successful in America. Education is a necessary path to success in this country." But, I was too clever and too smug in my own teenage delusional world. I was continually exhorted to get a job, any job, and stop sleeping into the late afternoon.

My well-worn path, however, led not to an employment agency, but rather, to the pool room on 160th street, some five blocks south of my home. I would slide the rusted, side Loew's Rio movie theatre door to the right, the one that displayed the coming, featured attractions. I then made my way up the back metal fire escape stairs. This rear entrance would allow me to bypass the dingy, water bug, infested bathroom, where queer Frankie, was always offering my friends five dollars if he could blow them. I never needed money that badly.

There were eight pool tables in the main area, and two billiard tables in the rear room. If I was early enough, Karl or Jimmy, the proprietors, would allow me to brush the tables for one free hour of pool. For extra time, I would dust the low hanging, fluorescent lights, nestled under a green, tin canopy that swung menacingly over each table. I soon became a good pool player, but paled in comparison to those who had high school careers similar to mine, some having commenced many years earlier. Karl, was an outstanding pool and billiards player, sometimes even running fifty and sixty consecutive balls. His position playing was extraordinary, thinking two or three shots ahead, and with soft, deft strokes the cue ball always seemed to defy Newton's law of Perpetual Motion, in perfect position for that next shot. When Karl played serious money games, with Big Mike, or some of the highly touted players coming to visit from nearby Harlem, he would make sure to keep his gun visibly tucked into the front of his pants, as did those protectors who accompanied the visiting players.

The smoke-filled pool hall became the center of my post-expulsion life. It was there that I became friendly with Julio, Jimmy, Tony, Ronnie and Kenny. I always remained on the outer circle of that bound for nowhere group. I consciously chose to remain on the periphery, as I was not drawn to their incessant preoccupation with pot. I felt different, perhaps as the only Jew in the crowd, or possibly because of my occasional foray into self-awareness and depression about the direction of my life. I viewed them merely as a means of distraction from my post G.Dub ennui. They comprised a formidable singing group that never cut a record. They did, however, provide ongoing entertainment for the neighbors, by crooning the newest rock and roll songs in local alleyways. I am not sure that the early-to-bed working class families appreciated the evening's song fest as much as I did.

Only Kenny became a popular singer, cut many records, and separated himself from the group, when his talent became apparent to agents in the neighborhood. Kenny's career was hampered by his drug addiction. The drug culture was a predominant hallmark of the neighborhood; the rough and tumble, Irish denizens eschewed the pot and heroin scene, opting instead for alcohol's mind-numbing state. Almost everyone else, was high on dope or pot most of the time. On some level, I found it amusing, that so much of the conversation in the neighborhood rotated around who was pursuing which drug deal.

But, Patti didn't fit the mold. He was a tough dude who somehow cut across all racial and social lines. Constantly bragging about his Irish pedigree, he proved to be the artificial stimulant anomaly: an Irishman who shot heroin and hated alcohol. Patti always sought me out as a friend, perhaps because he could trust me, as I was not a druggie, or maybe he had just never had a Jewish friend. He was forever rubbing his nose with his forefinger, a sign that he was high on something. "Patti, are you trying to hide your bad case of acne by using all of these drugs?"

His predictable and ludicrous answer was, that he had read an article contending that heroin would clear acne up.

"Man, I thought you Jewish mama's boys read these professional journals. You mean you never read about the positives of shootin' horse?" Patti could say anything to me and I never got offended. In fact, I often bought him lunch and lent him money, despite being certain of its ultimate destination. There was something that connected me with him emotionally. I was never quite sure from where my caring for Patti emanated, perhaps it was his neediness, of both having friends or a confidante. I often wondered if Patti helped me lay the groundwork for my future path in the service of persons in need.

Of course, I could never trust anything that he said, as supporting his increasingly voracious addiction, was all-consuming. In some ways, my combined warmth for him and my fear that his addiction to drugs might not always appear so repulsive to me, seem to have left an imprint on me. I wanted to help Patti, and continually urged him to seek professional help. His response was often: "Will you stop being such a Jewish know it all?" Neighborhood intelligentsia informed me that Patti died of a drug overdose before his twenty first birthday.

But it was Patti who introduced me to Leila. Leila was a tall, very attractive, olive-skinned Latina. She proved to be a young woman of insatiable sexual needs. It was almost intimidating. She lived in a tenement building on 138th street, an exclusively Puerto Rican, six story warren of decaying apartments, each with a battery of chains and security locks, offering an illusion of protection from the druggies who prowled the hallway. The cooking odors emanating from many apartments were heavenly. I could picture the *arroz con pollo* simmering on stoves, as I climbed the four flights to her apartment. Each time I visited her, I felt that my life was in jeopardy, but it was worth it. Because Leila really fell for me, she held out the hope, that she continually shared with me: "Every Puerto Rican woman secretly wants a Jewish husband."

"Is that a possibility for the two of us?" She peered directly at me with her piercing, iridescent, almond-shaped eyes, as she often did during tense or warm encounters. It was unnerving. "I am willing to convert to Judaism."

"Leila, can we put this off, until we are least nineteen?"

My modus operandi in my love affairs was quite consistent: I was an emotional wimp. I began perfecting my hasty termination of a relationship by disappearing from the scene. Leila, being more together and prouder than me, understood it, and after a few weeks, communication between us ended. About three years later, I heard that she had married a neighborhood guy, whom she had often described to me with lukewarm affection. Both, her marriage and ambivalence toward her new spouse, were confirmed for me, when I received a postcard from her while on her honeymoon. "Wish you were here," written in her unique scrawl, signed: Your Leila.

What transpired in the following months was a continuing honing of my skills at establishing ephemeral relationships, both interpersonal and in my employment. Relationships would begin, show promise and dissipate, fading into some dark recess of my unconscious. With women, they were suddenly too short, too loud, too abrasive, too whatever. In the workplace, jobs were too easy, too boring, and too dead end. Even my promising football days were compromised.

I had joined an inter-borough football team, which some used as a stepping stone to advancing in the sixties football world. I had promise. As the team's quarterback, I could throw a football fifty yards with ease. My coach, Eddie K., repeatedly praised my throwing arm. It meant a lot to me, but could not motivate me enough to overcome my resistance to discipline and a reluctance to accept compliments. It felt great, however, to know that opposing teams were watching me during warm ups. Maybe that's why I left the team.

But thankfully, I didn't end my relationship with Eddie K. Coach Eddie, was a unique, physical specimen. He had an outrageous physique to complement his athletic ability. He was the only Jew in the neighborhood who was truly feared. Even the tough, Irish gang members, who kept our local taverns in business, understood that behind Eddie's phlegmatic personality and warm, Mona Lisa-like smile, was unusual strength that was not to be tested. Often, after practices, Eddie would walk over to me, smack me on the back of the head, and then put his arm around me. He could, at the same time, admonish me for some unconscionable playing error, while complimenting me on elements of my technique. I hero-worshipped Eddie: his strength, his off the field warmth and consistency, and his ferocity on the field, before and during our games. I was certain, as well, that he understood the personal and unseen, demons that I was wrestling with.

I tried hard to uncover the magic of Eddie's physique. I regarded his muscular body as magic, because it had not yet occurred to me that years of hard work and sacrifice might have had some influence on such an outcome. One day, Eddie asked me to pick him up at his parent's apartment and accompany him to practice at our reserved Riverside Drive fields. He still lived with his parents, not so unusual in the 1960s. His mother greeted me at the door of their fourth floor walk up apartment, and ushered me into their modest living room, to wait until he finished breakfast. The polyethylene covering, preserving both the couch and the two cushioned, armchairs for decades to come, crinkled noisily, as I sat down and waited for Eddie.

"What's he eating?" I asked casually. I was hopeful that I was on the verge of unearthing a scientific revelation. "Two tuna fish sandwiches," she answered, with a hint of annoyance in her voice. "That's all he ever eats for breakfast...two tuna fish sandwiches." I imagined what the Philistines must have felt, when cunning Delilah delivered to them, that the secret to Samson's strength was in his hair. Two tuna fish sandwiches? Not as sexy, but certainly equally effective.

Unfortunately, my subsequent, rigorously adhered to breakfast regime, two tuna fish sandwiches, destined to create that chiseled physique, did little more than make me inordinately thirsty during the day. Maybe it took more than two tuna fish sandwiches for breakfast to look like Eddie.

Eddie called me one chilly morning in March and asked me to meet him at a bus stop near his home. It was a typical, blustery morning in New York's most fickle month, a point on the calendar designed, it seemed, to ensure that whatever apparel one selected was inappropriate for the rapidly changing weather. I had recently shared with Eddie that I had moved my draft notice ahead, and that I would soon receive my orders to report for a physical exam prior to joining the army. I felt rather aimless and had discussed with him that perhaps it would be a good two year experience for me. His only response to my announcement was a non verbal nodding of the head and a pursing of the lips, a gesture that I mistakenly interpreted as a tacit approval of my intention.

He was waiting for me on the corner of 160th street where the number four bus made its turn off Fort Washington Avenue to continue south on Broadway. "So, where to?" I asked.

"I'm taking you to tour some of the buildings at CCNY, City College, on 137th street and Convent Avenue," he responded. No explanation, no reason.

"What am I," I asked, "an architect on a tour of buildings?"

"Just be patient," he offered, "you might have fun."

Eddie did not have a historical precedent for entertaining me, or anyone else I knew of.

The number four bus ride, while no longer than fifteen minutes, was far from comfortable. The City Rapid Transportation System had recently introduced molded, plastic seats to replace the worn, often vandalized, cushioned accommodations. Unfortunately, the sculpting seemed designed to comfortably seat Quasimodo; concave seemed purposefully and generously to be alternated with convex in all of the wrong places.

As we pulled the bell cord to signal to our driver that we were approaching our destination, the bus lurched to a sudden stop. Somehow, it seemed that the New York City bus drivers were never in a hurry to keep to their posted schedule, but made up for lost time with a jolting stop, and an obvious eagerness for passengers to hurriedly descend from the bus. This was no exception, nor was the plume of black, acrid exhaust that our bus left behind as its calling card.

We were on 138th street and Broadway, greeted by those ubiquitous, damp gusts of salt-tinged wind, chilly reminders that it was March, and that the still frigid Hudson River was only a couple of miles west of us. We headed east toward Shepard Hall, City College's largest structure. As we walked toward Amsterdam Avenue, we passed Lewisohn Stadium on our left, an incongruous amphitheater in the heart of Harlem. The Doric colonnades were an appropriate prelude to the wealth of Neo-Gothic architecture that made up CCNY.

Once on Convent avenue, we turned north, for a block or two, and headed for Shepard Hall's main entrance on St. Nicholas Terrace, on 139th street. The architecture of the campus buildings was anomalous to the neighborhood's grungy, five and six story pre-war tenement buildings. It was as if the campus had been designed by an alien population; akin to the apocryphal origin of Stonehenge, attributed by some, to hosts from another world.

As we entered Shepard Hall, passing underneath an ornate archway, Eddie stopped just inside the main doorway. "Since your grades were not at the level to get you in as a student, you might enjoy seeing the inside of a university." I tried hard not to be insulted. Eddie was a motivator, but his technique took some strange twists every so often.

A well-lit, shiny floored, crazily packed, raucously loud, main floor hallway welcomed us as we made our way through the ten foot high entryway. I wondered whether Eddie had planned to introduce me to the tumultuous corridor just as classes were changing. We threaded our way through the hundreds of students whose grades were obviously at the level that allowed them to attend classes. They didn't look much different than me. And the women, oh my god, the women. Diaphanous blouses, tight knit sweaters, exposed navels; Is this what coming to college exposes you to? I must have been an obvious standout in my somnambulant meandering, as I tried to take it all in.

Eddie led as we wended our way toward the extreme southern section of the hall. "I'm taking you to our fraternity rooms to introduce you to a few folks. The fraternity that I joined is ZBT, the Greek letters of Zeta Beta Tau. The fraternity was established at CCNY in 1898, initially, as a Jewish frat, that soon thereafter did away with hazing." Eddie had played lacrosse in intramural games representing his fraternity, and was a city-wide star in that sport playing on the university's team as well.

Eddie introduced me to a number of frat members, many of whom seemed to adhere to the unwritten, CCNY dress code of drab and loose fitting cable knit sweaters with beaten up cargo pants of nondescript colors. Eddie was accorded the respect of a visiting dignitary. A line formed to greet him, while three girls standing no more than fifteen feet away whispered and pointed his way. He had graduated only five years earlier, but his reputation as a star athlete remained a seeming fixture in the frat rooms. CCNY did not have designated buildings for its fraternities, perhaps because of the geographical limitations of a hemmed in city campus.

We left the frat area and Eddie said, "let's head over to the campus dining area, lunch is on me."

I had only barely enough bus fare to get back to our neighborhood. We entered the dining area which was packed with students and faculty members. CCNY did not have a segregated faculty dining area. Eddie pointed out to me, that faculty had rejected that feature, believing that it would contribute an undesirable blow to their commitment to faculty-student egalitarianism. The area appeared to accommodate at least five hundred, uniformly dressed students. There were tables for two or four diners and booths prepared to seat as many students as were willing to squeeze together.

While raucous, the atmosphere was welcoming and relatively orderly. The walls were bedecked with posters of the school's sports teams. The welcome scent of brewing coffee was everywhere. Eddie was greeted by a number of faculty members and countermen working diligently behind steam-clouded, glass partitions. Ever hopeful, I ordered, yes, a tuna fish sandwich. We sat with several graduate students, friends of Eddie's. He continually introduced me as a friend, who was considering attending classes at the College. Our walk back to Broadway, to catch the number four bus, was met by a stiff westerly wind, that felt considerably colder than the gusts that had welcomed us on our arrival several hours earlier.

"So," Eddie asked, "what did you think?"

My answer belied the confusion and enthusiasm that I suddenly felt, "Made a great impression on me," was all that I could muster as an answer.

I negotiated the modest gradient from the bus stop to my street, with greater than usual ease.

For some reason the wind always seemed to be blowing in my face irrespective of which direction I was walking. Just then, it didn't bother me.

The next morning, a less blustery March Friday, I headed for the eighth avenue subway bound for Times Square. The Selective Service office, from where my army draft notice would emanate, was on 43rd street and eighth avenue. After waiting on line for a not too terrible period, I spoke with an advisor and asked that my draft notice be reinserted into the normal cycle, and that they cancel the acceleration request. The advisor informed me that it was within my rights to request this adjustment, as the accelerated notice had not yet been mailed out.

I asked, upon rising to leave, when my new notice would be mailed out, and she said, that she did not know, but in all likelihood, it would be within the next two years. My final question to her was, did she know when the accelerated notice would have been mailed? Her answer continued to reverberate in my head for years: "this afternoon," she said quite unemotionally, "it was going out with the batch of notices, this afternoon."

In one mid-March afternoon, Spring arrived early for me. Serving in the military remained on my horizon, but, in one, seemingly capricious moment, a response from a detached and uninvolved clerk, changed the arc of my life. The shift from the directionless path on which I had been wandering was seismic.

The near term, horizon became increasingly clear to me; there was nothing to stop me from applying to college, nothing that is, but what Eddie had so indelicately reminded me of: my grades were not at the level for me to have a remote chance of entering college. I was, however, seized with a Leibnizian optimism. I recalled reading an article, in which seventeenth century Leibniz and Spinoza, advocated that our universe was the best possible one that God could have created. The feeling of optimism and having found a direction out of my aimlessness, was strange to me...and energizing.

The next Monday, I enrolled in the College's evening courses. My high school grades were salvaged from the abyss of hopelessness, by my night school achievements, which when averaged together with my G. Dub disaster, raised my higher education potential to just above a glimmer of hope. There were minimal requirements to attending evening courses at CCNY. A "B" average was required over thirty credit hours, in order to matriculate to day classes.

I moved into a boarding room apartment in an area not far from CCNY. I would simply allow myself to be swept in the current of events which were dramatically reshaping my life. I couldn't begin to articulate why I was moving in the direction of college, away from my dear pool hall, where Frankie was undoubtedly still offering his five dollar deal to all of my shady friends. I knew that it seemed right, but I also felt that I was standing on the edge of uncharted territory.

Some years later, I was to again be swept along by a series of events with an inability to rationally explain what had unleashed them. Then married, my wife, Aviva, and I had decided to move to Israel, then a young and unstable country. When questioned for a rationale for causing this upheaval in our lives, we both were gloriously inarticulate, able to deal with our family and friends' angst with only the most platitudinal responses.

As I was preparing to challenge myself in college, a similar dynamic was at play: it felt like the right thing to do, but was fraught with many trepidations, not the least of which, was my history of abject failure in academic settings. There were unfamiliar forces that were compelling me to move downstream, whereas my history to that point, like a spawning salmon, pointed me upstream, against all currents.

Chapter Six

SEPTEMBER WAS UNUSUALLY warm that year. The tempering effect on New York City's summer weather, that is often heralded by Labor Day, was late in its arrival. The City College campus hallways were abuzz with students catching up with one another after a summer's hiatus; conversations were usually accompanied by kvetching about the hot weather. I felt like a guided missile negotiating those corridors, with the nose cone aimed at matriculating to day school classes with a "B" average.

I often looked at the students, many of whom seemed laissez faire about their studies, and thought that they did not know how lucky they were to be there. The zeitgeist, that had surreptitiously entered and conquered my being, found me extending it a warm welcome. I felt alive, focused and fortunate. While there were certain basic courses required in the mix that would constitute the thirty credit hours necessary to become a diurnal scholar. I leaned heavily on my blossoming interest in literature.

Professor Isaac's English literature class was extraordinary in many ways. His unassuming, diminutive stature, seemed paradoxically to house limitless knowledge. It was, however, difficult to forgive the plaid shirts and baggy pants that were his trademark. His encyclopedic knowledge of past and current literary trends and the social and political movements concurrent with the novels he assigned, was breathtaking. His class was both energizing and enervating at the same time (if that is possible). His breadth of knowledge was intimidating and immensely appealing. I asked many questions, some, just to hear myself talk, and some just to hear how he would answer; his answers always took the "scenic route," never the direct highway approach. I was inspired.

My increasing interest in literature, and my imperfect emergence into a more conventional life style, had much to do with Norman. Norman, was a nice, Jewish boy from Washington Heights, who happened to be six foot two, weighing about two hundred twenty pounds. That sizable frame was home to a zany, quirky, somewhat loony, incredibly creative counter-culture icon. He never attended college for it was, as he described it, "a conventional, unimaginative and stultifying experience." Not exactly what I needed to hear at this point in my life. But, he read like a madman and continually berated me for not yet having read Camus, Sartre or Baudelaire.

I met Norman quite coincidentally through our friend in common Robert Sussman. Robert was a strange, brilliant isolationist. He was more an acquaintance than a friend, as his only real relationship, other than with his even stranger, but strikingly attractive mother, was with Norman. Oddly, Norman was Robert's Ariadne thread to sanity, a state of mind Robert meandered into only occasionally. And so, after being introduced to

Norman by Robert in his dark, airless, ground floor apartment, I assumed he too was brilliant. I was struck by Norman's physiognomy: a receding hairline at age twenty one and a generous nose which was partially obscured by a bushy, jet black, nicely trimmed mustache. He was only one year older than me but, his mature countenance contrasted sharply with my boyish appearance.

I grew up in a home that cherished opera. My mother's father had been the Vienna State Opera's chorus master for twenty years and a tenor appearing with that opera company regularly. My mother often described her early recollections of growing up in Vienna, in an environment that put a premium on classical music and, most notably, opera. As I look back now, piecing together the historical patchwork of my family's history, it saddens me to think of how little value I assigned to their earlier years. In many ways, that is what compels me to chronicle elements of my life. Read it, if you will, but, it's there for anyone's review.

"Every Tuesday and Thursday evening my father would convene cellists, violinists, flautists and my sister Mela on the piano," my mother's blue eyes would mist over as she continued. "They would play the most glorious chamber music, Beethoven, Mozart and Dvorak...right there in our living room in the center of the Second District, in Vienna. My father would then sing an aria from Puccini or Verdi," her throat always constricted at the mention of her father. Her sister, Mela, had been an acclaimed concert pianist, before her tragic fate at the hands of the Nazi scourge. I suppose, given my consistent teen age rebellion against any and all things of value, opera and classical music assumed a negative valence. Until Norman.

While Norman and I both shared an iconoclastic view of our peers and a society that we felt to be abjectly hypocritical, we were both on a path of increased conventionality, he via his enrollment in art school and me as an evening student at CCNY. Our friendship deepened rapidly and was founded on a variety of commonalities: we both loved reading, we were both insufferable wise asses, taking joy in putting others in compromised situations, he loved classical music and I had begun to immerse myself in it as well. Norman, in his condescending manner, berated my love of Beethoven symphonies as adoring cacophony, while he relished, what he termed, more sophisticated, chamber music. Perhaps most importantly, we both loved women.

Visiting Norman at his parent's home was an other world experience. I would run up the three flights of stairs in his tenement building on Fort Washington Avenue. Invariably, upon my knock at the door, I would hear: "Mom, I've got it." He always wanted to intercept her greeting me, which was generally accompanied by her hug. It made him uncomfortable and, quite frankly, it made me exceedingly uncomfortable, mainly because she was unusually unattractive.

Norman was mean and derisive to her, and she just seemed to be oblivious to it. That behavior took some getting used to. While I was obnoxious and self-indulgent, parental denigration was not an attribute of mine. Mrs. Schwartz was always urging me to eat something which I occasionally, but quite reluctantly, accepted despite its emanating from a very untidy kitchen. "Harryle, I've just broiled a steak for Norman, you'll have half." "No, Mrs. Schwartz, Norman is a growing boy and I will not deprive him of his dinner." Norman had once opened the counter level cupboard drawer, to show me the hundreds of bottle caps his mother hoarded for some inexplicable reason. This, among other things, was not an incentive for me to enjoy a meal in their home.

I was accustomed to a meticulous home, which contrasted so markedly with Norman's apartment. I often suppressed a slight revulsion immediately upon entering his home, as I was growing increasingly connected to Norman and was inclined to overlook both her unkempt appearance and Norman's progressively annoying one-upsmanship.

While his mom was diminutive, about two heads shorter than me, I had no idea how tall his father was. A long time, neighborhood kosher butcher, his father was at home most of the times I visited Norman. Jack, his father, was always seated in the same cushioned arm chair, in the same corner of their tiny living room, under the same lamp, reading- I hope not- the same newspaper. Pleasant and phlegmatic, Jack was always courteous and soft spoken, even when his wife railed about Norman's dereliction of household responsibilities. He never stood up when I was there.

Norman, became my comrade in intellectual pursuits as well as my partner in asinine pranks. We decided, one boring weekday evening, that we would pose as contracted painters and paint the 178th street IND subway station black. We secured two painter's caps, a tall ladder and purchased two gallons of black paint. Brushes in hand and adorned with our caps, we marched into the station. "We're here, sorry to be a bit late," we informed the attendant in the change booth. "We've been contracted by the city and are ready to start painting the station." Thankfully, the alert attendant didn't buy it and we were turned away.

Norman constantly urged me to read more, appreciate modern art and continue to challenge mediocrity and convention. Armed with my newfound intellectualism, I visited a well-known artsy bookshop in Greenwich Village, on my way to a study group. As I entered the shop, I immediately noticed a lovely, young lady: tall and thin, with a long, brown pony tail. She was dressed in the popular village garb of a loose fitting, Indian blouse, with tassels dangling over her ample breasts, and well-worn jeans with the appropriate number of holes around her knees. I assumed, that she was open to spontaneous relationships, so prevalent in the Village. Somehow, probably all too conspicuously, I found myself browsing the books in the same area.

"Open for a recommendation?" I asked. She looked somewhat taken aback, and so I said, "I mean a book recommendation." Her "oh yeah" look was camouflaged by her pleasant response, "sure," she answered, looking directly at me with her head tilted slightly to the right. "Have you read 'The Rebel' by Albert Camus?" I thought that this was a great starter to a lengthier discussion. The problem was that I pronounced the cult author's name Kaymus. She smiled and responded smugly but politely, "isn't his name pronounced Ka'moo?" Of course she was right, I was mortified, end of discussion.

Laughingly, I related the embarrassing experience to Norman the next day. Not surprisingly, Norman did not find my crash and burn exploit funny. While possessing a sense of humor, he lacked what I had begun to cultivate: an ability to laugh at myself and not take my shortcomings too seriously. Norman, on the other hand, took himself very seriously, and generally wore a personal protective coat of armor, a shield, that he'd probably forged during his two months in the closed ward of Columbia Presbyterian Psychiatric Institute. I never asked him why he voluntarily chose to vacation in that somber environment, and he never offered a reason. He didn't hide it, nor did he discuss it. Frankly, I could both understand and handle his fits of anger or despair.

Generally, when listening to music in his twelve foot by twelve foot bedroom, I would be subjected to his quirky moods. "Because you think you are better looking than me, you believe that you should get to ball the more attractive women." "If you are so good at sports, where did it take you?" "Did you ever read any books before we met?" I listened patiently, and waited for the tempest to blow itself out. Friendship with Norman was often a chore, but worth it for me.

Trying to envision my growing up in his home, my vacation at PI, as the Psychiatric Institute was known in the neighborhood, might have been double his stay. I was less comfortable with his often trying to hit on the girls that I was interested in. But, we arrived at a modus vivendi about sharing. What we never got to share and what made me very envious, was his well-guarded trysts with Amy.

I was jealous, even though I had never met her. Amy and Norman had partnered during his stay at PI and, in his words, "screwed their brains out." Evidently, this "brain manipulation" continued sporadically after their graduation from PI. Norman would, on occasion, be unavailable to get together with me, as he had to make a quick trip to Amy. Considerably younger than her, Norman would extoll the virtues of sex with older women. "We both know why we are there, exactly what we want from each other. No bullshit, no phony wooing, no unnecessary dialogue, no duplicity, no conning."

He would then condescendingly inform me, that I might one day discover this as well. "Women, often like to have sex with younger guys, it may happen for you too." I so disliked that sermonizing quality, but it did sound like a potentially attractive possibility. In truth, however, it was hard for me to visualize anyone over thirty having sex. Nonetheless, I was envious, probably more for having to share my time with Norman, than his relationship with some mythological Brunhilde. In many inexplicable ways, I regarded my relationship with Norman as my salvation from the abyss of becoming eternally mediocre and inconsequential.

My relationship with my self-righteous, cantankerous friend, continued to deepen, and soon I found that I had lost contact with other friends with whom I had less and less in common. While Norman always had to prove that he was more successful, smarter, artistically knowledgeable and more sophisticated than me, I learned to become impervious to it. I focused increasingly on his immense and positive impact on me and my uneven trajectory away from a purely anti authority disposition.

While few people that I had met were as unshackled by cultural norms, Norman's range of interests highlighted for me, that being solely against things was not a meaningful philosophical approach to life. While Norman was opposed to almost any semblance of conventionality, he was devoted to his art, design and inventiveness. I struggled to understand what, if anything constructive, I was devoted to.

My academic performance at CCNY continued to improve, as I neared that hallowed thirty credit hours at a "B" grade level required to matriculate to the formal BA program. Perhaps I was becoming uncomfortable with my linear progression and an increasingly positive success path. Norman and I began planning an extended overseas trip prior to my entry into the BA program. My extensive travel experience had taken me as far away from New York City as Fort Lee, New Jersey, and East New York, Brooklyn. Influenced by my recently arrived cousins from Israel, we thought that Israel was as exotic a destination as we could hope for. My cousins were in the USA to study for their Masters and PhD in computer technology. So, with our penchant for long range planning, we decided over a cup of coffee, that we would somehow find our way to Israel. Upon our return, I would be able to cash in on my candidacy for the BA program.

We had a sum total of one thousand dollars between us. What proved to be only the first of many life-long, still-born financial schemes of mine, I convinced Norman that selling electronic equipment had great upside potential in Israel. We descended to New York City's Lower East Side, home of real and imagined deals on housewares and electronic equipment. We each purchased four Motorola portable radios, which we would transport in our suitcases and sell upon arrival in Israel. The substantial profits that were awaiting us, would enable us to eat and cover our other living expenses.

We arrived at the Yugoslavian freight and passenger company *Splosna Plovba* as a result of our adept, long range planning: a two inch, New York Times advertisement that we had randomly spotted a day or two earlier. Upon our arrival at the freight shipping company's office, we selected our preferred departure date and were intrigued that our initial destination would be Tangiers, Morocco. I had many fleeting associations with my parents arrival in Casablanca, Morocco twenty two years earlier. The fare was cheap, the agents were friendly and a cargo ship was leaving within a few weeks.

The cargo-passenger ship, the *Bohinj*, would ply the mysterious depths, beyond the Brooklyn Navy Yard, for thirteen days to arrive at Tangiers, and then terminate at some point in Yugoslavia. We planned to spend time in Spain and Italy as well. I read with relish and anticipation, Stendhal's accounting of his visits to Italy, "Rome, Naples et Florence." It never occurred to me to read anything a bit more recent than this early nineteenth century travelogue.

On the day of our departure, my cousins drove us to the ship's berth at The Navy Yard in Brooklyn. As we approached the loading dock, a small vessel bobbed in its mooring. I informed my cousins that this was probably the ferry that would transport us to the *Bohinj*. I was somewhat surprised when it became clear to me that this, indeed, was the *Bohinj*. "Oh well," I said to Norman, "what can we expect for a fare of two hundred dollars?"

We bade my cousins a warm farewell and told them that we would be so pleased to meet their parents in Israel. My parents were not able to join us at the dock. I had discouraged them from seeing us off, in part because I was hoping to avoid an emotional scene at our departure, but I was also averting displaying the internal tumult that I was experiencing. I had spent what seemed like seventy two consecutive hours assuring them that I would be safe. I think that I was convincing myself that all would be well, as I informed them that I would be in regular communication with them and I would be just fine.

As we boarded, what was to be our home for the next almost two weeks, we were greeted by an affable crew member who welcomed us in halting English and ushered us to our cabin. The accommodations were sparse, but clean and not uninviting. Norman and I looked at each other, we seemed to share a growing excitement. This was certain to be an extraordinary experience.

Chapter Seven

THE FOUR LENGTHY, booming whistle blasts from our floating home belied the very modest size of our ship, as we slowly backed out of our berth, and lazily swung to the southeast. The eight thousand ton *Bohinj* measured just over one hundred thirty six meters in length and a touch more than seventeen meters wide. There were thirty passengers and thirty crewmembers on board, twenty eight of the passengers were heading to Yugoslavia. The *Bohinj*, a shipmate related to us, was headed to the Yugoslavian city of Split on the eastern shores of the Adriatic Sea. Tangiers was a destination only for the loading of some equipment and supplies and the discharging of the two of us. Upon hearing this disembarkation schedule, I might have had a premonition of things to come.

As I sat on a faded, canvas deck chair breathing in a crisp October breeze, I thought about spending the next few months enacting what would surely be some form of a real time, picaresque novel. What might it be like, I wondered, to spend time with Norman, with whom, it had been clear to me for some time, I had a very ambivalent relationship. For the most part, however, his nuttiness, his willingness to partner with me in outrageous exploits, his sharp mind and what I believed was his caring for me, as much as Norman could care about another being, was all that I needed at this time.

The days passed pleasantly enough. Chugging through the Atlantic at twelve to fifteen knots, was not exactly stimulating although the weather was clear, crisp and exhilarating. Buoyed by the knowledge that I had anti sea sickness medication should I require it, we spent much time topside reading or planning our itinerary. About six days out I popped my first sea sickness pill; Norman had no apparent need, he had the constitution of an ox.

The sea was getting rambunctious. Meals were now served with dining room table slats raised about two inches, to keep the dishes from sliding onto the bleached, wood-paneled floor. Only a few of the passengers were at lunch joined by the ship's crew. In his generally genial and informal way, the Captain mentioned that we were heading into a storm that might make us a bit uncomfortable for a few hours. The Captain's calm demeanor made us feel reassured. "We always hope for at least one storm every time we cross the ocean," the Captain joked, "it makes us remember that we are sailors."

After another less than memorable lunch, we climbed the fifteen or so rusting metal steps to the upper deck which was the most significant open, public space on the ship. "This should be exciting," Norman smiled, the jury was out for me. Our ship, which now seemed like a little cork bobbing in the vast ocean, was beginning to dip its bow with more intensity into an increasingly frenetic sea. "Follow me," Norman was enthusiastic and a bit wild-eyed. We made our way forward toward the bow of the ship. The topside crew allowed us to move freely, but advised us to stay close to the metal railings ringing the ship. The boat was rocking and swaying and waves were breaking over the prow. Norman seemed exhilarated; I was considerably less impressed.

Drenched, we returned to the open area of the upper deck. Several passengers sat, huddled around a woman, who was lying on a chaise lounge covered with several blankets. The language barrier prevented us from social exchanges with most passengers, as many were Yugoslavian nationals. Norman's reluctance to extend himself in forming new relationships with anyone lacking artistic or other apparent intellectual qualities, isolated us even further. This was a unique social encounter for us.

We introduced ourselves, fully expecting to hear that the poor soul, pale and seemingly virtually comatose, was going back to the "homeland" to finally succumb to some hard to pronounce disease. I didn't want to pry, but I mustered the courage to ask the woman sitting closest to the assumed patient, "What is ailing this woman?" My query was fifty percent words and fifty percent hand gestures. She answered, by pointing her forefinger toward the darkening sea and then placing her hand on her stomach. The "patient" was suffering from acute sea sickness.

I reached into my pants pocket and extended the vial of pills that I now carried with me. "Please give her one pill and we will see how it affects her." My communication was augmented by my non-verbal pantomime. If it helped, I would share another of my more precious than gold sea equalizers. Voltaire's Candide, I recalled, when crossing the ocean, became violently ill and cried, that if he had been a king, he would give his kingdom to overcome his wretched, sea sickness.

Less than two hours later, the erstwhile cadaver arose from her crypt, and appeared cured. I am not certain how many people have had the rather dubious honor of being hugged by four Yugoslavian men and women simultaneously. I subsequently gave them three additional pills, which they carefully secured in a multi-colored, Yugoslavian handkerchief. Norman was not generally begrudging with his possessions, but he was somewhat taken aback by my gesture, and asked me why I had given a stranger three of my last, six sea sickness preventers? "It was the right thing to do, Norman."

My parent's Washington Heights tenement building, and most of our apartment windows, faced a bleak and generally deserted backyard. Several clothes lines crisscrossed the desultory space, with their attached, wooden clothes pins barely securing the sheets drying and blowing in the vigorous updraft. Cyclonic swirls of dust emanated from the few open spaces struggling for sunlight in a circle of brick warrens. The interconnected backyards were like sooty wind tunnels, frequented by strolling Gypsies, mostly Rumanian refugees, strumming their mandolins or extending and compressing their worn accordions with their sunbaked and withered hands. Upon hearing our backyard bandoliers, my mother reached into her pocketbook and fished out a nickel and wrapped it in a tissue. In my most mature, six year old voice, I asked her what she was doing. She resolutely answered, "I am sending them my best wishes," as she tossed the wrapped coin out of our third floor window.

"Mom, we have so little money, how can you just give it away?"

"Whatever we have," she framed her doleful response as if rehearsed for years, "they have less." I still recall a sense of pride that I felt for my mother's generosity. Maybe we weren't really that poor after all. They both were cut from the same cloth, my parents were: we had little, but others had less.

My father, an uncomplaining soul, worked in a women's rainwear sweatshop- owned by his cousin. His meager salary could have been augmented by his wealthy cousin, but unfathomably, it never was. All that brainpower, all that "Yiddishe sechel" kept under wraps for years.

One blisteringly, cold January afternoon, with large, crystalline snow flakes presaging a significant storm approaching, my father came home from work having traversed the three long and windy blocks from the 168th street IND subway station. As he entered our tiny, apartment corridor and removed his goulashes, my mother asked him if he had forgotten his winter overcoat at work, as he was only wearing his charcoal gray sweater.

"No, there was a homeless man sleeping on the park bench near the subway station. I saw the snow flakes accumulating on his hole-filled sweater, so I covered him with my coat. What a nice feeling it will be for him when he wakes up." We were somewhat surprised, but only somewhat. My father had again personified the family credo: "someone has less than we do." I didn't think Norman would understand.

The storm came and went leaving behind only a wave-soaked deck, a few nauseous passengers, and a profound feeling of the fragility and insignificance of our tiny vessel and the sixty crew and passengers aboard it in the vast, uncaring and now shimmering sea. Similar to Joseph Conrad's description in "Heart of Darkness," as his small boat made its way through foreboding African backwaters "...hugging the bank against the stream, crept the little begrimed steamboat, like a sluggish beetle crawling on the floor of a lofty portico." The last leg of our journey did, indeed seem that we were that "sluggish beetle."

We were bored and thankfully, vast schools of phosphorescent fish at night provided our evenings' entertainment, while dolphins, raced playfully alongside our ship during the day. We had befriended Ken, a marvelous, pointillist painter, and his gay entourage, headed to Yugoslavia and ultimately to Malaga, Spain, to paint. That relationship provided us with the sole, spirited conversation since my Yugoslavian sign language exchange on the ship's upper deck during our stormy weather saga.

Upon sailing north of the Azores, heading toward Tangiers, we knew that we were only a couple of days out. The sea was relatively calm and so, the inexorable chugging of our engine became more pronounced, I knew that I would soon miss that steady, subdued pounding of the engine. Like a universal heartbeat, it was always there.

On a clear and brisk Wednesday morning, day thirteen of our odyssey, we were greeted with another breakfast of watery eggs and some form of warmed over gruel. The Captain asked that we forgive his early departure from the meal as we were only about two miles off the Tangiers shoreline. Somehow, we tore ourselves away from our Yugoslavian repast. We had our luggage packed and ready and had completed the international debarkation forms required by customs officials.

With heightened anticipation and excitement, we flew up the metal staircase to the upper deck.

We had not noticed that our engines were suddenly at rest, the pulsating backdrop we had become accustomed to had ceased.

As we reached the deck, Norman turned to me and gestured out at the ocean. Our ship was flanked on portside and starboard by large French warships, probably cruisers or destroyers. Their prominent cannons glistened in the sun, while their white, red and blue flags flapped visibly in the steady breeze. About halfway between the *Bohinj* and the shoreline, a motor launch was heading toward us, with four or five men who, even from that distance, carried themselves with the officiousness of government personnel.

The Captain was gesturing to three or four crew members nearby. He abruptly ended his dialogue and approached us, with a sweet smelling, Gauloises cigarette dangling from his lips. Preempting any questions, he offered in his best and most precise English, "We have a bit of a problem that we will have to resolve, the Moroccan officials are on their way here to help us."

"What's the problem and does it concern us?" I asked. I was prepared to hear that it in no way did it pertain to us, but it did.

"The French, whose warships are just out there," he pointed left and right, "will not let us dock at the Tangiers port. "Since France had granted Morocco independence in 1956," the Captain continued, "we assumed that there would be no problem docking our communist country's ship at the port of an independent Morocco."

"Obviously," he continued tersely, "they have different ideas."

Catching the look that Norman and I shot one another he added, "Don't worry, we will figure it out." Somehow the more that someone tells me not to worry, the more I worry. The launch pulled up alongside our gently bobbing vessel, with its passengers now all standing up and preparing to ascend a multi-leveled, portable staircase that had been lowered on the port side of the *Bohinj*.

After a brief display of rehearsed pleasantries, the customs officials asked where a table might be set up, so that they could go about the business of customs officials, whatever that was. Approximately ten minutes later, a crew member asked that we join the newly arrived Moroccan officials, in the now vacated dining area. Norman and I entered the area to be greeted by a very cordial customs official, fortyish, nice looking and smartly dressed in a fitted tan, cotton suit. The customs official sported a pencil thin mustache and a full head of slicked back, black hair. He spoke English fluently, albeit with a French accent.

"OK, we have a little problem, but nothing that we cannot solve," he began. In New York that might sound like the beginning of a shakedown, but thankfully, it was not. "You understand, yes," he continued, "why we cannot allow the ship to dock in our port of Tangiers?"

"Yes sir, we do," Norman and I answered simultaneously, with Norman omitting the sir.

"Well, to begin with, you have two choices: get off here in a somewhat unorthodox way or continue to Yugoslavia."

"Must we walk the plank?" I couldn't resist.

"Not quite," the official answered, "but close." I felt my heart flutter at his comment. "Let's hold off on this part of the process. May I see your passports and debarkation forms? And do you have any electronic equipment or anything else that you wish to declare?"

After peering intently at our forms, he looked up at us and exhaled rather ominously. Norman and I had no idea what he was responding to, and returned his look with what must have been regarded as born yesterday, naiveté.

"I see that you have entered Israel as your final destination on this form, is that correct? Do you realize that Morocco is in a state of war with that country?"

Holy shit, how could we have been so stupid? He leaned across the table. "I will help you," he said, quite pleasantly, unperturbed by the extraordinary cluelessness of the two Americans sitting across from him.

Oh shit, I thought, here comes the strong arm stuff.

"I will allow you, in your own handwriting, to change Israel to España, thereby solving the issue."

"Really," I asked?

"Really."

A few strokes of our pens and it appeared that we had dodged a bullet. Almost. The official smiled...how did we get so lucky? "What kind of electronic equipment do you have that you will be bringing into our country?" he asked.

"Well sir, we have four portable radios each, Motorola portables to be exact," I tried to answer calmly. My tendency was to try to bullshit him, with some nonsensical story about our need to listen to radios stereophonically, or some such crap. I decided to level with this guy who, so far, had been so helpful. Norman peered at me with incredulity, as I continued. "We have very little money, and were planning to sell the radios in Europe or Israel, to pay for our lodging and meals." I held my breath and gritted my teeth awaiting all of the official rules and regulations to be quoted dispassionately.

"Good. Good thinking." He proceeded to stamp our passports and our debarkation forms. Phase one of a multi-phased disengagement process was successfully completed.

"Now," the official continued in a voice that might have been feigned sincerity, although I liked the guy and trusted him, "we must decide how to get you off this ship, and help you to visit our fair city."

Our formal business concluded, the official and his assistant rose and wished us a pleasant trip to España. We thanked him profusely for his assistance and creativity. He informed us that a boat would soon be alongside the *Bohinj* to ferry us to the port. We would not need to deal with customs again, as he had completed all of the necessary paperwork and formalities. Norman and I returned to our cabin, bid it *adieu,* and carried our bedraggled suitcases topside- each made infinitely heavier by four portable radios. I couldn't believe our luck. I had no prior experience with custom officials, but I had never imagined that they might be positive and flexible.

Thankfully, it was a pleasant, sunny day with a balmy, persistent breeze caressing the placid Mediterranean cove. The Captain approached us and thanked us for choosing his ship and wished us a good journey. He must have known, at that time, that the caique bobbing gently, some sixty or seventy feet below us, was to be our transportation to shore. Two pleasant looking, fiftyish or so, men sat on the six foot wide boat's slats, seemingly unconcerned that their red, tasseled fezzes might blow away in the stiff breeze. Our suitcases were lowered, one at a time, into the swaying vessel. We were then to make our way down the multi-tiered metal staircase, that our friendly officials had recently climbed.

As we slowly descended, I recalled working as a roofer's assistant for two summers. The roofers called my job the "mule's" job. I was to carry fifty pound bundles of shingles up to them, in what seemed like a never-ending Sisyphean task. The problem was coming down off the roof: getting back on the swaying ladder while looking down, sometimes from a height of three floors, and descending with aching legs. Each time I reached a lower rung, I thought: from here a fall might kill me, and then two or three rungs down, from here, I would only break a leg. I tried not to think about it.

But Norman and I, with the agility of fairly well-conditioned twenty and twenty one year old bodies, made it fine. Our water borne taxi, which had a small mast for its unfurled sail, set out toward shore about one and a half miles away. Why the chosen method of locomotion was rowing, rather than sailing, was not on a list of preferred questions with which we assailed our English speaking sailors.

Our bronzed and sinewy sailors skillfully delivered us to a cove adjacent to the main docks, negotiating what suddenly turned into a stiff current pulling us to the right. It was impressive for me, as my rowing skills had been refined at, and relegated mainly to, the Central Park Lake in Manhattan. Upon reaching the sandy shore, we gingerly stepped onto the beach and tipped our skipper and his first mate generously. They pointed us to a nearby hotel which they said was reasonable and clean. The port was grimy and chaotic, with vendors barking the freshness of a variety of fish displayed on blocks of rapidly melting ice. Young men sat in circles playing shesh besh and drinking tea. This was not exactly a place where two, light skinned dudes schlepping a suitcase each, would want to have an evening stroll.

The recommended hotel was clean and served our purposes just fine. The next morning, we left for a ferry across the Bay of Gibraltar to Algeciras, Spain, one of the largest and busiest ports in Europe. Our hotel in Algeciras, in a quiet neighborhood, was less than a mile from the port. We decided, with some reluctance, to leave our luggage while we took our day trip. Algeciras was to be our launching site for Gibraltar, our first stop on an itinerary that was, at best, a work in progress. We caught an early morning ferry from Algeciras to Gibraltar, with five minutes to spare, not knowing in advance that we had to pass through customs.

The crowded ferry moved swiftly over the open waters, with the back deck no more than a yard or two above water level. I kept telling myself and Norman, that the fins that appeared everywhere in the choppy Sea of Gibraltar, were clearly dolphins. I suppose this could be called an exercise in self-delusion. The one hour ride passed quickly and uneventfully. We entered the port of Gibraltar, with the quarter mile high limestone promontory seemingly guarding the Strait of Gibraltar.

Gibraltar, on the southernmost tip of the Iberian Peninsula, was considered by the ancient Greeks and Romans, to be one of the two pillars of Herakles (or Hercules to the Romans) that signified the boundary of the known world. It was nice to experience, first hand, what had been so intriguing to me in the Greek Mythology evening classes at CCNY.

We spent the better part of a day enjoying the island and losing our sandwiches to the marauding and ornery Barbary apes, Europe's only colony of wild monkeys. These pesky animals, while cute for about one minute, ran wild on virtually all of the walking and hiking paths, aggressively attempting to hijack a meal from anyone passing by.

My mother would have enjoyed the winding, flower-lined paths. She loved the outdoors, hiking in the woods, swimming in frigid lakes and similar activities that were available in inner city New York as frequently as a Perseid Comet shower. Family vacations for us had had been summer treks to the Catskill Mountain bungalow colonies in Uncle Lazo's 1954, light blue Plymouth. The greatest seasonal challenge of that journey, heading northward on the single lane route 17, was whether my sister, Josephine, could refrain from throwing up before getting to the Red Apple Rest Cafe, some fifty miles north, or about half of the one hundred mile journey. I'm not sure that Norman's parents were even that adventurous. His father was permanently affixed to his living room easy chair.

Toward late afternoon we made our way to the ferry docks heading back to Algeciras. The lines to the ferry seemed longer than when we had arrived, and we assumed that those on line with us, none of whom appeared to be tourists, were returning home to Spain after working in Gibraltar. This was in part correct, but it was soon apparent that there was a more intricate plan afoot. About halfway through the one hour journey, about one hundred young and middle-aged men began undressing, simultaneously...as if acting on some cue in the ether that we were not able to detect.

Bronzed, sinewy bodies abounded. "Norman, are we the only people dressed on a nudist colony ship?" As if in accordance with some time honored ritual or well-rehearsed ballet, choreographed to some inwardly inspired music, our partially clad shipmates reached into the shopping bags that each of them carried.

Soon the deck was festooned with cartons of cigarettes, toothpaste packages, packs of razor blades and other barely recognizable commodities. Norman whispered, "I think this is some kind of religious ritual. Maybe they are making offerings to their gods." Lastly, withdrawn from each shopping bag were thick, elastic bands. With great agility and purpose, they each moved quickly and wrapped the bands around their thighs, calves, biceps and chests. They then inserted cartons of the merchandise that they had purchased duty free in Gibraltar, between their tanned bodies and the elastic straps.

It became clear to us now why so many of those workers who had been on our outbound ferry seemed to have ill fitting clothes…all too large. Those additional sizes, not exactly a fashion statement, now easily accommodated what was going to be shuttled past custom officials greeting them in Spain.

Each worker, now with dramatically enhanced girth, kept several items handy. These unsecured cartons of cigarettes, in short supply and retailing for at least double the duty free price throughout southern Spain, were passed to customs officials. This rite of passage served as a thank you for not noticing that a previously one hundred thirty five pound individual who had left Spain that morning, now appeared to be returning that afternoon as the eponymous, muscular hero of the Pillars of Herakles.

The officials greeted many of the returnees by name and, with finesse and rehearsed slight of hand, accepted the largesse of so many workers.

Chapter Eight

WE MOVED NORTHWARD through Spain over the next two or three weeks stopping in Malaga, Toledo, Madrid and Barcelona. Barcelona of the 1960s, was a far cry from the modern, vibrant, art hub of today; we opted for a somewhat extended stay there. The Funicular brought us to a park some hundreds of feet above sea level. Always in the market to meet attractive women, we connected with three young women who had never been outside of Barcelona's suburbs. After several hours together they, with a surprisingly casual air, asked us what our nationality was.

They knew that we were American, as we had conversed in elementary English and worse Spanish. When we informed them that we were Jewish, they at first, thought that we were teasing them. When they realized that we were not, they shared, that we were the first Jews that they had ever met. They had been taught that Jews had tails and horns. That was it for us, as we rather abruptly bade them farewell, we turned to show that we had no tails or horns. Not an easy task for us as they were very attractive and, we surmised, very receptive to our advances. Quite an eye opener, coming from Washington Heights, home to so many Jewish refugees, many of whom held positions of political prominence.

Our goal was to reach Naples, Italy and from there find some nautical means to reach the port of Haifa, Israel. Based on our ever-dwindling financial capacity, we booked inexpensive tickets on a Spanish passenger-cargo ship to the Port of Naples. The twenty four hour ride passed uneventfully, although we were in constant anticipation of another tobacco smuggling enterprise. We reached the Port of Naples, passing north of Sardinia into the Gulf of Naples. Mount Vesuvius was visible, somewhat to the east of the city of Naples. Naples appeared tranquil and benign.

Our ship docked at around noon in the northernmost sector of the port. Passing through customs was surprisingly quick and easy, with only a minimal amount of the customary shouting and organizational tumult that seemed to accompany most Italian gatherings in excess of four people.

We wandered through central Naples until we happened upon Pensione Maria, just off a main thoroughfare. It suited us just fine. The front desk staff of the quaint, family run guest house, was friendly enough. The staff spoke a modicum of English and seemed pleased to get the business. The Pensione Matriarch, Maria, had what appeared to be one glass eye, as did the young man showing us to our room, who was her youngest son. There must have been a congenital hand-me-down, but, it made me uncomfortable.

I was besieged by a sudden and thankfully, short-term, anxiety that perhaps there was some contagious bacterium in the water. Norman would have no part of any discussion about this, as he had probably, I concluded, seen far worse residual DNA anomalies during his stay at PI.

Having grown accustomed to the modest size of affordable accommodations, we settled in rather quickly and turned our attention to what remained of our rapidly dwindling finances. We had enough remaining cash for about one week's lodging and modest meals. The greatest expense was to be our lodging and we felt quite at ease negotiating a lower rate with Maria, as we were staying with them for several days. "Maria," I began, "as we are staying here for many days, we are asking you to give us a discount of fifty percent." I was hoping for ten percent. Maria, after endless gesticulations and undecipherable and frenetic sentences in a surprisingly attractive Italian, acquiesced and lowered our rates by fifteen percent.

Notwithstanding Maria's magnanimity and our main meals, which now consisted of a shared salad and a thin-crusted pizza each, we were on the verge of international bankruptcy. So, we both agreed that we would look to the sale of our combined eight portable radios as an immediate financial bailout. "Harry," I was waiting for this comment, "what happened to your money making scheme?" The best we could do however, in the impoverished city of Naples, was to sell our radios through the commissioned services of Maria's son- for the amounts that we paid for them. We knew that we were being taken advantage of, but we had no alternative. The proceeds from the sale of the radios proved to be a welcome, but short-term relief. A portion of these funds did allow us to visit Pompeii, to witness what an agitated Vesuvius was capable of.

Within a few days, we found ourselves in the all too familiar situation of having insufficient funds to pay for our board, but this time with no radios to sell. We were left with our dedicated reserve funds to purchase a one way ticket home- from wherever. "OK, Norman, my business venture is defunct, so, I volunteer to contact my parents in New York, to 'borrow' some funds." Our hope was to subsist for a few more days and make our way across the Mediterranean Sea to Israel. Once there, we would be fine, as I had many relatives living there, and I was certain we would be accommodated.

Norman was pleased, both in my admission of failure and of avoiding a confrontation with his father. His father, the calm and phlegmatic individual, who ground chopped meat in a kosher butcher shop, had been vehemently opposed to Norman's apparent frivolous and wasteful trip to Europe. Sitting in Norman's dimly lit living room, with its long overdue and peeling tan paint job, we discussed our planned trip with his father. His mother sat in her perennially nervous state to the right of Jack, repeatedly folding, then unfolding, her gnarled and sweaty hands on her lap. This was one of the few times that I had seen Norman's father somewhat animated. "Why this trip Now? Where is the money coming from? If you've saved a few dollars, why not go to college?"

Norman was as courteous to his father as he was dismissive to his mother. My parents had very little excess funds, but they were incredibly generous and protective of their three children. I was certain that if my father did not have the three hundred dollars that I was going to request he cable us, he would borrow it from his brother Lazo, who did have the funds.

We walked about five blocks to the bus stop that would take us to Piazza Municipio, where the American Express office was located. The office was remarkably modest and was tucked away neatly down a pleasant, quiet street. It was bordered on its southern side by a small pizza and pasta shop with outdoor tables, covered with checkered table cloths, and unevenly matched, wooden chairs partially obscuring the office entrance. On its northern front, a green grocer was stacking Italian eggplants and green and red peppers.

Upon entering the office, we were casually greeted by a lethargic security guard who, after hearing us speak English, most likely deduced that we were not major security risks. I asked him where I could send a telegram to the States. He pointed to one of the four gated windows behind which sat a cherubic, young woman no more than twenty years old. This was a dramatic departure from so many of Naples' post war clerks and store employees, many of whom were considerably older and often appeared birthed in a petri dish of antipathy. This clerk was on the ball. What luck.

Her English was passable, but I was more interested in her olive complexion, smooth skin and dark and urgent eyes. When I slid my passport under the brass gate separating us, she looked at it with some interest. I was hoping that she was enthralled by my picture, but it appeared that she was more taken by my name.

"You are Harry Stern?" she asked with some interest. "Yes," I answered, wondering if any of my high school teachers had besmirched my reputation internationally. "Why do you ask?"

"We have been hoping you would come in and have been waiting for you for a few days." I was puzzled as she handed my passport back to me informing me that I would need it at the cashier's window. She pointed to the window opposite her compartment. "Come back when you finish there and we will continue with the cable to America," she called out as we crossed to the cashier's gated window. I loved how she elongated the second syllable of America.

The cashier's compartment was, perhaps appropriately, the most dimly lit area of the office. Naples seemed to be mired in a postwar budgetary morass which weighed down what appeared to us nevertheless as a vibrant, fun-loving city. Shady deals seemed not only possible, but preferable and intense bargaining for everything purchased was universal. So, it was little wonder to me that the cashier's window was located in the darkest, gloomiest and shadiest looking sector of the office. Passport in hand and a foreboding feeling slowly overtaking the fine mood that our first American Express contact had stimulated in us, I marched across the tiled floor with a false air of joviality.

As expected, a dour looking, slightly pudgy fiftyish woman, probably counting the days until her retirement, asked in a surprisingly pleasant voice if I was Harry Stern. I answered affirmatively and thought of extending my hands outward to facilitate the placement of handcuffs on them.

"You have a letter here from professor Villet of Berne, Switzerland, and with it the three hundred fifty American dollars he has sent you. We have had this deposit in our office for almost three days," she soon finished her mild reprimand for my tardiness. As I handed her my passport for verification of my identity and her immediate stamping of what seemed like one hundred duplicate forms, I thanked her and offered a weak *mea culpa* for my late appearance. She asked me if I wanted the funds in dollars or Italian Lira. I determined that I was not strong enough to carry three hundred fifty dollars in the Italian currency, and opted for greenbacks. I thanked her profusely and caught a glimpse of Norman's face, frozen in shock and incredulity.

As I turned from the cashier, funds in hand, I whispered to Norman that I would explain outside. We nodded farewell to the guard. Thankfully, the lovely signorina, who was so determined to help me send a request to my father in New York, was not in view behind her caged window, and we left the storefront office.

We closed the exit door and were once again headed toward Piazza Municipio.

"Who's Professor Villet and what's up with the money?" "I can't explain it, I have no idea who that professor is, I know no one in Switzerland and I am thankful that God put another Harry Stern in Naples at this time."

Our pace quickened, we tried not to run, as we made our way to the bus stop. This ill-gotten gift allowed us to pay our patient hotelier and have meals that thankfully, did not include pizza or a shared salad. I did feel pangs of guilt for accepting funds that to me were a gift from heaven, but to the other chap of the same name, might have resulted in his eating small pizzas and shared salads. I tried hard to suppress those feelings.

Many years later, while living in Washington, D.C., I received a call asking if I was Harry Stern.

When I responded affirmatively, the party on the phone asked for my address as he wanted to send me a check for the sale of "my" strip mall in Maryland. My Naples adventure flashed before me as I informed the caller that I had no strip mall and he must have the wrong Harry Stern. I later met the caller, who informed me of the seven figure amount of the check in question. I was so relieved to simply tell my mystery caller that he had the wrong party.

We were careful to reserve enough of our treasure trove to cover our fare for the twelve hundred mile journey by sea to

Haifa. To this date, I cannot fully understand precisely what happened in Naples to delay my arrival in Israel by eight years. It seemed that in a series of cascading, mysterious and cataclysmic emotions that converged simultaneously and, for which, I had no understanding or defense, I was overcome by an all pervasive sense of panic. I was sitting on one of the two beds that comprised about fifty percent of the area of our hotel room, when there was a knock at our door.

Emilio, Maria's youngest son, entered to ask us a question about the radios that we had sold through his negotiations. While not an aggressive person, his rapid Italian, dappled with heavily accented English phrases, suddenly seemed confrontational and threatening. His blue, tinted glass eye appeared foreboding and menacing. I had enjoyed nothing but pleasant conversations with him for days preceding this encounter. But now, I felt a pervasive nausea and an intense claustrophobia. I felt impelled to leave the room, virtually gasping for air, only to feel more suffocated in the dark, winding, suddenly threatening corridor that had been a friendly home away from home to me for days.

I believe that Norman's "been there done that" approach to psychological distress was helpful.

He clearly understood that the demarcation between real and imagined fear was at best unclear and intangible, and for all intents and purposes, not very meaningful at this point. In what seemed like a millisecond, I had morphed from a mercurial, independent, seemingly daredevil individual, to an anxious, twenty year old who had already quietly determined that his European jaunt was at an end. I shared this with Norman and conveyed how upset I was at cutting our trip short, but I knew that I had to return to the States.

I understood, on some level, that what I was feeling was not short term. Once again, Norman was understanding and supportive, and I believe that he was also prepared to declare our almost two month sojourn over. "Hey man, whatever you need to do now, I'm OK with it." Norman's first hand experience with psychological tumult could have evoked multiple responses from him, such as: "get it together," to his more empathetic response of support. I welcomed his unemotional caring.

I sent a telegram to my parents informing them that we were aborting our plans to visit Israel and would be returning to the States in the next few days. I was suddenly struck with a wrenching concern for their safety: Had my father's heart condition worsened? Had my mother's depression and anxiety returned? On some murky level of my tumultuous unconscious, I understood that it was I who needed to be taken care of, it was concerns for my own safety that I was transferring onto my parents.

How much of this susceptibility to my panic reaction was lurking in some sub dermal region, waiting for a crescendo of confusion to emerge? Was the anti authoritarian bravado, the tough-minded, adventurous and independent guy that I appeared to be, I asked myself, simply camouflaging faults in an outwardly appearing granite facade?

I grew up in a house of mixed metaphors. When my parents arrived after their narrow and harrowing escape from the Nazi killing machine, the U.S was still accepting new immigrants. The U.S. had yet to enter World War Two, which would bring the immigration flow to a virtual halt. My mother arrived at

Ellis Island from Casablanca quite traumatized, having lost key members of her family in the Holocaust.

On very rare occasions, after living in New York for several years, she would recount to us, teary eyed, how, while still in Vienna in 1938, she had urged her sister Mela, an acclaimed Viennese concert pianist, not to board a train that was bound for Salzburg, Austria. Mela assured my mother that all would be well and that she had to honor her performance engagement. My mother's vivid description of her smiling sister, waving to her from her open train compartment's window, has stayed with me until today. Her sister never arrived at the concert hall and was never heard from again.

The horror of the disintegration of her famous, tightly knit and beloved family weighed on her heavily. Her inner strength, ferocious love of life and my father's resourcefulness and intuitive judgment, carried her through their flight to safety. Once in the States and no longer fearful for her life, she became quite agoraphobic, never wanting to leave the house, needing constant communication with my father. She was affected by a debilitating, ever-present and prolonged stream of anxiety. She referred to the psychiatrist, that she was fortunate enough to be in therapy with, as her saving angel.

Columbia Presbyterian Hospital, just across the street from our apartment building, was funding a research project which studied victims of the Holocaust and the psychological impact wrought on its survivors. Her angel, Dr .Cotton, an independent practitioner participating in the research project, offered my mother ongoing, supportive analytical treatment for over three years, at no cost. He reviewed his diagnosis, and the progress made treating my mother, with the psychiatric division of the hospital. She made rapid and extraordinary progress, although any televised or radio mention of the Holocaust would cause her tearful departure from the room.

My father never really exhibited overt, psychological symptoms resulting from their almost two year escape journey. His photographic memory could, had he chosen, have provided all of us with the details of their harrowing escapes, information my mother was unwilling or unable to retrieve. He rarely spoke of the obvious bestiality of the Nazi regime, the complicity of the German nation and the eager accompaniment of too many European nations as well. As a coda to any of the rare direct or oblique references to the Holocaust, he always counseled us to remember that the Poles, his homeland folks, and the Ukrainians were not far behind the Nazis in their determination to eradicate Jews.

Entry into the United States for refugees from Europe required an American sponsor. The financial commitment of the sponsors seemed to vary on a case-by-case basis, but their primary responsibility was to ensure that the immigrants would find employment and would not be a burden to the American economy. My father had, through endless communications with his brother Lazo, who was already living in New York, secured a sponsorship from Mr. Margaretten, a partner in a significant Jewish matzo company: Horowitz-Margaretten. My father described, in his laconic and humorous way, his April, 1941, visit to the Vichy Government office in Casablanca, in order to secure a visa and a permit to leave the country.

As he entered the clerk's office, he was greeted with a disdainful scowl.

"So, Mr. Stern," the aspiring Nazi sneered, "you people seem to be so eager to leave us."

"The weather doesn't agree with my infant daughter." The clerk ignored his response.

"So, you managed to secure yet another sponsorship from that Margaretten man. You know that there are many of you Jews that he is vouching for."

"Yes, I know that this gentleman is very kind."

"You know that he is quite old, what if he dies when you get there?"

"In that event, I will go to his funeral."

The clerk quickly, and disdainfully, signed the papers and called out to the next person on line.

From my earliest recollections I admired his cool, level headedness- except when it came to dealing with my unruly teen years. For the most part, those were the only days I remember him losing his cool. Otherwise, he was a rock of logic and rationality. He often joked about his five European passports and credited his Czechoslovakian passport with saving the family on numerous occasions. He would sketchily discuss his father's and brothers' smuggling business before the war, which was a source of great amusement for us.

He could have been a greater source of support and stability for my mother, who certainly needed it, had their relationship allowed. They argued incessantly and it was not until many years later, that they seemed to eke out some warmth and happiness from their relationship. With great urgency, I worried if my foray into the world of seemingly uncontrolled anxiety was genetically transmitted to me from my mother. Was that possible? Why, I quietly bemoaned, did I not acquire the rock solid approach to adversity that my father epitomized?

Now, I needed the familiarity of home and, like that proverbial homing pigeon, that was where I was heading. Within two days of the onset of my continuing panic, we were packed, had paid our hotel bill, and were on our way to the airport. We had booked an afternoon flight; I had withheld precisely enough to pay for my flight to New York. What I did not account for was an embarkation fee that amounted to about fifteen dollars. No amount of bargaining, promising or cajoling was going to get me past passport control. As yet another example of inexplicable good fortune and funds spontaneously materializing, as if through the design of some unseen celestial force, a gentleman on line behind me tapped me on the shoulder and said, "I've got it." He handed the agent a handful of Italian Lira, which I assume totaled the amount necessary to get me past him. He then handed me a U.S. ten dollar bill.

"In case," he said, "you need a cup of coffee along the way." He gave me his business card, Vice President of Hormel Meats, and held his hand up in front of him as if to say, "thanks are not necessary." Or, maybe it was to protect himself from what he feared might have been my attempt to kiss him on the cheek. Norman was clever enough to have withheld some funds for embarkation fees.

Chapter Nine

JFK INTERNATIONAL AIRPORT failed to meet my unrealistic expectation that it would be a familiar, safe haven and would end my acute anxiety. I was experiencing so many conflicting feelings. My all-encompassing fearfulness had not dissipated. Additionally, I was now gripped by a sense of shame and cowardice: I had cut our trip short for some undefined reason, and I now felt an inexplicable emotional void. I was happy to be home in New York, but, I felt only unrelenting anxiety. The *sturm und drang* around the baggage claim area, and the hundreds of faces moving in random directions, added to my distress.

Upon retrieving my sorry-looking suitcase, I told Norman that I would call him soon. With about two dollars in my pocket, I entered a New York City Yellow Cab after waiting on line for an eternity. The Taxi headed toward my parent's home in Manhattan. Everything was familiar and yet it seemed like I was dreamily experiencing all anew. The cab driver was garrulous and thankfully, not very interested in my responses, which was good, because I wanted time to think.

About forty minutes later we reached 165th street, and it was then that I began wondering how I would pay the almost twenty three dollar fare that the meter ominously displayed. "Twenty three dollars?" I asked, as we stopped in front of my building. "Excluding one dollar and twenty five cents tolls and, well, you know what else." I hesitatingly told the driver that I would be back in a moment, as my parents would give me the fare.

"I will leave my suitcase here just in case you want a guarantee that I will be right back."

"OK kid, but I got the meter running." I jogged up the three flights to my parent's apartment and rang the bell as I could not locate my house key. I rang it several times and to my dismay, there was no answer. I flew down the stairs and rang Mrs. Strom's bell. She was a virtual recluse, who lived alone in apartment number one, just inside the building's entrance. She always liked me. As a kid, as I would go shopping for her at Lena's, the neighborhood produce store, and Daitch Dairy, three blocks away, for creamed butter and pot cheese. As I would never accept a tip from her for years of deliveries, I felt comfortable asking for a loan until my folks returned. Thankfully, this was not one of her half hour weekly forays into the wilds of Broadway, and she answered on the second ring.

Accompanying her unwelcome hug and declarations of how she, and my parents, had missed me, was a positive response to my unusual request. She withdrew three crumpled, moist, ten dollar bills from her well-worn purse, and thrust them affectionately, into my hand. "Don't worry," she said, "your dad will pay me back."

"And dad will pay me back for this frivolous waste of money," I thought. I raced outside, gave the surprisingly patient driver the whole thirty dollars, and made my way up to the third floor walk up apartment. I sat on the nearby staircase for about a half hour before my mother and sister Melinda came walking up the steps. My mother had kept my eleven year old sister out of school, in anticipation of my arrival. She knew that Melinda wanted to be here at this time. My mother got teary eyed and Melinda jumped in to my arms. While happy to see them, I felt hollow, empty, emotionally dried up. With each familiar, retraced step, I experienced a new disappointment. I kept expecting all to be better, but, to my dismay, the all pervasive and inexplicable sadness that came upon me in Naples, did not dissipate with the return to familiar terrain.

Perhaps most unnerving to me was the impatient and cool response I had to Melinda, whom I loved dearly. With a reckless abandon and tears of joy streaming down her face, she leapt into my arms. I embraced her, but suddenly felt a recurring, breath depriving claustrophobia. We were standing in the third floor hallway, where I said hello to Mrs. Engel every school day morning for almost fifteen years; where I carried the grocery packages for Mrs. Lindt, living one flight above us: but, now it was all dark, strange and foreboding to me.

I had, for the eleven years of her life, felt increasingly connected to Melinda, abundantly protective, deeply respectful of her unbounded intelligence and amused by her joie de vivre. Now, Melinda sensed that I was different, something had changed. "Did you not miss your beautiful sister?" She was probing and probably felt that something was amiss. "Of course I missed Josephine," was my lame response. Our older sister, while very attractive, was where the family united in its communal depression.

It dawned on me that I had a different kind of journey ahead of me, one that did not involve international travel, passports or foreign languages. I wasn't sure what that experience would look like, how I would undertake it, or whether I would ever again feel free of this enervating anxiety. I think Melinda and my mother understood that something had happened that altered my wise-guy demeanor. My mother seemed to be assessing my frame of mind and was hoping for some breakthrough explanation. Melinda eagerly awaited my familiar jokes and stories about what I had seen and done. Melinda understood that something quite impactful had occurred to me. They came about their observations from their individual perspectives: Melinda, from an understanding of behavior that was unusual for someone her age, and my mother from a "been there, done that" vantage point.

My mother was approaching forty four years of age when she gave birth to Melinda. My parent's dysfunctional discord occurred with the regularity of Big Ben's hourly chime. My mother would continually flaunt my father's alleged insistence that she abort her pregnancy. "I believe," she would share with us with a worn out bitterness, "your father really did not want another child." They lived from week to week financially and had a tiny, one bedroom apartment. My mother contended, that my father feared that the family could not be supported, even at our current level, for long. I never corroborated this accusation with my father, and never felt an inclination to discuss it.

I never fully fathomed the need for this occasional, spontaneous maternal reportage, except that it was designed to solicit support for what appeared to be their Washington Heights version of the Hatfields and the McCoys. Whether this discord was real, imagined or a combination of both, Melinda's birth was special to all of us. Melinda, we had decided, was God's gift to the family.

While I was subjected to my high school excommunication, Melinda was entered into unique, educational institutions for "gifted children." Thankfully, she brought our sibling educational achievement average up to mid range, as Josephine and I performed academically at basement level. Melinda was named after my mother's sister Mela, whom my mother often described as brimming with vitality, humor, intelligence and an unquenchable zest for life.

An astute, sensitive and gifted pediatrician in the making, Melinda's graduation from Mount Sinai Medical School augured well for a bright future. Her medical school graduation reception was held on the Columbia University campus, where I had spent four years studying for my doctoral degree. I was standing with Melinda chatting when our mother called us over to introduce us to an old friend of hers. She first introduced me as her son, and then introduced Melinda as the "real doctor."

Several hours after my European return, my father came home from work. Many embraces followed with some attempt on my part to describe some of my two month journey. I tried, with limited success, to explain why my adventure had been cut short: "Dad, honestly, I don't know what happened to me in Italy. One day, I was fine and planning our continued trip to Israel, the next day I was in a state of terrible, ongoing panic." It was very hard for me to admit failure or emotional tumult to either of my parents.

They were supportive and tried to offer some guidance. My mother suggested that I seek therapeutic intervention, if only for a short period. Whereas, in the recent past I had regarded my father's calm and rational approach as too devoid of emotion and probably replete with denial, I now found it helpful and comforting. He had been down this well-travelled road before with my mother.

The starting gun had sounded for my race to find a therapist that I could relate to and trust. I had, to this point, little regard for therapy or therapists. While I was certainly aware, that it had helped my mother through endless and seemingly bottomless crises, her flair for histrionics and her complete and public deification of Dr. Cotton, her psychiatrist, created for me a reaction formation regarding therapy. I spent the next weeks getting past this dilemma. I have to assume that those therapists that I did subsequently develop a therapeutic relationship with must have dealt with my aversions successfully, as I spent forty years of my professional career in the "helping profession."

The therapy search process was, thankfully, short and successful. Dr. Weiner was smart, real, empathic, and not a pushover. I was fully prepared to dump my anxiety and newly developed dependency on his doorstep. He wasn't having any of it. He handled my vulnerability and need to know his whereabouts and vacation schedules at all times, with a straightforward and calm demeanor. All of my demands for this breach of his privacy were met with: " Harry, what might happen to you if I am unavailable? What are your fears about?" I fought through my embarrassment and shared with him: "I would feel abandoned, and overwhelmingly bored. Just now, I feel that when the person

I rely on for help is unavailable, I might go into a state of permanent panic, irreversible panic."

It was becoming increasingly clear to me that, even before our European jaunt, the anxiety that I felt, when Norman was unavailable or visiting his PI lover Amy, must have been connected to my fear of being alone with my aimless self. The need to feel that I could reach Dr. Weiner, even though I never attempted it, became increasingly important in the first several months of our year and a half relationship. The conclusion of each session, in the early stages of our therapeutic meetings, brought about increased anxiety. Weekends, when I felt that I was out of communication with him, seemed interminable. I never quite adjusted to the prospect of meeting another patient in Dr. Weiner's waiting room. I often felt the need to announce, to anyone in the waiting room, that I was delivering an important parcel to him or that I was a distant relative visiting from out of town. Not that anyone really cared.

Twice weekly, and then one therapy session per week, proved to be a significant budgetary challenge. I was now getting closer to receiving a Bachelor of Arts degree from City College and had been paying for my therapy with part time work and student loans. Dr. Weiner was careful in sharing his opinions with me. "Harry, it would be good to continue treatment for a while longer, but the resentment that you are feeling, about such a large part of your weekly budget dedicated to treatment is not helpful in our process." We explored other alternatives. And so, after a year and a half, our relationship concluded. I arranged interviews with a number of psychoanalytic institutes that Dr. Weiner recommended. I was no longer feeling acute anxiety and felt increasingly stable and rational. I continued, however, to be afflicted with an intense claustrophobia and a not-very-well disguised need to be symbolically in the vicinity of a protective authority figure.

For several years, prior to our European excursion, I worked in the Wall Street area of New York. My morning commute from upper Manhattan, was a forty five minute compressed, sweaty, eminently forgettable ride on New York's IND Eighth Avenue subway line. Despite, mid-tunnel delays, often lasting fifteen minutes or longer, no air conditioning and the luck of the draw with your crammed in neighbors, I felt nothing but an eagerness to get to work on time. Now, I was reluctant to step on to an elevator, for fear that it would stall. I often carried a tranquilizer wrapped in a crinkled paper napkin as security, should I encounter a feeling of inescapable closure- I never used it, but, it was comforting to know that it was accessible.

It was my luck, that New York Psychoanalytic Institute offered me an opportunity for ongoing and dramatically subsidized analysis, if I would commit to a two year period of five day per week analysis. I agreed to this arrangement, which actually lasted three years, although I had ongoing reservations about this process assuming such centrality in my life.

The hiatus between my therapeutic relationship with Dr. Weiner and his very full time replacement, Dr. Glass, proved to be brief. Aside from providing me with a legitimate cover for strolling on Park Avenue, where his office was located, Dr. Glass added an enormous amount to my life. I had become an avid reader, often reading three books at time, and had absorbed a great deal from texts of Freud, Jung and Joseph Campbell's treatises on mythology in many cultures and locales. I was hoping to impress my new therapeutic ally with my ability to intellectually interpret dreams. He would gently, but firmly, channel my discussions back to my associations and feelings.

One afternoon, some six months into our relationship, I entered his office, received his perfunctory greeting nod and, for a change, eagerly strode to the blue, sloped couch. It was that azure blue couch, where I lay facing away from him, where so much of my monologue emanated. I struggled to understand how my vapid comments and uninspiring daily life could be, even remotely interesting or helpful. Until today. I felt energized, and was eager to share my dream of the previous night.

"So, I was on this blue raft floating down a fast moving river, heading toward roiling rapids. I was able to steer around them and evade dangerous, mysterious fish and rocky shoals. I felt pretty capable and reasonably secure of my navigational skills. But, there was this pervasive feeling that more danger was just around the next bend. I held onto that blue raft so tightly."

"What are your thoughts about that dream?"

"Lots of dangers being overcome by me and many more out there on the horizon."

"Have you thought about the color of the couch that you are lying on?"

Lying on a couch with Dr. Glass sitting behind me, out of my line of vision, took some getting used to. I often imagined that he was working on his grocery shopping list. When I would share these thoughts with him, he would always bring the conversation back to me and my feelings. "Dr. Glass, I always resented, or so I thought, being the center of attention for my mother, growing up on 165th street. I often felt that she used me as a vehicle for antagonizing my father and making him feel rejected. I don't mind, however, being the center of attention here." Discussing my feelings about every seemingly inconsequential utterance I made got a bit annoying at times, but was very helpful as it continued to shed light on my feelings about just about everything. This helpful, three year relationship ended with the mutual agreement that I had benefitted substantially from the therapeutic experience. And, I was about to embark on a new direction in my life: marriage to Aviva.

Within weeks after entering City College as a matriculating day student, I met Merle. Merle was smart, attractive and had a wry sense of humor. Our relationship lasted two years and was highlighted by, and perhaps most interesting at, its denouement. At Merle's urging, I applied, together with her, for a summer position as a counselor at Camp Surprise Lake, a Jewish summer camp at the foothills of New York's Catskill Mountains. I loved the outdoors, could play sports for hours non-stop, liked the prospect of working with teens and welcomed getting out of the city and away from the sweltering New York summers. I got the job after a less than scintillating interview and settled on a compensation sum of one hundred ten dollars for the three camp sessions, each one lasting three weeks.

Two weeks later, I arrived at the designated gathering spot in the Bronx, where we would be met by the camp's assistant director. We were then to board a bus for the hour and a half ride to the camp grounds. My packing consisted of cramming some baggy shorts, tee shirts, and shredded underwear, into a well-worn duffle bag. It was surprisingly mild for an early, New York June day. As I rounded the corner from the public bus stop, I saw a group of twentyish men and women waiting at the designated spot. Merle was already there and greeted me with a hug. This was intended to be a mini vacation and an opportunity for continued bonding between us. It turned out to be anything but that.

Standing off on the periphery of the assembled counselors-to-be, was a shy-looking, delicate featured, young woman. Her brown, almond eyes, and delicate cheek bones highlighted her gentle features. Her slender, regal neck was partially hidden by a flowing mane of wavy, brown hair. She caught my involuntary fixation on her. Charles De Gaulle's famous, *"tout est perdu,"* all is lost comment, upon realizing that France would fall in World War Two, flashed through my mind.

As I think back today, I am struck by the instantaneous eradication of my two year relationship with Merle. When does the notoriously unreliable chemical attraction trump all reason? Is it, that in retrospect, we only retrieve the success stories? To this day, I clearly recall the first visual contact with Aviva; the demure curling of her lips in a begrudging, barely perceptible smile. I was captivated.

I could not take my eyes off her, and worked hard to keep it from being obvious to Merle. Aviva was to be the camp's dance counselor. As fate would have it, Merle and Aviva were assigned to be bunkmates for the duration of the summer. They became chummy during the first week of camp, while my complete infatuation with Aviva intensified. I found myself avoiding Merle and looking for every opportunity to communicate with Aviva. I was only too happy to learn that the feelings were mutual. We moved at warp speed to begin a torrid love affair. I was completely enthralled and could think of little else.

A week's training passed quickly, and we soon found ourselves waiting at the designated arrival area for the campers of session one. To my surprise and chagrin, my group was comprised of twelve teens, ages twelve to fourteen. These were not the young men that I had hoped for: malleable, craft-oriented, and most importantly, interested in, or at least curious about, dance classes. Aviva, the dance specialist, would conduct one hour classes with groups that selected dance as an elective activity. My assigned group was straight out of the tough, Brooklyn, Red Hook neighborhood, complete with rolled up sleeves to their shoulders, long, slicked back hair and budding, serious physiques. I could relate to these kids, but my primary motivation had become how to get this anomalous group to select dance activities so that I could spend time with Aviva.

After a brief tour of the camp grounds, I reviewed a schedule of core and elective activities with my likable and funny group. I knew that we would get along fine. Before deciding definitively on week one's activities, I asked, "O.K., guys what is it that you would like to do most often while here at camp?" After the expected macho banter of: "gettin' togeder with some of those nice lookin' broads," they answered in virtual unison, "playing baseball."

"Okay, guys, here's my offer: you come to dance classes twice a week, and I will play baseball with you through every lunch period for three weeks. Lunch sucks anyway," I added. They agreed with my proposal, but they looked perplexed and suspicious. Upon leaving our first dance session, one of the group members said, "Hey man, after seein' Aviva, we all understand your bargain with us. She is hot." I did not have lunch once during that three week period, and was commended by administration for my dedication to the group and for spending valuable lunch breaks with them.

Merle, however, was not as effusive in her accolades. She put Aviva in a difficult conundrum. Merle confided in Aviva, her bosom bunkmate, "I sense that Harry is attracted to another woman in our camp. I'm really not sure how to handle it. Should I just confront him?" I was ecstatic to be nowhere near that conversation.

When that Pandora's Box was opened, and the truth revealed, Merle, to our great relief, packed her bags and left camp that same day. I believe that I still have the book, by Jules Feiffer, "Harry the Rat With Women," that Merle sent me at the conclusion of the summer. As retribution for sending that book, or as the subplot of a cosmic comedy wrought upon Merle by unknowable forces, she found employment at another Jewish camp and was assigned to a division named: "The Aviva Division."

Chapter Ten

MY RELATIONSHIP WITH Aviva was now unencumbered and devoid of any sense of rational, dignified reserve. As our affair preceded "Downton Abbey," who knew from reserve? Had I committed myself to my nascent football career with the same total immersion that I'd committed to this relationship, I might have progressed further than I did. Young, beautiful, vital and in the camp spotlight as a performing dancer as well, others tried to hit on Aviva, including the much older, married, camp's assistant director. I weathered that storm and our relationship intensified. I owe much to that Red Hook Dozen, as they loved playing an hour and a half (half hour, post meal rest time, included) of baseball seven days a week for three weeks. They tolerated the twice, weekly dance classes with silent dignity.

The three week session flew by and Aviva and I developed an itinerary for the three day, mid- session, break from camp. We planned a day in Cold Springs, the nearest town to camp, and two days in New York City. Our loosely wrought schedule included a visit to Aviva's West End Avenue apartment, a quick tour of the furnished room which I had recently rented, and lunch with my parents (I had yet to notify them).

I don't recall leaving our Cold Springs motel room, even for lunch. We laughed at Aviva's description of our rented room: "Let's call this, our thirty dollar a day mildew special." Even the peeling wallpaper, incoherently hung photographs of quail hunts, and the amateurish oil paintings of bounding deer, managed not to affect our aesthetic sensibilities. We were not there to remodel the accommodations. I do recall, however, how silly I felt registering as Mr. and Mrs. Stern: Aviva was nineteen and I looked about the same age, although I was three years her senior.

Reluctantly, we set out the next morning for New York City from the town's central bus station. The one hour ride to the George Washington Bridge Port Authority bus terminal brought us in around mid day. It was pleasant, and so Aviva and I walked the thirteen blocks to my parent's apartment building. We had no luggage, having crammed a backpack with minimal necessities.

We arrived at my parent's street and as usual, Mrs. Strom (famous for her thirty dollar loan to me), Mrs. Ligum and three or four other beach chair regulars, were reclining in their chaise lounges in the area shaded by three broad, cherry trees. The hospital's garden, just across the street from my parent's building, provided shade and relief from the summer heat. They, and several other neighborhood fixtures missing that day, formed the gauntlet that I had to negotiate on an almost daily basis, during beach chair weather, from May through September. I often wished for inclement weather just to avoid answering: "Harry, that was pretty late that you got in last night, no?" "Who was the girl we saw you with on Thursday…Jewish?"

I was gauging Aviva's first impression of the neighborhood. The only buildings on our block with elevators, were the book ends on Broadway, to the east and Fort Washington Avenue, to the west. Our tenement was one of the interior pages to those book ends, a five story walk up. I pointed up to our front windows on the third floor, the ones with the corroded, metal, child window guards, there to ensure, that all of the adult tenants of apartment thirty two, would be safe when they looked out of the windows.

Aviva's apartment was on The Upper West Side, in a traditionally middle class neighborhood. It struck me as elitist that, despite my parent's building being some five miles north of that more affluent neighborhood, and on the actual, upper west side of Manhattan, the more prestigious neighborhood was called, the Upper West Side. It almost seemed as if our working class neighborhood was an unimportant appendage to Manhattan.

Unexplained goose bumps came over me as we climbed the three flights of stairs, but I shook them off. Aviva would certainly wow my parents, and they would be as happy to see me as I them. I had not visited them for a while, as I had moved into a furnished room in the Columbia University area. It was only a few steps to apartment thirty two once we arrived at the third floor landing. I rang the doorbell and soon understood why my prescient anxiety was well-founded. My mother answered the door, and greeted us with a concerned frown and a nervous smile. She hugged Aviva warmly. My father welcomed us with a wrinkled brow, that I recognized as his concerned look.

Missing was the unmistakable pungent aroma of sauerbraten, smothered in caramelized onion and red cabbage with plump raisins that generally greeted my visits. My mother would bake a heavenly, angel food cake and top it with whipped cream when she knew I was coming for lunch or dinner. Something wonderful that she would casually prepare, even for my surprise visits, didn't seem to be on her radar screen today. Nothing. No aromas. I was on guard.

My sister Josephine's presence was a surprise, as was the accompaniment of her two toddler children. She had appeared at my parent's home that morning, with no notice of her pending arrival. She had decided, unbeknownst to her husband, to board a bus and escape the horrid marriage that she had naively inserted herself into. This was merely the prelude to the three additional times that this escape occurred. Each new episode found her carrying one additional child, as she boarded that same New York City-bound bus from a small town in rural upstate New York.

Aviva sat on the love seat, diagonally across from the pink, living room couch with its familiar rose colored, floral patterns. I kissed Josie, as she preferred to be called, and hugged my two adorable nieces. Josie was still pretty at twenty-six, but was already succumbing to the ravages of an abusive and lonely, mountain top life.

Growing up, we had never been close. Her three and a half year seniority seemed like an impassable mountain range between us. The essence of our relationship in our youth, was her benign neglect. We mostly went our separate ways. I would become the center of attention when she would complain to my parents about my rudeness. Our relationship began inauspiciously, when my parents had the temerity to bring me home as a newborn infant from Beth Israel Hospital.

Our Aunt Valli, in half German and half barely, decipherable English, recounted to me one Sunday afternoon, how, when visiting our parents, she'd intercepted Josie heading toward my crib brandishing a pair of scissors. That incident pales in comparison with my mother's description of an act that made her very wary of the degree of Josie's jealousy and her creativity in displaying it. On a late, autumn, Sunday afternoon my parents, Josie, then five, and me, in my baby carriage, stopped in front of Hanscomb's Bakery Shop on 163rd street.

My parents, upon entering the shop, asked Josie to watch over the baby carriage which was parked perpendicular to the bakery, as it was situated at the top of a steep slope. To my father's shock, as he looked out of the large plate glass window, he saw Josie release the carriage brake and aim the carriage downhill and toward Broadway's traffic. My mother describes my father's surprising athleticism as he bounded out of the crowded store, raced into the street and grabbed the carriage's front handle as it was gliding toward a trafficked area. I have never asked what happened after that as I am certain that it was met with Josie's protestations of innocence.

I felt a sense of sadness for her now, mixed with my love, as she was the victim of her own impetuous and irrational decisions. Aviva must be thinking, I feared, that we were a pretty crazy family. Josie's resolve never to return to her brutalizing husband had already begun to erode. Our parents were supportive, as she unburdened the misfortune of her unhappy marriage. After an hour of reviewing Josie's litany of complaints about Fred, it was becoming increasingly apparent, that she would return to her mountain enclave. It was fruitless, at that point, to have any meaningful dialogue with my parents, although I wanted them to get to know Aviva. They appeared emotionally drained, and focused exclusively on Josie.

Aviva and I received warm hugs goodbye and left my parents apartment, assuring them that we would return for a long, and less adventurous, visit at the end of the camping season. I kissed Josie and told her I would be around to help her and would come to visit for a week after camp. Aviva and I left and made our way toward Broadway and boarded the number four bus heading for my 112th street residence. I wanted to show Aviva my newly rented accommodations and stop for lunch at the 111th street luncheonette. I was determined not to be apologetic about our family tumult, but I did want to offer a brief explanation.

"It is hard to call Josie's marriage to Fred purely catastrophic, as they have produced two lovely children." I wanted to give Aviva a brief review of that fateful decision of my older sister. "Fred, a burly, handsome, bachelor moved into apartment thirty five just across the small hallway from our apartment thirty two. He was thirty-six and Josephine was barely eighteen. We had no reason to suspect that a sexual relationship was flourishing no more than twenty five feet away from apartment thirty two." Aviva listened attentively. "Not long after that unwelcome revelation, they eloped and moved to a small house on a three hundred acre farm in rural New York, that Fred had purchased for a pittance." It was easier to suppress most of these details, but I wanted Aviva to have a better understanding of what she had witnessed.

"Fred had been a boxer in the Merchant Marines, was an avid hunter and, on occasion, had shared with me some details of his Harlem, bred background. With great pride he recounted how he often had to protect his rooftop pigeon coops by firing his

Winchester 30-30 at those he suspected to be the raiders of his territory. I can only surmise what the results were, as Fred had demonstrated to me his uncanny marksmanship, on my visit to their mountain home. With a calm, sure aim, he hit a small woodchuck at over four hundred yards distance with a high caliber rifle. He drank, and would become quite abusive to Josie. Her current flight from her home may have been the result of one of those episodes."

"Why did she ever enter into this relationship and why stay?" Aviva asked.

"Josie always had an overriding need to be loved and needed. Those traits are dangerous for a very attractive, blonde, teenage girl continually searching for personal validation in her home. Josie was not one to share her feelings, and kept much of the usual teenage tumult bottled up. I am not sure how much the stress of the first two years of her life spent fleeing the Nazi killing machine, one formative year as a refugee in Casablanca, and my mother's emotional paralysis, for the first three or four years after their arrival in the USA, ultimately affected her."

Aviva was an attentive listener and asked insightful and incisive questions. My answers to those inquiries were generally anything but incisive. I too often took the "scenic" route as a response as opposed to the more direct "highway" approach.

"How did your parents respond to Josie's eloping and marrying Fred?" "My father didn't speak to her for one year, and said that he regarded her as having died." Even saying this made me shudder. "My mother, on the other hand, took a more balanced and liberal approach, and hoped for the best, despite her foreboding feelings. It took my father's dear brother, Lazo and me, several heart-to-hearts, to convince him that this was not what he really intended. His love for his eldest daughter eclipsed his disappointment, and that she needed a strong relationship with her father, now, more than ever." "In truth," I concluded, as we were arriving at the 113th street bus stop, "our younger sister Melinda was always closest to Josie and was her confidante. I was never sure how much of this saga Josie shared with her in later years."

   The bus driver pulled his number four bus close to the curb, and impatiently allowed us about ten seconds to make our way down the steps onto the street. We proceeded south one block to my new address on 112th street and walked up the two flights. This was the first apartment building that I had lived in that had an elevator, it would be weeks before I began using it. As I fumbled in my pocket for the keys, I was hoping that none of the five, young women living in similar accommodations across the narrow hallway, would open their apartment door to greet us. Not yet, anyway.

   If Aviva was impressed with my sixty square foot room, she did an excellent job concealing it.

   We walked down the dark, narrow apartment corridor past four other rooms, rented as well, but currently vacant. After a brief look at the communal kitchen, we left and headed east toward Broadway and the luncheonette on 111th street.

   An intense and unwelcome nervousness gripped me as we entered the restaurant. I had no idea how I would be able to overcome the queasiness that had overtaken me. With no external distractions and no sexual encounters expected during lunch, I was fearful that Aviva would find me boring and pedestrian. I fought off my anxiety-induced nausea with determination. Somehow, our time together at camp seemed surreal, with an other world reality. Now, thrust back into my "real" world, the anxiety that continued to debilitate me at the most inconvenient times, reappeared. A familiar wave of stomach churning was gripping me. I hoped that the beads of sweat on my forehead were attributed to poor air conditioning.

We sat at a booth and were greeted with feigned conviviality by our past-middle-age waitress. I was thankful for this brief interlude as it offered me a few moments to try to calm myself.

Aviva ordered a salad. What else would a dancer do? I ordered a tuna fish sandwich and asked the waitress to hold the mayo. Aviva later told me that she had never heard anyone say, "hold the mayo" before. What she did not tell me then, was that she was turned off by what sounded to her like a boorish, uneducated comment. Many of our friends would later say, that living with me for so many subsequent years, only validated her initial concern.

We hurried through our meal and left the luncheonette heading south, having agreed that we would walk the mile or so to Aviva's 89th street apartment. As we turned west on 90th street and then onto West End Avenue, Aviva pointed to her building. I was impressed. I had never been in a building with an entrance canopy.

The fifth floor apartment's layout was nicely designed: a modest living area, a spacious bedroom and a small kitchen with a minuscule dining area. Framed photographs of New York cityscapes were arranged in asymmetric patterns at the entryway from the corridor. A rattan chair had a colorful, woolen, Mexican blanket draped over it. There was no couch in the living room, but the two tan, love seats, at forty five degree angles, made for an attractive arrangement. We spent the evening in her apartment and set out the following morning for the bus terminal at Penn Station and the hour and a half return ride to Camp Surprise Lake.

The remaining weeks of the summer passed quickly. Aviva performed in several camp programs. I was impressed with her grace, fluid movement, and professional stage presence. During that same period, I had two additional eminently forgettable groups of twelve campers. The challenge, humor and raucous, street banter of my first group, was missing. I counted the days until the season's end, trying to imagine what my post summer relationship with Aviva would look like. Aviva was for me, the ideal woman who, to this day, made other relationships seem tenuous and meaningless.

We returned to New York City in mid August, Aviva to her apartment, and me to my Holden Caulfield-like room. Over the next month, I stayed with Aviva almost every night. She introduced me to her mountain lion-like cat with the misnomer Grushenka. Years earlier, upon retrieving him from the humane society, Aviva and her mother believed the cat was a female. Their first visit to the vet for shots, disabused them of that modest error, but they liked the name and so, some ten years later, he was still named Grushenka. As if through some preternatural sense, Grushenka knew what page of the newspaper I was reading and claimed it as his territorial resting place. I would continually ask Aviva how I might preserve my right to the New York Times sports section, as I had paid for the paper.

"Shoo him off," was her answer. "Aviva you have to understand my reluctance to 'shoo him off'. I regard him as a home grown Tyrannosaurus Rex. I've never been accustomed to so large a house pet." My sole experience with a pet had been a one day, disaster with my parents. I was about seven years old when Giovanni, the friendly, Italian peanut vendor, with a beautifully arched handlebar mustache, asked me if I would like a small dog. Giovanni was a fixture on the corner of 165th street and Broadway for years. With his well-worn peanut cart with an American flag painted on both sides, and its familiar, steam-powered whistle, he sold bags of warm, unsalted peanuts in the shell for ten cents a bag.

In many Eastern European households, a house pet was unthinkable. A household animal was thought to be unclean and, with so many shtetl families impoverished, the thought of feeding a pet was looked upon as frivolous. The association with dogs for so many Holocaust survivors was that of baying German Shepherds, that often accompanied the Gestapo, as they rounded up Jews for eventual deportation and execution. Little of this registered in my seven year old mind, and I answered, "Sure, we would like one." "I will bring it tomorrow," Giovanni said happily.

Well, he did bring the cutest, brown, long-eared puppy the following day. I thanked him and carried this gentle, squirming bundle of fur, licking my hands and face, home to apartment thirty two. My mother wanted to know if I had totally lost my mind, but held the dog warmly which attested to its incredible cuteness. When my father came home from work, he was less amused, but agreed to give it a try. To the puppy's misfortune, it cried all night long, and peed in several spots other than the Daily News sports sections spread out on the floor to absorb those puppy miscues. The following morning the puppy was on a return path to Giovanni, who reluctantly agreed to take it back.

Until that evening in Aviva's home, the extent of my domicile pet experience had been that one fateful experience. I soon mustered the courage to gently and beseechingly ease Grushenka off my reading material. By the time I felt sufficiently comfortable with my newfound feline facility, my relationship with Aviva was to experience a sea change. The month since we had returned from camp passed quickly and seemed only to solidify and intensify our relationship, which, as it turns out, was our temporary undoing. For that short period, we proceeded with our individual lives, Aviva with dance classes and rehearsals and me with my CCNY classes in full swing. We had breakfast and dinners together and spent evenings side-by-side.

One morning, Aviva was prepared to leave for a two day performance gig in Pittsburgh. I remained in bed for a while longer. The previous night I had left Aviva an amateurishly worded note which ended with, "…I love you too much." Her written response on the note read, "…and that's what worries me. Let's back off." I was dumbfounded, as I had fully expected a similarly, gushy response, although that would have been out of character, as Aviva was more visceral than verbal. But, I got it. In yet another inimitable personality foible, I had allowed my passion to override the reigns of restraint. I loved her to distraction, and felt that it might even be mutual, but for Aviva, at nineteen years of age, it might have gotten scary. That morning was the last time I saw Aviva, for almost two years.

Chapter Eleven

MY AVIVA-LESS LIFE was about to begin. The only contact that I had with her was through the pay telephone that the landlord of my apartment recently installed. I hoped to hear that perhaps I'd misinterpreted her response to my saccharine note. She reiterated her belief, that one day we would be reunited, but not at that time. My response was defensive, "How frivolous I was to have initiated an affair with a nineteen year old." The fact that she was more mature than I, at three years her senior, was not factored into my thoughts. Upon the conclusion of that call, I knew that I would be navigating uncharted waters, that for now, did not include Aviva.

I began to make as much hallway noise as possible, fumbling for my keys, inadvertently banging my grocery bags against the door of the five women living just across the hallway. My determination to carry on with a passable social life surprised me, as I was bereft at the loss of Aviva. My day classes at CCNY were now met with a renewed dedication and intensified focus. My good fortune was evidenced by my rarely crossing paths with Merle and that I had no reason to believe that she had taken out a contract on my life.

I secured a three quarter time position at the American Numismatic Society, a venerable coin museum, then located on the Audubon Campus, at 155th street in Washington Heights. My position, assistant to the museum's photographer, brought me in contact with two people of importance to me. Mike, the photography department director, was a very unusual synthesis of an Italian, blue collar personality and sensitive and extraordinary photographer. Mike could make two thousand year old Roman coins come to life through his lighting and photographic genius.

Of greater interest to me, and to him, was his abstract photography, which was exhibited in many prestigious galleries across New York. Mike was effusive about his work and confrontational when I would naively ask him what the photograph represented. He would prod me about what he termed my "somnambulistic state," failing, he would say, to be sufficiently inquisitive and creative. He would cite, in his criticism, Gurdjieff, a Russian occultist, who espoused "enlightened Christianity," and lectured that the average person sleepwalks through life. My two years with him unshackled much of my provincial thinking about modern art. In many ways Mike confronted my conventional thinking about art and my misguided need to continually identify images in his abstract photography. "Harry, you are so blocked from allowing yourself to absorb the emotions stimulated by art. Why can't you let go and allow yourself just to experience things without your internal censor?" Questions I often asked myself.

During the years of my employment at the museum, I spent many lunch hours wandering through the beautiful, Audubon campus that also housed the American Indian Museum. Frank, who worked as an administrative assistant to the museum Director, would often pass by me in the outer courtyard eating a sandwich, in the shadow of the ten foot high statue of El Cid astride his horse. On other occasions, I would lunch leaning against the bronze statue of Don Quixote and his bedraggled steed, Rocinantes. I often wondered why, given the brutal New York summer heat, I was subjecting myself to lunch in the sun and to this self-flagellation.

My ongoing association was with my father and his working conditions. I had recently visited him at work at the women's rainwear sweat shop that his wealthy cousin owned. It was a sweltering, summer day. As I entered his work area, the cutting room, I breathed in deeply, trying to catch my breath in the suddenly oppressive heat. No air-conditioning, only several, free-standing industrial sized fans, ensuring that the hot air of the shop was evenly distributed. I was so saddened that my brilliant and cultured father was working in such primitive and uncaring conditions. My throat tightened and I could feel tears threatening to make a most unwelcome appearance.

My father came to greet me wearing an undershirt and a plaid bandana around his neck. No complaints, no apologies. It would be difficult for me, from that day on, to enjoy my lunch in the nicely, air-conditioned museum lunchroom while my father and his fifty co-workers had appreciably less comfortable arrangements. When I discussed this with Dr. Glass, I say discussed, but it was yet another soliloquy, as he would ask me what I made of my lunchtime sunbathing. "Dr. Glass, I just couldn't bear to see my father suffering."

My furnished room, which faced a rear alleyway, was not air-conditioned either, but it mattered little, as the months that I lived there were the autumn and winter months of that year. I had introduced myself to Fraser, a nice looking guy, who had a similar room rental arrangement, but with a front exposure. More interesting to me, however, was Jane, one of the young ladies from across the hall, who knocked on our front door one evening.

"Can I come in?" Jane, attractive in a mid-western, wholesome way, had large and mournful brown eyes. I had become aware that, every time I clumsily, but purposefully, banged against their door as I pretended to fumble for my keys, she appeared to ask if I needed help. She had long, wavy, brown hair, that streamed halfway down her stout frame, which bordered on chubbiness. Her round face seemed pulled taut, highlighting her beautiful, clear and virtually translucent complexion. I was disconcerted as she locked her stare on me. I informed her that I was alone as all the other tenants were out, but I was pleased to formally make her acquaintance.

I wasn't really surprised, that within a half hour we were involved in an athletic, sexual encounter that belied the brevity of our acquaintance. The rapidity with which this occurred made me think that this had been a virtual scenario that she had rehearsed for some time. Our one dimensional relationship continued for several weeks. It might have been the best and the worst of all worlds combined. What could be better than saying goodnight and having your partner walk ten feet to her apartment; but then, what could be worse than saying goodnight to your partner and having her walk ten feet to her apartment?

An evening in September found me sitting on my bed reading. As I had no chairs in the room, my bed served as a chair, couch, storage unit, bed and dining room table. A knock on the apartment's front door had more urgency than usual. I took that to be a good sign, as Jane often came to visit me just after dinner. "I hate to be a bother, but I've got to talk with you." Jane often seemed apologetic about something, but I rarely asked her about her feelings or concerns, for fear that she would respond. This was different. No niceties, no greetings, just a morose look on her face. "Have you been hurt? Are you ill?" "Harry, I've missed my period." Jane paused and looked down at the tattered, checkered, six by six foot carpet and slowly and wistfully whispered: "I'm pregnant." I couldn't speak. My stupidity, my naiveté, my immaturity and my near the surface anxiety all merged simultaneously.

"I've talked this over with two of my apartment mates and I've decided that I'm going to get an abortion." Her friends had experience with a sympathetic, Cuban doctor in the Bronx, where he would perform the procedure.

I was in shock. "Why," I kept asking myself, "would this happen, just because we had unprotected sex almost every night for a month?" My worldliness was a thing of beauty.

Recovering slowly, I asked about some logistical matters and the cost.

"Three hundred and fifty dollars." About six times my week's museum salary. I had only the thinnest of emotional connection to Jane beyond our two hour evening soirees, but I now found myself canvassing my inventory of gallantries to reassure her. I swallowed. "We're going to do this together, Jane." I put my arms around her warmly, told her that we would overcome this, and that I would provide all of the funds required. I certainly wasn't feeling warm, as simultaneous with my outwardly supportive response, was my more practiced and well-worn reaction of fleeing from an emotional scene.

After two days, all the support that I had garnered was a commitment from my down-the-hall neighbor Fraser, to drive us to and from the doctor's Bronx office. My cash reserve was comprised of a week's round trip bus fare on the number four bus to The Numismatic Society and enough for a deli sandwich for lunch. As if by a divine sprinkling of angel dust, Frankie and I entered the museum together on the third morning after my seismic shock. Frankie, or Frances to his mother, came from my old, Washington Heights neighborhood. There were positives and negatives about the nature of our relationship. Frankie always regarded me as a hustler.

This perception was undoubtedly formed as a result of the cast of characters that I associated with when I was still in high school and shortly after my ignominious ending at G. Dub. Many of those neighborhood friends were familiar to Frankie, who knew that they were potheads, who later graduated to more sinister stimulants. Frankie was always on the periphery of neighborhood cliques, and I often wondered who his friends were. I went out of my way to chat with him then; I liked him, as he had an intelligent, wry sense of humor.

Frankie, a devout Catholic, graduated from the neighborhood Christian oasis, Saint Rose of Lima, Primary School and then, All Hallows Catholic High School. With his father no longer on the scene, Frankie and his mother attended Sunday Mass and other church functions with regularity. When I would pass them on Broadway on their way to church, Frankie's limp was barely discernible. The hitch in his gait, was the result of being struck by a car on Broadway and 163rd street.

That Frankie was never short of cash, and often pulled out a roll of bills to pay for his deli sandwiches, lent credence to the neighborhood lore, that he had received a substantial insurance settlement for his street crossing misfortune. A prolonged hospital stay only added fuel to the neighborhood pundits' debate about the size of his insurance settlement. My rough and dirty estimate was that the three hundred fifty dollar loan I was about to ask him for, would make only a modest impact on Frankie. After all, he had many thousands of insurance dollars, that the neighborhood intelligentsia had estimated as Frankie's net worth. As usual, I had both an inside and an outside track.

Frankie liked me and I genuinely liked him. We found ourselves working in the same museum albeit, on different floors. Over the next few days, I would ensure that Frankie had an amiable lunch partner...me. On each of those lunch days, I chatted with Frankie about some new college friends that I had met, in particular a young woman named Jane, who had no contact with her parents for years. Sadly, she now required immediate, but unspecified, surgery. Frankie was intelligent, friendly, lonely and generous. His religious beliefs were in conformity with the rigorous doctrines of Catholicism. His slightly tarnished silver cross had been dangling prominently from the same chain around his neck for years.

On some level, lying to someone so devout in his religious beliefs, offended my rather malleable sensitivities. But, urgency trumped my reservations. I knew that, neither Frankie nor his mother, would be even moderately swayed by a young woman's need for an abortion. Catholic doctrine was eminently clear on this subject. I summoned up the courage to ask Frankie for the short term loan to help pay for the lifesaving surgery required by Jane. The following Monday, Frankie arrived with the exact amount, and required of me only a handshake and a verbal commitment that I would repay him as soon as possible.

The following Tuesday, in an intermittent cool rain, Fraser drove Jane, her friend and me to the physician in the Bronx. After what seemed like an interminable wait in Fraser's car, both women emerged from the clinic, Jane looking as if she'd been in a barroom brawl. The doctor assured them that Jane needed only two days rest. On the drive home, they informed us that there were no complications, other than their revelation that the Cuban doctor was not allowed to practice medicine in New York.

My mind was already a thousand miles away, thinking of a payment plan to Frankie. I was pleased and relieved that there were no physical complications. Jane was a lovely, trusting, needy woman for whom I had a rapidly dwindling reservoir of empathy. We had both entered into our ephemeral relationship with needs emblazoned on our foreheads, and a grand abundance of myopia and naiveté. Upon learning that Jane was physically OK, what was left for me was bidding adieu to those sad, puppy eyes.

Shortly after that eventful ride to the physician with Jane, I moved to an apartment in the Bronx, just across the 181st street bridge connecting upper Manhattan to the Bronx. The apartment, (I rarely stayed overnight), was rented for one year and was a stone's throw from the bridge. I enquired several times about Jane's health and state of mind, both of which appeared on the mend, while all that I could think about was Aviva and how to "accidentally" come in contact with her.

I was fortunate that the apartment in the Bronx was only a modest walk from my parent's home. My father had just suffered a heart attack in October of 1965. Thankfully, he survived and was in a ward at The Columbia Presbyterian Hospital just across the street from their apartment. He remained in the hospital for two weeks, after which he would participate in physical therapy sessions. I visited daily, to shave him, as he felt unclean if he had not shaved and was too weak to shave himself.

While visiting him on a blustery November evening, the lights throughout the hospital dimmed and noisy emergency generators rattled throughout the corridors. Elevators stopped running, my mother and Melinda were passengers on one of those suddenly motionless elevators. Thankfully, I had finished my father's daily shave, when we received the news that all of New York State, most of New England and cities in Canada, were affected by a cascading series of transformer shutdowns. The east coast had experienced a major blackout, and we were uncertain when the grids would be repaired.

I left my father, who took it all very calmly. I could not find which elevator bank my mother and sister were stuck in, but was comforted that many maintenance attendants and police were on duty, safely and calmly extricating the elevator passengers. I stepped outside, into an eerie blackness, with only car headlights and the occasional flashlight as the sole illumination.

I had not gotten the full impact of the blackout until arriving at the street level. No house lights, no store lights, no traffic lights, no lamp posts. I proceeded to walk north on a darkened Broadway toward 181st street. All subways were out of operation. City busses had pulled over to the side of the road. People were cordial to one another, helping the elderly and calming people's fears that this was not the prelude to a Russian army invasion. Transistor radios picked up some details, generally from unaffected cities, as many local transmitters were also non-functional.

Shortly after the repair of the power grids, a process which left hardened New Yorkers somewhat shaken out of their insularity, I moved once again, this time to east 92nd street in Manhattan. While an address on the upper East Side of New York generally carries with it a panache, indicative of swanky, high rise buildings with snooty doormen, this apartment was hardly in that category. Ancient three and four story walk ups were still to be found tucked in among the patrician's high rises. My new dwelling was a railroad flat, basically, one long room with arbitrary divisions each serving as a separate room. One needed a vivid imagination to visualize these room separations. The front room was sloped at a rakish angle and the area designated as the bedroom had a grimy, rear window facing a shaft of some sort. The sixty dollar a month rent was barely worth it.

The location was acceptable as it was a short walk to the more accommodating Third and Lexington Avenue shopping areas and the 92nd Street YMHA. All that was required of me to arrive at that venerable cultural hub, was that I bravely traverse the perennial seepage, searing odor of hops and yeast, and the armada of giant, black water bugs that had acquired a taste for the Knickerbocker Beer brewed right there, in the heart of Manhattan. This challenge remained formidable until the day I once again moved. The Y was important to me, as I had left my position at the museum, and I would inquire about a summer day camp position with that institution.

I received my B.A. degree in Language and Literature from CCNY in 1966. Had the degree been awarded some ten years later, I might have identified with a verse from 'Chorus Line,' "....Gee, I'm almost ready, but what for?" I certainly felt buoyed by the degree but, I was quite directionless professionally. Working as a day camp counselor for the summer was familiar to me and would, I hoped, give me some time to think of next steps. I had no problem with the interview and was asked to report to counselor training and orientation in two weeks.

I arrived early for that training session and had a chance to meet some of the other counselors attending orientation. Karyn, cocky and attractive in a Waspy way, sat next to me. Her speech brought Bryn Mawr or Vassar to mind, and her arrogant demeanor spoke of east side money. A few coffee rendezvouses later and I was able to pat myself on the back: she had graduated from Vassar and her father was the Chairman and founder of a well-known, stock exchange-listed company. Karyn soon became my latest diversion from my continued obsession with Aviva. Her Madison Avenue apartment had only the City in which it was located, in common with my east 92nd street sloped abode. For the next few months, I faced the difficult choice of living together with her in the luxurious apartment on the eighth floor as opposed to a daily crossing of the Knickerbocker Brewery moat.

Karyn was a bright, testy woman, who was searching for an independent identity. Her rich and powerful family was a source of financial, but not interpersonal, security. Her acceptance into the Adelphi University PhD program in Psychology appeared to me as the irony of the century. It was hard for me to imagine her in a helping profession as a compassionate and sympathetic therapist.

The few months that I enjoyed as a denizen of Madison Avenue, had produced several highlights in my life: Karyn was a fun, physical and intelligent, but emotionally fragile companion; shopping at the vastly, overpriced Gristede's Grocery Market on the corner of Madison Avenue, and charging it to Karyn's account, was nothing short of miraculous for me; and finally, having the doormen of her building refer to me as Mr. L, her family name, always made me smile. Our separation was inconvenient, not at all traumatic, and thrust me back into my sloped floor reality. I had no notion that Aviva was soon to re-enter my life.

Chapter Twelve

I MAINTAINED A TENUOUS, but as it turned out fortuitous, relationship with Howard. I first met both Howard and Zita in the weeks after we returned from Surprise Lake Camp, when it appeared that Aviva and I were destined for a long term relationship. Howard and Zita, Aviva's mother, married several years after her divorce from Aviva's father. He was a Professor at Columbia University's School of Social Work, had written numerous articles and books and, at six foot six inches, was imposing at the tennis net. Zita, recently awarded a PhD in psychology, was now focused on caring for her new born son Joshua. Howard and I shared an interest in Israel and discussed current social issues including President Johnson's recent declaration of "War on Poverty."

My discussions with Howard helped to provide some trajectory to my careening professional interests. He had just made a splash in the social work arena with his very interesting book, "Cottage Six." The book, a study of the culture formed in a residential treatment center for delinquents, maintained that life patterns that are developed in their neighborhoods, were replicated in an institution. That is, the tough individual in the outside world became the bully in the institution, the picked-on youngster assumed a scapegoat role in the residential setting. The research maintained, that a youngster being remanded by the juvenile justice system for therapeutic intervention, had their deviant behavior unwittingly reinforced in the institution that was treating them.

Howard arranged an interview for me with the research project director for the sequel to his seminal work, which was to be: "Cottage Seven." The research was conducted at Hawthorne Cedar Knolls Residential Institute, in Hawthorne, New York, about thirty five miles north of the city. Upon securing the position and a one month hence start date, it was evident that I would need a car. The new position, as a daytime cottage worker, and the need for a car, both proved to be of future importance to me.

And it started with Roger. He had been my friend for almost a decade. His parents had migrated from Puerto Rico some years prior to his birth. His father, a gruff, uncommunicative man, was the long-term superintendent of their building on 161st street and Riverside Drive. His mother was petite, friendly and smiled sympathetically when I conversed with her in my horrid Spanish. Roger was tough, immensely strong, and had two older brothers, one a neighborhood hustler and the oldest, a local union boss. No one in the neighborhood would knowingly cross his family.

Over the many years of our friendship, I had never been in Roger's apartment, located at the end of a dark and cavernous tunnel in the basement of their building. Only our mutual friend, Jackie, had been brave enough to knock on their door and was rewarded by their fearsome German Shepherd biting him on the calf. I regarded that creature as Hade's many-headed guard dog, Cerberus, and generally kept my distance.

Roger influenced my life in several unique and direct ways. In at least one instance, he may have actually saved my life. Perhaps the most dramatic incident occurred some years earlier in McGuire's bar on 162nd street. When I was eighteen, I barely passed for fifteen. Being served in a bar required continually keeping my identification handy, as I was frequently required to produce proof of age. By some ill-defined genetic mutation, I was able to win in almost every arm wrestling match I participated in. These tests of testosterone and machismo were frequently on display at McGuire's.

Roger, who was stronger than most human beings are supposed to be, couldn't beat me. Roger could easily lift a one hundred fifty pound metal ash can filled with ashes, that his father had shoveled out of the building's coal burning furnace. I was never sure whether my skill was a leverage issue or a cosmic determinant. One evening in McGuire's, Roger and I stopped in for a beer. The bar was a rowdy place, with the crowd's behavior held in check by the two burly bartenders, who made sure that the baseball bats behind the bar remained visible until closing.

Three men entered, clearly friends of many of the guys in the bar. One nicely dressed newcomer, sat next to me with a cast on his left arm. There was an arm wrestling contest that commenced. The new arrival, sitting next to me, asked me to move as he was arm wrestling. I asked if he would like to arm wrestle me. He smirked and said, "sure, Jew Boy." How did he know I was Jewish? I looked directly into his eyes, as I easily forced his arm down onto the counter, and held it there. He snarled, "do you know who I am? I'm Davey Brock."

As he angrily announced his name, Roger grabbed my left arm and started pulling me to the door. Thankfully, the bar was packed and Davey's angry announcement of his name was muffled in the drunken din. As we hurriedly exited the bar Roger said, "run as fast as you can, that guy is a connected mobster. I'm surprised he didn't shoot you on the spot." "Roger, you're joking, right?" No answer. We were both running as hard as we could. We raced into an apartment building a few blocks away and hid under the steps. That I am writing this account today, bears testimony to the fact that Davey and his associates' investigative skills were heavily influenced by their excessive alcohol consumption, and we managed to elude their angry chase.

Roger influenced the outcome of my life in a less direct, but for me, equally important manner. I was certain that his union connected brother would be an excellent recommendation source for a purchase that was to be of great significance to me.

I asked Roger if his brother had any connections with car dealerships where I might get a good deal. He gave me an address on Tremont Avenue in the Bronx. He forewarned me, that it was "not your traditional car dealer," and advised me that I would need to mention the referral from his brother. Despite Roger's instructions, I found myself walking up and down Tremont Avenue looking for something that remotely resembled a car dealership.

The address proved to be a full, covered parking lot that extended about a half block in length. I had passed it by several times before stopping in to ask whether this was the dealership. Standing at the entrance was someone who more closely resembled Godzilla than a car salesman. But, salesman he was. Had I known about the Sopranos then, I would have imagined that I was in the midst of a New Jersey episode. The burly, cigar smoking hulk standing between me and the entrance asked: "Why do you want to know about a car dealership?"

Choking a bit on the cigar smoke, I answered, "I'm interested in buying a car. Angie (Roger's brother) told me this was the place to come." I guess that Angie was the magic word as his demeanor and tone changed radically and he became more accommodating. "How much you wanna spend on a car?" "Three hundred is all I have," I answered. With my meager financial capability now divulged, he ushered me over to a row of cars, many with a variety of out-of-town license plates. Slowly, I reviewed the row of about thirty cars that were designated in my price range. Halfway down the aisle of cars, I stopped at a lovely, white, Karmann Ghia convertible.

"You like that one?" Godzilla asked.

"Looks pretty sharp, can I take it out for a quick spin?"

"Kid," he replied, not overly concerned with how I felt about being called 'kid,' "You gotta tell me if you want the car or not. You can test drive it all you like, but, once the car leaves here, it don't come back."

I didn't require inordinate analytical skills to understand that the conversation began and ended with my answer. I pulled out three one hundred dollar bills, leaving me with about two dollars for gas and said, "we got a deal." No paper work, no tax, no receipt, he handed me the owner's document and the keys and said, "Careful backin' out."

It was that spunky Karmann Ghia, my first car, that transported me to Hawthorne Cedar Knolls for my first day as a residential cottage worker. With a full tank of gas that left me close to penniless, I arrived at Hawthorne ready to begin my new job. My co-worker, Steve, was waiting for me in the administrative offices and escorted me to cottage seven. He had been a minor league pitcher whose baseball career had been shortened by a severe elbow injury. He seemed like a great guy, completely unpretentious and open.

The peeling, clapboard exterior of cottage seven screamed for a new paint job, the front flower bed resembled the Gobi Desert and the screen door was torn in two or three places. Twelve young men, ranging in age from fourteen to sixteen, were informally assembled in the spacious, but sparsely furnished, living room. My initial reaction was one of surprise, as only one of the residents was African-American. Later that afternoon, in response to my query about my surprise finding, Steve succinctly summed it up this way: "this is a residential treatment center that focuses on therapeutic intervention that is expensive. Sadly," he observed, "it seems that most juvenile courts will remand minorities to lock-up facilities."

The weeks passed quickly and I established a friendly, but not overly warm, rapport with the residents. I liked them and I think they thought I was well-intentioned and supportive. The great emphasis on documentation helped me to focus on patterns of relationships: who associated with whom mostly, and which of the residents were the alphas. Equally important, was the identification of the resident most likely to be scapegoated, remaining on the periphery of the sub culture of the cottage. Clearly, the latter category belonged to Denny, a portly, freckle-faced, redhead.

Denny was deeply disturbed and prone to violent outbursts, which I encountered in about week five on the job. Having been provoked for one reason or another, Denny picked up a wooden chair and charged at his tormentor, ready to break it over his head. I had no time to reason with him and had an empty quiver of social work skills. I tackled Denny about two feet away from inflicting serious damage and pinned him to the ground. At that point, holding him to the carpeted living area, I tried to calm him down. The empty glaze in his pale, blue eyes was that of someone in a trance, a million miles away and seething.

"He gets this way, sometimes," several residents mused, as they stood around calmly; they'd seen this before.

"Well," I responded, "being angry is OK, but hurting someone isn't."

This uncomfortable, somewhat intimidating and quite tiring juxtaposition went on for almost twenty minutes, until Denny convinced me that he was back to only his traditionally abnormal state. Holding Denny in this compromised position was both physically draining and enlightening. As I was searching his eyes for some sign of composure, I had a vivid flashback to so many of my youthful rebellious activities that might very well have had me as a Hawthorne resident, undergoing what passed for rehabilitation. Maybe, it was that unconscious connection, that facilitated my rapport with these hard to manage young men.

About halfway through my four month contract, I was, as usual, a bit late in getting all twelve members of my cottage to lunch on time. I told those who were ready, to make their way to the dining room, a sign of my faith in them, as all groups were to have a staff member accompany them at all times. Sitting in the small cottage kitchen were Derek, handsome, muscular and the cottage's only African-American and two of his cottage friends. I told them that we were late and asked that they accompany me to lunch. The two friends got up and made their way to the door behind me, while Derek slowly rose from his chair and walked toward the kitchen sink. In what was certainly a pre-planned action, both boys came up behind me each grabbing one of my arms. Derek produced a long kitchen knife and held it to my throat.

"Now, you in a big hurry?" he snarled.

"Derek," I said, in a calm voice that I generally kept under lock and key, "I'm going to count to three and you will put that knife away and you guys will let go of me. You do that and we're OK and we go to lunch. You keep this up and you will make me mad."

To my substantial relief, Derek smiled and backed off, "just messin' with you man," as he returned the knife to the sink. I never mentioned it again, did not put it in any of my documentation and did not have a similar event for the remaining two months at Hawthorne. Of course, I had no idea what I would do if the "count to three" thing didn't work. The only time and place that this event reemerged was in my analyst, Dr. Glass's office.

"How is it," I asked him, "that I remain calm in a scary situation like the Derek episode, and suffer from anxiety for no discernible reason, or when I know that you are going on vacation?" No answer, of course, only a redirection back to me.

The four months passed quickly and I soon bade all the residents a warm goodbye. I would miss them…even nutty Denny. I accepted a position as a caseworker at a foster placement agency, Brooklyn Home for Children, which was, paradoxically, located in Queens. I seem to have had the ability to establish a rapport with hard-to-manage clients despite my lack of formal, professional training. And Warren, presented a significant challenge in my new career direction.

The agency was located on a campus of about ten acres with six residential cottages. Youngsters from eight to sixteen years of age resided in the well-maintained cottages until a foster family could be identified and vetted. The foster families would, we hoped, provide the kids with a warm and inviting new home. Contrary to Hawthorne, most of the eighty residents were African-American or Hispanic. Some of the residents had been at the agency for months, even years.

Caseworkers tried, often in vain, to locate the biological parents of the residents. Once a parent was identified, the worker was to either assess their readiness to assume responsibility for their child or rule them incapable or unwilling. My job was to meet weekly or twice weekly with the fifteen youngsters assigned to me. I was to connect with them and ensure that they were being well cared for in their cottages, or if they were fortunate, to prepare them for placement in a foster home. It appeared that I always ended up with the most challenging and confrontational clients. That was Warren.

Warren was the most troublesome by far of my caseload. He was fourteen years old, thin as a broom stick and given to constant violent outbursts in his cottage and in organized, peer activities. He was as bright as he was violent and our twice-weekly meetings started out as fun. He was inquisitive and always asked intelligent questions. I was expected to conduct five to six counseling sessions daily in my comfortable office, housed within cottage number three. I would join the kids in that cottage for lunch, sitting at different tables daily, although there was a staff lounge where most of my colleagues enjoyed their sandwiches and a forty five minute respite. Working with these youngsters was as intense as it was rewarding.

The problem with Warren began about a month after my arrival. He was assigned to me with all of the prerequisite caveats, all of the social work jargon that I had begun to abhor: perseveration, dementia, psychosis, paranoid outbursts. I would ask Mrs. Kirsch, my supervisor, if all of those descriptions could fit into so thin a body as Warren's.

My absurd questions to her were often met with a nervous smile. She was trying to figure out when I was just naive or being a wise guy. "Who diagnosed Warren as psychotic?"

"The psychiatrists at Creedmoor Hospital."

"Mrs. Kirsch, most of those shitty doctors are psychotic themselves. Is there one doctor who treated Warren, who comes from a country that you can pronounce? Would you send your child for treatment or diagnosis at Creedmoor? We both know that Creedmoor is a snake pit." She looked peevish, but unrepentant.

Warren was at one end of the hit parade spectrum while Ulpiano, a fifteen year old Hispanic young man who was as tough as he was soft spoken and pleasant, was at the other end, the pleasant one. Ulpiano spent much of his free time weight lifting and he looked it. Like Derek at Hawthorne, Ulpiano, by virtue of his physique, rarely had to prove himself, and almost never raised his voice in anger. They didn't have to, they were a form of residential royalty.

And, if Ulpiano was royalty, Warren was the knave. He was cultivating the unpleasant habit of not wanting to leave at the end of our one hour session. Initially, some convincing and cajoling was sufficient, but it took time, and the other youngsters I was scheduled to meet with had to wait in the corridor. It wasn't fair to them, and it got worse. I believe that Warren was intent upon proving to me that all of the lovely psychological adjectives that adorned his personal charts were, indeed, earned and justified.

At the end of each new session it became progressively more difficult to extricate him from my office until one day, he grinned at me and with as much menace as he could muster said, "You want me out, Mr. Stern, you gonna have to throw me out."

As tempting as it was, all I did was play social worker. One session was extended by forty five minutes because of his manipulation. I was convinced that Warren was angry, disturbed and violent, but not psychotic. I decided to see just how irrational Warren really was.

My strategy was simple: just change the schedule of appointments. Every session with Warren was now to be followed by a regularly scheduled appointment with Ulpiano. Two days later, I had my now highly anticipated appointment with Warren. It was quite pleasant, until the last five minutes. The by now familiar mantra of "throw me out" reared its ugly head, this time with an even more menacing tone. I calmly asked Warren if he could do me a favor.

"What," he grunted in his most belligerent tone. "Would you please tell Ulpiano, who is waiting outside my office for his session with me, that we will be delayed and he will miss weight lifting? Tell him that I apologize, but that you don't want to leave."

Warren looked shocked and said, "no need, I gotta go, when is our next session?" His angry outbursts with me at session's end quickly disappeared. It seemed his decision making was quite appropriate and rational. Perhaps all of that social work jargon really didn't fit into his thin body.

I had another goal, an overarching, aching goal that never left me for a day. That was to reconnect with Aviva. I continually visualized my histrionic note to Aviva declaring my overbearing love for her. My absurd phone call to her upon our one-sided separation, bemoaning my falling in love with a nineteen year old, was quietly repeated verbatim in my spare moments. It was clear to me that every woman that I met subsequent to our glacial divide, was unfairly and unfavorably compared to Aviva.

It had been almost two years since we last spoke. Aviva was living in an apartment in Hempstead, Long Island, and was attending classes at Adelphi University. I felt that her whole family: her mother, Zita and Aviva's dear aunt Carol and her wonderful husband, Richard, were rooting for us to get together. All I needed now was to add Aviva to that distinguished list. Fearful of rejection, or worse yet, to hear of a competitive relationship, I called Aviva and asked if we could go to a movie. Innocuous and public enough. To my surprise and delight, she agreed and gave me the address, which included a twenty five mile ride on the crowded and reviled Long Island Turnpike. I was so thrilled that even my exposure to the highway, known as the "world's longest parking lot," didn't faze me. And so, that Friday night I set out, in my trusty Karmann Ghia, on the one hour trip to Hempstead.

I was nervous, excited and deeply apprehensive of her rejecting me again. I followed Aviva's directions and neared the exit which was about two miles away. I cruised at about sixty miles an hour with my convertible top up, despite the warm evening.

The noxious gasoline fumes from the heavy traffic, necessitated a closed top, and windows completely shut, despite my lack of a car air conditioner. It was at that point that my bright, red, check engine light flashed on, indicating some automotive malfunction. I had no idea what it might be as my mechanical aptitude rivaled my academic achievements. Thinking it too dangerous to pull over on the busy exit ramp, I decided to push on and assess the nature of the problem while at Aviva's house. Thankfully, her apartment building was very close to the exit ramp.

As I pulled off the highway, the car bucked a bit and then, the engine became menacingly quiet. I coasted for about a block and a half before the car rolled to a lifeless halt. I managed to guide it into a parking spot only a few blocks from Aviva's building. I set out on foot and continued following Aviva's directions. It was only a few minutes walk to her building. I was increasingly nervous as I rang her bell, about what was left of our tattered relationship, and how expensive it would be to repair my car.

Aviva answered the door looking radiant and as beautiful as when I last crashed and burned with my dulcet note. We greeted one another cordially and conservatively. No kiss, no mush. To my chagrin, lurking in the background, was her black and white mountain lion, Grushenka. I never quite trusted him. He hadn't forgiven me for my intrusion into their lives. I informed Aviva about the fate of my suddenly moribund car. She said that she had an excellent and trustworthy car mechanic, an oxymoron? Vinnie, the mechanic, had a repair shop nearby, which was certainly closed at that time. We agreed that I would stay over that night, and I would sleep on the living room couch.

After a friendly, but unfortunately, quite uneventful night, Aviva drove me to Vinnie's repair shop in her ancient Nash

Rambler, with its shaky front hood held in place by a thin chain. Vinnie appeared competent and above all else reasonable. His relatively quick diagnosis pointed to a faulty starter, which he replaced. As was my wont, I was generally quite short of cash. Vinnie, agreed that I could send him a check or come out again and pay him at a later date. Within a couple of hours my car was up and running. Aviva and I agreed that we would meet again next Friday evening, I was to visit her in Hempstead again. We had broken the almost two year breach in our relationship and I was cautiously optimistic.

The following Friday I set out again on the Expressway at pretty much the same time as the previous week. We had agreed that we would keep the same plan and have dinner out and then go to a local movie. My trusty Karmann Ghia had at least half a tank of gas and I felt great about seeing Aviva again. Within about two miles of my exit, the red light on the dashboard began to flicker, just as it had the previous week, and my check engine light lit up. At virtually the same spot as the week before, the car bucked and soon quit altogether.

This week, I was able to coast about a half block further and glided into a parking spot within walking distance of Aviva's building. I couldn't believe my bad luck, which turned out to be my good luck. Aviva greeted me, and I almost gleefully told her what had happened, and we would need to pay Vinnie the mechanic another visit in the morning. I think that to this day Aviva has some serious doubts about the truthfulness of the car gods smiling upon me.

Aviva was certain that I had somehow arranged for this repeat performance. In truth, I would not have had the slightest inkling of how to orchestrate such a car event, after all, I was Jewish and a relatively new driver. What could have been the unfathomable determinant that caused a car breakdown at virtually the same place in two consecutive weeks? I had driven the car with no discernible problem for the entire week prior to my repeat breakdown. Vinnie, the mechanic, replaced my alternator the next morning and all was, once again, well. This sleepover date, thankfully, proved much more eventful, and clarified for both of us how important we were to one another, and how we would not allow another painful separation.

Within a period that seemed to move at meteoric speed, Aviva and I planned that we would make changes that would ensure close contact with one another. I moved to the Lower East Side, with my furnished room friend Fraser now living in an apartment above mine. Aviva transferred from Adelphi to New York University School of the Arts, located on 5th Street and Second Avenue, which was only a few blocks away from my apartment. I luckily discovered, that a young woman I knew was moving out of her apartment, directly across the street from my building. Aviva, shortly thereafter, moved into that apartment. She was able to walk the few blocks to her NYU classes from her new apartment.

Both Aviva's and my apartment featured precariously sloped and warped floors, peeling paint, endless varieties of wildlife, dingy hallways and bathtubs resting on four sculpted, cast iron legs in the kitchen. If we turned the volume up on our small black and white televisions, we could hear our programs over the din of the many Hell's Angels' motorcycles parked just up the block near Second Avenue. They all seemed determined to rev their engines twenty four- seven.

From my rear window, Fraser and I were able to see the wooden railings encircling the ancient, tiny, neighborhood cemetery in the backyard, just outside my third floor apartment. The flat surface of the fenceposts offered a platform for the coke bottles that Fraser and I would place there, trying to hit them with my Remington thirty-thirty. Gunfire was not a rare sound in our neighborhood, and so, we were never reported to the police authorities.

The local police precinct was located a few blocks north of us on 9th street. While I continued to tell my parents, and anyone who would listen, that the neighborhood was going through a slow gentrification, there wasn't much visual evidence to support my contention. Fifty, or so Hell's Angels motorcycles parked just off Second Avenue, was not a picture that Hallmark would commission for a neighborhood greeting card. There were generally two or three overflowing garbage cans in front of each building, and it appeared that the favored neighborhood pastime was burglary.

My first contact with our neighborhood police guardians came one evening, when Fraser and I were visiting the fourth floor apartment of a young woman Fraser was hitting on. Just outside her bedroom window, one of the two windows in the railroad apartment, we heard voices on the fire escape, facing the rear courtyard. Without any hesitation, she called the local police precinct and reported the incident, and that she feared whoever was on the fire escape might intrude into her apartment.

Within a few minutes, she answered a knock at the door. Two burly, uniformed policemen stood in the doorway. She thanked them for their quick response and ushered them into the apartment. Probably forewarned by a lookout, the uninvited fire escape visitors were nowhere to be seen. The policemen were pleasant and courteous and joked about needing a traffic light on the rear fire escapes in our neighborhood to help control the traffic. Then, to my surprise, one of the officers asked me: "Do you have a gun?" I answered, that I had one rifle and one shotgun.

"Even better," he commented, "the shotgun is the weapon of choice." I was listening. The instructions were soon to come: "Never shoot anyone on the fire escape. Wait until he has one foot, that's all you need, one foot, inside your apartment, then you can legally shoot him. Or you can march him or them at gunpoint up to the roof and push them off. That will save us a lot of effort."

I had a day off from my Brooklyn Home job having worked the previous weekend. I was able to sleep late and needed some time later that morning to do some grocery shopping at our outrageously overpriced, second avenue grocery store. I left my apartment with my plastic shopping net and was surprised by two uniformed, policemen racing past me up the stairs, guns drawn. One of the officers stopped and looked at me, and continued to race up the steps to the floor above me. Not being a stranger to mayhem, I continued down the three flights to the street, exiting through the narrow front entrance. The street was blocked off by three police cars, lights flashing. A small crowd had gathered to catch today's live entertainment.

As I emerged from the entrance, a uniformed officer walked up to me and asked me why I had been in the building. I told him that I live in the building. "Oh yeah, the front or the back?" was his less-than-friendly question. "The front," I answered, "apartment 3D." "You got your name on a mailbox?" he inquired. "Yes I do." I guessed that satisfied him, and I proceeded to walk to Second Avenue to shop.

Having purchased what I needed, I headed back toward my apartment, hoping that whatever had happened was now resolved. As I started crossing the avenue, I noticed a police patrol car slowly proceeding my way. The patrol car passed me and quickly backed up to block me from crossing the street. Calling at me from an open window, one of the officers said that he had seen me emerge from the building. He asked me in a quite belligerent tone, "What were you doing in that building"?

"I live in that building, officer," I answered.

"Oh yeah," he asked, "the front or the back?"

"The front," I answered, "apartment 3D."

"OK, get in the car," he sounded angry. I really, at this point, was not sure what he was annoyed about and whether they were going to drive me home. Instead, they made a U turn and proceeded a block north against traffic before heading north on First Avenue in the direction of the police station. The squad car pulled up in front of the police precinct and the three officers and I got out of the car, just as another patrol car pulled up behind it. Two police officers emerged and stood next to me. I recognized one of them as the officer who raced by me on the staircase of my building, gun drawn: the one who stopped to look at me as I left my apartment. He walked up to me, looked at me, and said to the others, "that's him." The humor of the situation had suddenly dissipated into the Second Avenue ether.

Three police officers escorted me, along with my grocery bag laden with perishables, into the precinct. Immediately to the left of the entrance was a ten foot desk on a raised platform. The Sergeant on duty was sitting behind the desk, a red-headed, Irish looking officer who, I surmised, was not about to welcome me to the neighborhood gentrification committee. One of the officers who had accompanied me into the station told the Sergeant that I was a suspect.

The Sergeant looked at me sternly, and asked me what I was doing in the building. Obviously, I thought, this was some kind of rehearsed interrogation pattern which seemed absurd and comical. When I informed him that I lived in the building, his next question not surprisingly was, "Oh yeah, the front or the back?"

I told him that I lived in the front, apartment 3D. I began to feel that I was an unwilling character in a Kafka novel, caught in a web of circumstances beyond my control and understanding. I asked the Sergeant if he could tell me what I was suspected of doing. He responded that there had been a burglary in apartment 3D of my building. He had not made the connection that I had just told him that I lived in apartment 3D.

"Sir," I said as calmly as I could, "I live in apartment 3D. Am I suspected of burglarizing my own apartment?"

He corrected the error, unapologetically, and said that the apartment was 4E, our friend's apartment. Minutes later, a Hispanic man was led into the precinct handcuffed. The accompanying officer informed the Sergeant that this was the perpetrator, not me. The Sergeant looked at me and, after an unconvincing apology, asked me if I would like to be driven home.

Despite my unique exposure to NYC's police force, which was highlighted by the advice given to me on how to impact drug-related traffic on our rear fire escapes, I had grown fond of the neighborhood. Raoul's intoxicated, night time wandering through our hallways brandishing his handgun, certainly added a dimension of originality that I could have done without. Nonetheless, I continually scanned the horizon for signs of gentrification, which never seemed to appear. The best part of living there ultimately was that I was just across the street from Aviva's building.

However, The daily commute to my work in Queens became burdensome. I often left for work early in the morning and came home after dark. I began planning yet another peripatetic crisscrossing of Manhattan. My relationship with Aviva had deepened and I was increasingly confident that, despite moving to a neighborhood further uptown, we were both determined not to allow any backsliding again.

The move northward in my living arrangements was prompted by another important event in my life. I was accepted into Columbia University's Master of Social Work program for the Fall semester of 1968. With little fanfare, and even less furniture, I got ready to vacate my apartment. I broke my east 3rd Street lease, paid my last month's rent, disregarded my thirty five dollar security deposit and, with Fraser's help, moved to east 83rd street and First Avenue. Despite living on the top floor of a five story walk up, my rent increased by thirty dollars a month, which added stress to my astonishingly precarious financial situation.

Several days after moving into my new apartment, the downstairs call buzzer sounded. I was expecting the telephone company to install my new telephone and activate my new number. Five minutes after I acknowledged the buzzer, I answered the door, barely hearing the faint knock. The telephone installer appeared, huffing and puffing, and informed me that I needed an oxygen tent more urgently than a telephone. I decided, that a trip to the store to shop for groceries, would come only when my pantry was empty, and I hadn't eaten for three days.

After the successful installation of my new phone, I made several test calls to give my new number to family and friends. Fatefully, one of the first incoming calls that I received, was from Melinda, who informed me that two detectives had just left my parent's home, asking if they knew of my whereabouts. Melinda informed me, that they were both from the thirty second precinct, located on the periphery of Harlem. She had no idea why they were looking for me. I joked with her and said that perhaps they wanted to give me an additional medal for averting a robbery when I was fifteen.

That not-so-pleasant incident occurred, one summer day as I was walking south on Broadway, near 163rd street, heading toward the pool hall. It was hot, and the streets were fairly empty, when I heard an elderly woman scream for help. She was pointing to two teens running away, having snatched her pocketbook. The two were running across Broadway toward Harlem. I had a good angle on them and ran after them and tackled the biggest kid. As he fell to the ground under me, a large pair of shears fell out of his hands near him. His compatriot reached for them and in my best John Wayne imitation, I said, "That may be the last thing you do."

I had no idea where all of my bravado came from, but he hesitated, thankfully, just long enough for a passing squad car to take over. I received commendations from the police, a reward offer from the victim, which I refused, and a visit from representatives of the police department. They met with my parents to tell them how proud they should be of me. All of this occurred about one year before G. DUB tossed me out of school, something my parents were not so proud of. Melinda laughed, and doubted that the most recent detective visit, had any remote connection to that incident six years earlier.

Having recently been spared from the Lower East Side Gulag for burglarizing my own apartment, and wanting no further complications with the men in blue, I called the number that the detectives had left with my parents. My mother refrained from asking the question that she really wanted to ask: "what have you done now?" as she recited the detective's phone number. I called, spoke to the detective, and, after providing him with some identifying information, he told me why they had paid me that unsolicited visit.

"The City is cracking down on scofflaws, those who violate traffic laws and disregard the penalties," he explained. "My partner and I are assigned to track down the biggest violators in our district, and you are right up there." I was really surprised, but, in retrospect, I shouldn't have been.

"What shall I do to satisfy you?" The detective informed me that a court date had been set for me to appear downtown, and that all I needed to do was show up and address the complaint. I thanked him and noted all of the details. He said that he would be notified by the court when I had resolved the complaint. Before hanging up, I asked the detective, "How many outstanding traffic violations are there against me?" "Sir, I don't have the exact number but, I believe that it was over two hundred." The number was shocking. Over two hundred traffic violations?

My traffic court cameo appearance was scheduled six days later, in the municipal court, in lower Manhattan. I entered the poorly lit, musty, court room reeking of stale tobacco and cheap after shave lotion. Or was it disinfectant? It was packed to the rafters with about one hundred invited, but equally reluctant guests, sitting in no particular order, across the splintery, wood benches. The judge appeared bored and eager to move from one traffic violator to the next. The bailiff called one name after another with an air of artificial efficiency, and instructed the person appearing before the judge where they must stand and that they must face the judge. I became uneasy when the bailiff read out the charges of another invited guest and the judge scowled if the list reached five or six violations.

My turn came, the bailiff read my name out loud to the Judge who seemed to be intensively scrutinizing unrelated papers scattered before him on his cluttered desk. I surmised that his personal utility bills were somehow mixed in that mound of papers. As the bailiff began reading the violations: parking meter infractions, illegal parking and other nonmoving illegalities along with the date and place for each incident, the judge seemed to awaken from his judicial slumber. When the bailiff reached ten violations read out loud, he asked the judge, "Your honor, shall I continue, or would you prefer that I summarize this rather extensive, list?" The judge seemed to have now emerged from his torpor, and appeared energized. His voice was surprisingly deep for such a slight man. "Proceed, until every last infraction is read into the court record."

The next ten minutes were humiliating. If I had been a turtle, my head would have long found a hiding place inside my shell. The bailiff read each violation, complete with descriptive details to the delight of the hundred plus persons sitting on the hardwood benches, happy to be entertained. At about the twenty fifth violation, those in the front rows of the gallery started chuckling; by the fiftieth, they were roaring with laughter. And the bailiff kept reading. Everyone was amused, except for the judge and me. I was embarrassed and not too eager to see the impact that this laughter had on the judge's demeanor and, ultimately, his ruling.

I stood before the judge, looking as humble as I could, shoulders stooped and head slightly bowed, hoping that he would recognize how contrite I was for this unconscionable, example of my disregard for the City's parking regulations. Would he understand and take into his deliberations that, of all of the two hundred plus violations now being recited chronologically for all to hear, not one was for a more serious moving violation? Certainly, that had to reflect positively on my good judgment and character. In truth, I was now being compelled to account for the two years of blatant disregard for parking restrictions in New York City.

When the bailiff concluded reading the list of my infractions, and the amused laughter began to subside, the judge peered at me, not with anger, but with a look of scorn and perhaps, pity. I noticed that his name plate indicated a great likelihood that he too was Jewish. That made me feel some sense of unwarranted comfort. In a calm, but sarcastic tone, he asked me, "Mr. Stern, do you work for a living?" "Yes, your honor, I do." With restrained disdain, he asked, "What do you do to earn a salary?" "Sir, I am a social worker, helping disenfranchised children and their families." I was hopeful that he would conclude that I was a devoted social servant, who has simply been at fault for occasional, poor judgment. He looked at me derisively. "No wonder our social service system is so messed up, it's in the hands of irresponsible people like you."

Not waiting for a response from me, he barked to the bailiff, that I had to pay double every fine plus fifty dollars, or ten days in jail. Luckily, I remembered to bring my check book, which, while attractive in its brown, faux leather casing, generally featured a balance of ten dollars or less. I post-dated the check, and managed to borrow the money to deposit into the account that evening. I left the courtroom relieved, but under increased financial duress. It was shortly after this unpleasant experience faded into my memory bank, which was, unfortunately littered with similar incidents, that the best event of my life occurred.

The most important contribution that my fifth floor, East Side, Alpine perch made to my life, is that it served as the venue where I proposed marriage to Aviva, and she, with no hesitation, agreed.

While I have always been, a sentimental gusher, my proposal was quite simple, unadorned with schmaltz and confident of the response.

Chapter Thirteen

THERE IS NO clear evidence that connects my marriage proposal to Aviva with my first impressions of her beautiful, Aunt Carol. For years, Aviva and I have joked, that my intent to marry her was the belief that she carried Carol's genes. Aviva's mother, Zita, was also very attractive, but her sister Carol, was a knockout. Aviva had been very close to Carol, and her husband Richard, since her infancy. They were like second parents to her. I was so pleased that I became intertwined with that loving relationship, one that lasted for many decades and continues with Richard until today.

Aviva and I agreed that we needed to coordinate our marriage announcement so that, within milliseconds, all parties concerned: Zita, my parents, Melinda, Josephine and Carol and Richard, would be notified. We both knew that my parents would feel hurt if they were to receive the news on the rebound, as they often felt that they were the 'B' team. So, after coordinating our watches with Greenwich Mean Time, we started with my parents.

My parents were thrilled, they loved Aviva. My mother, who really adored Aviva, had the universal my-son-is-leaving depression, despite my having lived independently for several years. My father was ecstatic. Perhaps, he was surprised that I had somehow convinced Aviva to marry me; or maybe he was thrilled that I might actually settle down and become partially normal.

Zita, Carol and Richard were equally effusive. Perhaps most ambivalent, initially was Melinda. She adored Aviva, and was tickled that many people had observed how she and Aviva, with strikingly similar features, were often taken for sisters, and on one occasion as twins. Melinda often joked, that this "coincidence" might be of interest to my therapist. Melinda, the youngest sibling in my family, must have felt abandoned by me. Despite her closeness to Aviva, she often spoke of our new directions in life in a wistful way. In her usual forthright and no bullshit manner, she warned of growing apart unless we worked hard to avoid any distancing of our relationship.

We shared our good news with Zita, who was pleased, but not surprised. We drove to Franklin Square, Long Island, where Carol and Richard lived. They were effusive. Carol offered their home as the wedding site. "We can rearrange our living room in any way that you guys would like. I can visualize the chupah at the far end, over by the bay windows," typical of Carol and Richard's never ending generosity. Their house was a modest, Levittown home, located in the pleasant middle-class neighborhood of Franklin Square, and it seemed just fine to both of us.

We very much loved the intimacy of their home as a marriage venue. Aviva and I both shared a general dislike of commercial wedding establishments. I had never been to a commercial site wedding and did not yet understand how even the most neutral of sites may actually be transformed into a warm and inviting location for a simcha. We were very pleased at their offer and said that we would get back to them very soon.

We planned to get married about six or seven months hence. We discussed possible dates with my parents. There were some religious holiday restrictions as we had hoped to get married in March. There are certain periods just before and after Passover, where weddings are not allowed in the Jewish tradition and finding a Rabbi would be difficult. My father guided us to an acceptable date, a window on the calendar on which weddings were allowed, which in 1968, was March 24th. With the wedding date fixed, Aviva and I set two near-term goals for ourselves: to locate and select a ceremony site that we both felt strongly about and to once again, alter our living arrangements, this time, under the same roof.

Aviva and I had enjoyed several dinners at an unusual restaurant about forty five minutes north of the city. The restaurant, The Old Stone Inn, was perched atop a hill, overlooking a rolling valley, dramatically sloped toward the Hudson River. The patio dining area, enveloped by lilac bushes and multi-colored bougainvillea, was a terraced pavilion with an unobstructed view of the valley and the river. We both agreed that this would be an idyllic location for our wedding and reception. We visited with my parents shortly after our decision and wanted to share the news with them. My mother was pleased, my father was decidedly unhappy. "Dad, you seem disturbed about something (as if I didn't know)."

"Is the restaurant kosher?"

"Why, does that matter? We never had a kosher home." I gulped. I knew he would never buy it.

"A wedding must be kosher."

In the third grade, while a student at the Yeshiva, in an inexplicable reversal of my disdain for the rigid rules and regulations that guided a Yeshiva student's life, I requested that we keep kosher at home. My mother, a staunch, left wing, liberal, socialist from Vienna, frowned, shrugged her shoulders, but acquiesced. It all must have been music to my father's ears, being a product of a religious home in a small town in rural Poland. My deeply held, devout conviction lasted about three weeks, when I furtively informed my mother, she no longer needed to shlep to the kosher butcher in order to pay double the price of the non kosher product. She was ecstatic, my father wasn't. But, he went along with my whims and the subject did not reemerge, until now.

"Dad," I really hated to upset him, "What if this is where Aviva and I want to hold our wedding, and it's not kosher?" My inclination was to tell him that this was our decision-take it or leave it. But, on occasion, reason prevailed- even with me.

"Then you will have to have the wedding without me," he said with calm conviction. My father's regarding Josephine as no longer his daughter, when she eloped with her misanthropic lover, and moved to the remote Catskill Mountains, bore testimony to his inclination to irrationally reject. She was the family's first born and my father loved her dearly...so, how will this play out with us? First, the shtetl ethos, that's probably just the way it was. Perhaps even trumping that shtetl history, was my father's wealthy and orthodox cousin, Mailach, who also happened to own the women's rainwear factory that employed my father.

Mailach's whole wing of the family was both wealthy and orthodox. It would have been a shameful announcement, had this influential wing of the family been unable to attend because of the kashrut issue. Aviva understood, and we agreed that we would comply with my father's request. "Dad, we cannot have the wedding without you and, if it is that important to you, we are OK with it." My father was thankful, my mother was in shock at the ease of our acquiescence. She attributed my incremental approach to rationality as a testament to Aviva's tempering influence.

We put the wedding venue issue on the back burner for a short period. We were now resolved to live together and we set out to find an apartment that we would share. Since I had developed a significant expertise in breaking a New York City apartment lease, the prospect of moving yet again was on my near term horizon and posed no worry for me. After a prolonged search, we both agreed upon a single family, freestanding home in a working class area of Jackson Heights, Queens. Within a few weeks, once again with Fraser's truck and muscle power, we moved into our new, and now, shared home.

The house was divided into two floors. The main street level entrance was hedge-lined, with three brick steps leading to the front door. Immediately upon entering the home, we found ourselves in a spacious living room, that featured arched, wooden beams. To the left of the entrance, we entered a kitchen and breakfast area. Approximately forty feet from the entrance, at the far end of the first floor, was a large, bright and airy bedroom. The bathroom featured an arched skylight, a novelty for me, as most tenement buildings were lacking such a quaint amenity. The apartment was very cute, but our landlady-to-be was the closest being to Medusa that I could imagine.

Mrs. Bongiorno, our future landlady, was the personification of a misnomer. She lived alone on the floor beneath ours, in a basement apartment. She always wore black, the Italian garb for mourning, and in her case, it also reflected her perennially scornful and dour demeanor. The interview process made Aviva and I feel that we were already guilty of some egregious crime. Despite her sour disposition, we both stayed calm during our entrance interrogation and did fine with posing as Mr. and Mrs. Stern.

We did not fully realize just how important the false representation as a married couple was, as her austere persona, and her rigidly devout Catholicism, would never have allowed a sinfully unwed couple to live together in her building. Despite the many times that we had significant disagreements with her, we overlooked them as the location was convenient and the apartment living space was perfect for the three of us: Aviva, me and her begrudging cougar.

Despite living in the apartment below us, it was as if Mrs. Bongiorno resided on an eagle's perch, able to observe all events with clarity. One such observation came on the evening of our wedding. After a lovely ceremony, we returned to our Jackson Heights home in the early evening, preparing to leave for our honeymoon the following morning. It was only after joyfully entering our apartment, that we looked out of our window at Aviva's newly acquired white Volvo, and saw what turned out to be Melinda's and Aviva's cousin Judith's handiwork: scrawled in large, red lipstick letters, one could easily read, "Just Married." Mrs. Bongiorno inquired about this, and we quickly, if only partially, dispelled her suspicion, and maintained that this was the work of neighborhood vandals.

While still at Adelphi University, Aviva had become friendly with a faculty member who offered to sell her his used Volvo. The car was in excellent shape, but our finances weren't. Aviva and I had agreed that we would sell the Karmann Ghia, that four wheeled miracle that had brought us together, and would borrow the money to purchase the newer, more reliable Volvo. Zita loaned us the money for the Volvo and we sold my car.

The months sped by as we approached our wedding day. We had agreed that we would take up Carol and Richard's wonderful offer and would have our wedding ceremony in their home. We had compromised with my father, and we would have a dairy and fish menu for the reception, avoiding kashrut issues. Mailach and his wing of the family could now attend. Mailach did not attend, but, his equally orthodox son, Dave and his wife did.

My mother was very pleased with the proceedings although it was clear that having the wedding at a site connected with Aviva's side of the family was causing her some pangs of jealousy. While my mother very much liked Zita, Howard, Carol and Richard, there seemed always to be a reemergence of "are we the 'B' team?" Especially joyful for her, was that her dear brother Karl, had informed us that he would be attending our wedding. He was to arrive from London one week before the ceremony. I was thrilled, as I had never met Karl, but had corresponded with him by air mail letters. I was really honored that he would attend.

Just after New Year's Day, our planning went into high gear. We were fortunate that our good friend Bob was an extraordinary help to us in the selection of excerpts for our wedding music. The music, to which Aviva would be escorted down the yet-to-be-designated aisle, was most challenging for us. Bob had been a child prodigy and had, at age eleven, performed as a piano soloist with the Chicago Symphony Orchestra. Neither Aviva nor I were novices when it came to classical music, which would be integral in our wedding ceremony, but Bob added a dimension that was very helpful. Ultimately, we selected segments of Shostakovich's Fifth Symphony and the second movement of The Brahm's Violin Concerto for Aviva's graceful entrance.

Some twenty years after our marriage, life's meanderings had brought us back from halfway around the globe, and then across the breadth of the US to San Diego. We had maintained a relationship with Bob: through his announcement of his preference for men, his subsequent divorce from Anne, his wife of fifteen years, his narcissism, his obsession with his male suitors, and the geographic challenge of living three thousand miles apart. Bob was to visit us in San Diego, we set the date and he purchased the airplane tickets. In the interim, one of the most profoundly difficult and emotionally wrenching events in our lives occurred.

Our lovely and spirited sixteen year old daughter, Lora, while returning from a visit to her boyfriend's house in a San Diego suburb, was in a serious car accident. She was extricated from her car by a terrific fire department crew and helicoptered to a well-equipped Torrey Pines hospital. She arrived in a state of semi-consciousness and was attended to in the emergency room. The attending neurologist calmed us and reassured us that, as sassy as she had been a few hours earlier, she would, within a number of weeks, return to form. The reassurance was indeed welcomed, but we were in a state of code red anxiety.

Even as she progressed and began the difficult but steady rehab process, I could think of nothing else; and Aviva and I had trouble sleeping and eating. But, Bob had his air tickets purchased and wanted to come visit despite our mental state. I thought, perhaps Bob, a trained psychotherapist, might even prove to be a source of comfort to us. As usual, my naiveté shone through and my self-delusion once again overshadowed my veneer of realism. Bob arrived, not quite at the apex of our anxiety about Lora, but only a click removed from it. He proved only to be a self-absorbed burden.

With Brahms and Shostakovich as the musical centerpieces for our wedding, we began choreographing our ceremony. As usual, Carol and Richard were wonderful and flexible co-planners.

Together, we redesigned their living room with an appropriate division for an aisle and a chupah at its far end as Carol had envisioned. With one month to go until our wedding day, we began serious rehearsals. We drove to my parents house in our shiny, white, free and clear Volvo. Zita, much more generous with tangible gifts than with the gift of her emotions, forgave our loan to purchase the car, as an engagement present. There was a great deal to love about Zita, despite her sparing (until much later in our lives) emotional support of Aviva.

After dinner with my parents, we began to review the flow and pacing of the wedding. My father absorbed the details rather quickly, while my mother, an unsurpassed admixture of good humor, impatience and an all encompassing bundle of id energy, wanted to get on with it. "Brahms, I understand, but Shostakovich?"

"Whose crazy idea is this…a Russian?" I had no answer for this. Then, in her uniquely hurried style, although we had all evening, she offered: "OK, so finally, you put on the ring, smash the glass and then, who plays the traditional wedding music announcing the march down the aisle as husband and wife?" At that point, she hums what was to have been Mendelssohn's traditional wedding music,… she unconsciously, perhaps, hums the funeral dirge.

"Mom, that's for a funeral, this is a happy occasion, our wedding." I am not certain that she really was embarrassed, but, she offered some tepid apology. Throughout my youth, she maintained that she was "part witch" and had the misfortune of sometimes seeing into the future. Unfortunately, her unconscious melody switch was a harbinger of an event soon to unfold.

My mother's brother, Karl, arrived about eight days prior to our wedding day. He was a nice looking fiftyish, redhead, which explained the red highlights in my mother's hair, that she always defensively maintained were natural. He was intelligent, energetic and had a jovial quality to his character which seemed somewhat uncharacteristic, as this was not my mother's hallmark-humor yes, but not joviality. His British accent was a novelty, as it was so uniquely different from my mother's heavy, Viennese delivery and my father's mish mash of Viennese and Polish inflection. Karl's visit was in its fourth day when he complained of intense indigestion. He jokingly blamed my mother's cooking, but when it persisted, my father escorted him to the Columbia Presbyterian Hospital emergency room only three blocks away from their house.

The attending physician diagnosed the ailment as acute gastric indigestion and prescribed medication to reduce hyperacidity. Karl and my father returned home with the medication. Within twenty four hours, my uncle Karl suffered a massive heart attack and died.

He was buried in our family plot in New Jersey two days before our wedding. My mother was crushed, we were dumbfounded. At the funeral, I embraced my mother and whispered: "Mom, Aviva and I have decided to postpone our wedding until an appropriate period of mourning has passed. You and dad will tell us when that time has come."

She would not hear any of it. She said with unadorned clarity, unusual for her, "a simcha must never be postponed because of a tragedy." She, and my father, despite the devastating loss, were united in their insistence that the wedding be held. Aviva and I acquiesced. Viewing the photographs of the wedding, the sadness on their faces is imprinted for posterity, despite their herculean effort to suppress it on our wedding day.

March twenty-fourth brought with it blustery winds, cool temperatures and snow flurries. The Bobbes' home was totally transformed and looked marvelous. In addition to the sixty or so neatly arranged chairs, there was a beautiful chupah bedecked with a myriad of white Baby's Breath and Alstroemeria, Aviva's favorite flower. The first time I saw Aviva that day, was when Brahms dramatically announced her arrival and she was accompanied down the aisle by Zita and Howard.

Zita had identified a local rabbi, whom we had not met until the ceremony. Rabbi Widam was warm, intelligent and pleasant. He conducted a touching and thankfully, short ceremony. Carol and Richard and Zita and Howard were very helpful in ensuring that the reception, held in the Bobbe's finished basement, was as festive and joyful as it could be under the circumstances.

This was not an easy task as Karl's wife, Piroshka and her sister Etelka, had flown in from London in time for Karl's funeral. They attended the wedding ceremony dressed in black, with Piroshka wearing dark sunglasses. My mother, who generally shared her more emotional reactions with Melinda, sadly told her, "On some level I know that Piroshka blames me for Karl's untimely death. Perhaps the strain of the travel was too much for his diabetes." In truth, Piroshka was immensely jealous of my mother, who was still attractive and had a deep and special relationship with Karl.

Piroshka was a concentration camp survivor and had the reviled blue serial numbers for the Sobibor death camp, tattooed on her left forearm. She complained bitterly to the sky and the wind, at Karl's funeral, that he had left her all alone. Hearing her heart-rending request for some form of heavenly intervention and the desperation in her voice, as she sobbed about her being left alone in the world, was sobering. I couldn't help but feel guilty that Aviva and I were now inextricably and joyfully welding our lives together. It was painful. My stomach was churning and I felt my throat constricting repeatedly.

Despite the challenges, the ceremony and the reception were lovely, very much in line with our modest tastes and dislike of ostentation. We left the Bobbe's home, after all of the guests had departed, and headed back to our Jackson Heights home. We were planning to leave for our honeymoon the following morning. We had booked a hotel in the quaint town of Port Antonio, Jamaica. Since Aviva and I had eaten nothing all day, we decided that we would have dinner at The Tavern on the Green, in

Central Park, before turning in early to prepare for our trip to Jamaica. After cleaning off the "Just Married" lipstick graffiti, compliments of Melinda and Judith, and under the watchful, landlady eyes of our own Cruella De Vil, we changed clothing and headed into Manhattan. To our dismay, The Tavern was closed for renovation.

"Aviva, I hope that this is not an indication to you of my planning ability." She smiled, perhaps knowingly. We decided that we would snack somewhere and go to a movie. As we were close to Times Square, we parked our car in a lot and checked out what was playing. Aviva selected "Camelot" and I spent the next two hours in the theatre, berating myself for not checking out the availability of The Tavern and worse, agreeing to see "Camelot" on our wedding night. Aviva sobbed throughout most of the heart-wrenching love and abandonment scenes. I kept asking myself: "Could you have somehow engineered a worse start to our marriage?"

The next morning's flight to Jamaica was, thankfully, uneventful. As we emerged from the airport in Kingston, we waited for a taxi on a line that appeared designated for tourists only, as no locals paid it much mind. We were headed to our Port Antonio destination. As we stepped into the cab and announced our destination, the driver's response was quite unexpected: " Mann, why you want to go dere?" he asked. "Why not?" we asked, in unison. "Port Antonio is boring mann, dere's only a nice waterfall and some rafting. Dat's it mann."

"More a place for older folk, not you," he continued. "If you trust me, I'm gonna take you to a beautiful place for your honeymoon," and he paused. Aviva and I looked at one another and told him, "OK, go for it." The next two hour drive, through winding mountain roads, past small villages with roosters and goats patrolling central town squares, had me visualizing fending off saber wielding pirates...or some such enemy. The drive and the driver, however, were both pleasant enough.

We arrived at a gorgeous, dazzlingly white hotel, perched on a promontory jutting out above the Caribbean Sea. The nearby town of Ocho Rios and the small, quaint and friendly hotel looked absolutely perfect. We thanked the driver for the effort, and the excellent deviation from our prior plan. As he pulled out of the driveway, he stopped and shouted, "Don't forget to try the homemade coconut ice cream. Oh mann, delicious." Our stay was wonderful and a dual testament to our naiveté and spontaneity.

Our idyllic week soon ended and we returned to New York as the now legitimate Mr. and Mrs. Stern. Aviva was attending classes at NYU School of the Arts on east 5th street. She was also dancing with a Yiddish dance company that appeared at the adjacent theatre quite regularly. I would often drive her home in the evening after performances. I enjoyed arriving early, as I loved watching Aviva performing. She was so poised, graceful and moved with such fluidity across the stage. I wanted to yell out: "that's my wife." I sat in the generally packed theatre and appeared to be the odd man out, as each seat was occupied by a grey haired, older adult. The intermissions were among my most enjoyable theatre experiences, the stage became a quasi, borscht-belt venue, with skits and comedic acts in Yiddish.

The first five years of my life were heavily influenced by my German speaking parents, to the detriment of my writing, as I continually fight off my tendency to punctuate my sentences with a verb. I was fluent in German in my early youth, which helped me to understand the Yiddish skits that I enjoyed while I waited for Aviva. I often wondered what those elders sitting near me thought, when I laughed at the Yiddish jokes. I was certain, that they believed that this black-haired, mustached, olive-skinned guy was an off duty, Puerto Rican, maintenance man.

Several months later, both Aviva and I were driving in to Manhattan daily, as I now attended classes at The Columbia University School of Social Work. Classes were moderately interesting. I felt that I was reading vanilla material. The students were constantly challenged to identify theories and link them to social work practice. So much of what I was learning theoretically had been elements of my instinctive practice for a number of years.

Toward the end of the first year of the two year program, I approached Aviva with a mantra that was to reappear many times over the course of our lives together: "Since we have so little money, let's visit Israel and England and France on the way back." Aviva had been, for the years that she lived independently, using the "envelope" method for paying her utility bills. Each of a dozen envelopes was designated toward a utility bill or other monthly obligation. Every week, she would dutifully insert one quarter of the anticipated bill into the envelope. "Aviva, that disciplined approach is so boring." My suggested trip was a paradigm shift of great magnitude. Thankfully, my illogic prevailed.

Our airplane tickets to Israel were purchased through a student organization. For two hundred dollars each, we soon found ourselves on a Pan Am flight directly to Tel Aviv. Arrival in Israel proved to be an unanticipated and laborious act of love. We disembarked on a blisteringly hot tarmac, were welcomed, so to speak, by soldiers armed with automatic rifles, scrutinizing each passenger's steps as we cautiously descended the rickety gangway. The air was oppressively hot, with not a trace of the scented floral breeze of our imagined arrival.

My cousin Zvi, who was in America completing his doctoral degree at MIT, made his apartment available to us during our stay in Israel. Located in a lovely part of Upper Haifa, it had not a stick of furniture in it. Zvi's mother Pnina, and her husband Adolf, my father's brother, lived in a lower section of Haifa. They provided us with a small, electric grill and bedding, which we used as a makeshift bed on the floor, for the duration of our five week stay. We hitchhiked across the country, slept on the beach in Eilat, our small suitcase tied to my wrist, and endured what seemed then to be a favorite Israeli teenager's pastime, rolling Coca Cola bottles down the aisle of movie theaters.

Without exception, every visit to a restaurant, motel or family gathering was punctuated by an all out effort to recruit us to make Aliyah to Israel. A significant branch of my family had fled the Holocaust, or anticipated the dark clouds soon to enshroud Europe, and emigrated to Palestine. Despite my family connection to Israel, and Aviva's and my strong sense of Jewish identity, we were not raised on the Zionistic dream of carving out a life in the Promised Land. We both loved the pervasive excitement, the challenge that lay ahead of building on a utopian dream, and the raucous frontier-like quality of Tel Aviv.

What we didn't like was the jostling to get on any public bus. We were unaccustomed to the asymmetric warfare, with the battle hardened elbows of all women, it seemed, over sixty, vying to push ahead of anyone on any line. We stood on what passed for a line, one blazing summer afternoon, in Tel Aviv's center, waiting for the number five bus on Dizengoff Street. Some twenty five persons were on the Israeli version of a line, which bore a resemblance to fidgety cattle, nervously grazing. We were third in that assemblage, having waited about fifteen minutes for the bus. A palpable tension seemed to energize the group as the bus neared. As the bus came to a jerking halt, the scramble began with the semi-orderly queue now more akin to a frenzied shark feed. After what seemed like a millisecond, the bus pulled away with Aviva and I still standing at the bus stop, now first on line, and waiting for the next bus.

As we made our way from one street kiosk to another, we were only slightly taken aback by the cursory rinse that any glass received just before one ordered a drink from the multitude of street vendors in Jerusalem. Virtually every driver that stopped to pick up the two weary hitchhikers, either in the middle of the Negev Desert, or the back hills of Tiberius, functioned as an ad hoc recruiter for Israel's Immigration Bureau. Inexplicably, we both loved Israel, our family encounters and the belief that anything was possible in the building of a new, egalitarian society.

Leaving Israel left us with conflicting emotions. Israel had aroused in us, a yearning for an opportunity to contribute to the development of a Jewish State, that welcomed immigrants from so many disparate lands of the globe. We also left with a profound sense of how difficult living in this twenty year old state could be. The contrast with the apparent civility and orderliness of British life, on our next itinerary stop, didn't make the prospect of living in Israel any easier.

Folks at London's, Heathrow Airport were mindful of a queue. No one pushed to get ahead, people seemed to be patient almost to a fault. Our cab driver was pleasant, and seemed not to be overly burdened by the daily rainfall that London had been subjected to for two consecutive summer months. We slept at our aunt Piroshka's home in Cotswold Gardens. My association with her continued to be the graveside wailing over the loss of her dear husband, my uncle Karl, about one and a half years earlier. She was pleasant and inviting, and insisted that we stay with her while in London.

The sun reappeared on our first day's visit, after a two month unwelcome absence. Piroshka warned us of too much exposure to the sun and the heat with temperatures expected to rise into the low seventies. She darkened the house with drawn drapery, and would hear none of our protestations, that this time of year produced temperatures twenty five degrees higher in New York. The local newspapers treated the reappearance of the sun with jocund headlines, entreating the public not to be afraid of the strange, yellow orb high in the sky.

On our second day in London, we rented a car and drove to Stratford on Avon, Cambridge and other lovely, green towns outside of London. Courteousness and civility was the norm; the expansive greenery of the English countryside highlighted the pastoral setting. We contrasted the idyllic, five days spent in England with the raucous, dusty, unhygienic, rude and cacophonous five weeks in Israel and concluded that there was no way that we could ever consider living there. Less than one year later, we arranged to have our mail forwarded to our new mailing address: Absorption Center Dora, Dora, Netanya, Israel.

Chapter Fourteen

IT WAS A bit more than one year after our marriage and we were perceived as running out on our family and friends. Upon our return from five weeks in Israel it was as if an internal, unrecognizable force possessed us. Aviva and I often shared with one another that Israel was not a viable choice for the raising of our future family. As if propelled by an unfathomable force, we began planning for Aliyah to that unlivable country. We had such mixed feelings about living in Israel: daily life fraught with anxiety about terrorism, acculturating into an alien society and a life so far away from loved ones. Yet, for some unexplainable reason, we set our minds to live in Israel.

No sooner had we announced our plans to move to Israel in the early summer of 1970, when the head scratching began in both of our families. For my father, understanding our decision was somewhat easier, as his mother had moved to Palestine before coming to the States in the 1950s. His brother, Adolf, lived there having left Europe ahead of the Nazi takeover of sanity. I had three wonderful, first cousins living in Israel: Zvi,

Igal and Ari. Nonetheless, the loss of Aviva and me weighed heavily on him.

For my mother, it was, as were most emotional events, much more difficult. It wasn't enough that she had "lost" her son to marriage, now she was being separated from him by seven thousand miles. She was convinced that Aviva had influenced me to move to Israel, which really pained her, because she adored Aviva.

Perhaps most difficult for me was leaving Melinda. She was too strong and too proud to try to dampen our plans. I knew it was a profound feeling of abandonment that she felt. And for me, leaving her was difficult. She was my closest friend, my ally and my most forthright critic. I knew never to ask her a question, unless I wanted an unvarnished answer. She was insightful and honest and possessed a rare ability to cut through the morass of fuzzy thinking that I was so proficient in. She took the scenic route when talking to me, perhaps because she understood that it was intimately tied to my non-linear thought process.

It was hard to read Zita's feelings about our upcoming move, she was involved in her psychology practice and was raising, quite late in life, a five year old son, Joshua. Carol and Richard took it very hard. Richard wondered why not Vermont for adventure, why Israel? And the truth is, neither Aviva nor I could rationally answer Richard's or other similar questions. What was it that was drawing us like a powerful lodestone, to move to a dangerous neighborhood, with no jobs, no real friends there, a few family members with whom we had only tangential relationships? Neither of us were victimized by anti-Semitism. The inevitable Jew Boy that I was called as a kid was answered by,

"Fuck you, Irishman." And that was it, we all moved on. There were occasions, bordering on anti-Semitism, that were more trying, but generally, inconsequential

It wasn't the anti-Semitism of incidents such as my barroom encounter with Davey Brock, that was propelling us toward Israel. Neither Aviva nor I could rationally explain why we were intent upon moving to Israel. We didn't understand it- until we were living there. There was something so energizing, so complete, so meaningful, so soulful, that we felt upon arriving in Israel. The country with all of its imperfections, naiveté and blemishes was spectacular in its potential, as well as its challenges.

The year before we moved to Israel was emotionally draining for both of us. My parents had lived in the same apartment for about twenty five years. It was comforting for them to be so close to a large and excellent hospital, Columbia Presbyterian. The neighborhood, however, was changing, with waves of Hispanic and Haitian immigrants flooding the area. Stores catering to Hispanic tastes were everywhere and my parents felt increasingly alienated. Shops that had been stalwarts of the neighborhood were closing or moving to other neighborhoods.

Leaving my parents weighed heavily on me. We had socialized with them quite a bit since our marriage. We had dinner with them, either in their apartment or in local restaurants. Their favorite was "Sizzler," an inexpensive, neighborhood steak house. They had really taken to Aviva and she to them. Now, we were leaving. Melinda was enrolled at the University of Chicago and Josephine was, now with her fifth child, enmeshed in a marriage that could only have been designed in the netherworld, still living on a mountain top in rural New York State.

Aviva and I spoke to my parents frequently about their moving, perhaps to Queens, near my father's dear brother Lazo, and into a neighborhood with a significant Jewish population. Despite initially regarding this discussion as blasphemous, their resistance was eroding.

My father had recently retired from his sweatshop women's rainwear position as a pattern cutter. This would mean an end to the occasional conversations that he and my mother would have about Moishe the Samplemaker. I never quite understood what Moishe did, but, whatever job he performed, it had provided material for animated discussions between my parents. I was worried about how my father might spend his retirement years and feared the effect of an ever-closer intrusion on my mother's private life to their already caustic relationship.

Neither of my parents had ever driven an automobile, certainly not since their Stateside arrival in 1941. Summer vacations were coordinated with Lazo, until I was old enough to drive or had friends with cars. When my parents planned a trip, either for a vacation, a day's outing or to visit Josephine, it was coordinated through me. If my car was on one of its frequent visits to the local repair shop, I would entreat my friends to drive my parents to their destination. Fortunately, I had good friends, all of whom were very fond of my good-natured parents.

One such driving venture involved only my mother and me, as my father was working, as he had not yet retired. My mother wanted to visit Josephine on a mid-week day trip. I arranged a day off from work in order to drive her in my car. My mother was annoyed that it would be a curtailed visit. I would have to stop in Woodstock for a short while to pay a speeding ticket fine at the office of the Justice of the Peace.

A year earlier, while driving to visit Josie, I was caught in a speed trap that I had been aware of for years. A less than pleasant State Trooper, whose motorcycle emerged from behind the Texaco gas billboard, made his unwelcome appearance. No sooner was I one mile away from the point of the infraction, when I completely locked the issue out of my mind. The issue became quickly unlocked in my mind, when the annual renewal of my automobile registration was rejected because of an outstanding speeding ticket. I called the Woodstock office and informed the administrative assistant that I would be there at a specific date and time to pay for my ticket.

Upon leaving Josie's house on the afternoon of our visit, my mother and I proceeded to Woodstock to pay for my speeding ticket. We entered the small, chilly, empty courtroom and sat on a wooden bench. Three fluorescent bulbs were the sole lighting, two vases filled with artificial flowers framed the Justice's desk. The nameplate on the slightly raised, blonde oak desk, informed us that the Justice of the Peace was Rudy Baumgartner. Minutes later Rudy entered in his Chevron gas station uniform. No smile, no greeting, just a question: "Are you Mr. Stern?"

"Yes sir, I am," I replied already feeling uneasy.

"One year since the infraction, any reason for the delay?" he asked.

"No sir, my apologies," I answered meekly.

"That'll be two hundred dollars cash, or fifteen days in jail," he stated in a matter of fact tone.

"Sir, I have a checkbook, but do not have that amount in cash," I pleaded. Without looking up Rudy, picked up the phone and called the State Police and informed them that he would need a patrol car at his courtroom as soon as possible. "Sir, may my mother and I attempt to cash a check at a nearby store, as the banks are now closed?" His rude, impassiveness was disconcerting. I could feel my stomach knotting up. Rudy granted us fifteen minutes.

The first store we tried would not cash an out-of-town check; neither would anyone else in town, they informed us. My mother freaked out. I thought for a moment. "Mom, I need your best Sarah Bernhardt acting. As soon as the patrol car arrives at Rudy's shop and the State Trooper enters the courtroom, you need to pretend that you are having a heart attack." It was all that I could think of to extricate us from Justice Rudy, who seemed intent upon showing this "city slicker" what rural law was all about. "Harry, are you sure it will work?" "Mom, I am only sure what will happen if it doesn't work."

We returned within fifteen minutes and informed Rudy that we had not succeeded in securing the cash. He didn't answer. Two minutes later the rear door opened and a straight-backed State Trooper entered and strode toward Rudy. On cue, my mother outdid herself as an actress. Certainly the many tragic operas that she had enjoyed over the many years in Vienna and New York, had modeled for her how to enact a death scene. Verdi himself, would have been proud. She clutched at her throat and her chest simultaneously and began gasping for air. Rudy bought it. He was really undone. I "begged" Rudy to please accept a check, so that I could get my mother to her medication and a calmer setting, she was in grave danger. He agreed, and we were out of there in two minutes flat. I counseled my mother, as I helped her exit Rudy's party, that she must not smile until we were five miles away from Woodstock.

It worried me that, with our leaving for Israel, my parents would become virtually homebound. They both had never flown on an airplane, had no personal means of transportation and seemed to have no ability or desire to travel independently. They were reluctant to consider moving to a new neighborhood and seemed always to be on a financial precipice. My father had few discernible interests outside of his daily work routines; and my parent's relationship was mercurial at best.

My father was probably the primary reason that our branch of the Stern family existed. He had navigated the treacherous shoals of a continent under Nazi siege through countries that were often complicit in virulent anti-Semitism. He was as cool as could be under duress. My mother had thrived after her debilitating initial years in America. She was the product of a highly cultured Viennese family. Somehow, she had managed to nurture her mountain dwelling daughter, her perennially problematic son, and her academically gifted youngest daughter.

It was only after several months in Israel, that I began to comprehend that I had unwittingly infantilized and underestimated them. Somewhere in that mix, I had also overestimated their dependence on me, perhaps as a way of unconsciously maintaining an acceptable tie between us. Or, perhaps as a camouflage for my own dependence on them. No sooner had Aviva and I boarded our one way flight to Israel than my parents were on their way to vacation in Puerto Rico, their first ever flight. My father soon became a head volunteer at The Metropolitan Opera, which allowed both of them to attend dress rehearsals of the many operas that they loved and were intimately familiar with. They booked trips to Austria, Switzerland, Costa Rica and made arrangements to visit us in Israel. They moved to Rego

Park, Queens, a Jewish neighborhood close to Lazo. As I analyzed this spurt of *joie de vivre*, I began to assess that I may have been holding them back, rather than facilitating their activities.

How often in life, do we delude ourselves that our overbearing protectionism is exclusively for the good of our children, parents, loved partners? More-often-than-not, our excessive caring comes with a healthy mix of personal dependency and insecurity. Anyway, that's what I concluded about my behavior.

For several months, we had been repeatedly saying goodbye to our friends and families. In early June, our furniture was removed from our apartment, taken to a warehouse to be waiting for us at our absorption center destination in Netanya, Israel. We really had only a very superficial understanding of what an absorption center was.

On the day of our departure to Israel, my parents, Melinda and our cousins Zvi and Sima, accompanied us to JFK International airport. Because of the nature of our trip, the Jewish Agency arranged for our entourage to accompany us to an area not far from the El Al airliner, which was situated on the tarmac, some distance from the main terminal. I had never seen an El Al plane before and looked with pride and wonderment at the Magen David and the flag of Israel displayed on the side of the fuselage. That swirl of a personal and secret personal anti-Jewishness, that the dogmatic and rigid Yeshiva had scarred me with, finally gave way to a sense of power and pride in viewing the airliner, even from a distance.

After an abundance of hugs, kisses and wishes of good luck, which in retrospect, probably meant: "come to your senses soon and return to us," we boarded a shuttle bus that would transport us to the plane. I stood by the window, looked out at the tarmac and felt my first real pangs of remorse, as the bus slowly wheeled to the left, and I saw my sister, Melinda, jogging alongside waving goodbye. I was suddenly riven by a range of feelings that I had suppressed for the past year.

I would be seven thousand miles from watching Melinda grow into a young woman. My parents were getting on in age, how could I be there for them? I wasn't sure when I would see Josephine again. "Tell me again," I asked Aviva, "why are we moving to Israel?" I pulled Aviva closer to me, as many tears welling up in her eyes, as in mine.

We arrived at the airliner after the brief shuttle ride. The seven forty seven sat alone in a circle of light standing out proudly, it seemed, in the midnight hour, despite its isolation. The bus came to a halt near the parked plane, we descended, and unenthusiastically walked toward the waiting gangway.

After yet another review of our boarding documents, we ascended and found our seats. How many others in our plane were experiencing similar emotional gyrations? Soon the flight was airborne; no turning back. I hoped for some recognition from the attendants, that we were on our way to live in Israel, family upheaval and all. It never came.

Chapter Fifteen

WE WERE MET at the airport in Israel by Jewish Agency representatives, transported to our Absorption Center where we were registered and perfunctorily welcomed. We were soon assigned an apartment, and informed that our furniture would remain in its wooden lift for several months, safe and secure in a guarded warehouse. Finally, we were tested for our knowledge of the Hebrew language, so as to be appropriately placed in a language class. The Center had the visual gestalt of a summer camp that seemed unconcerned with its appearance and was missing the playground, horseback riding stables, and zip lines. Despite being less than one mile from the azure, Mediterranean Sea, the landscape was bleak, scraggly, and poorly maintained.

Aviva and I tried hard to overlook the dearth of basic amenities and the aesthetic neglect. We reminded ourselves of what we soon learned to be the universal Israeli mantra, an excuse for virtually every problem: "We are only a new, poor country, barely twenty years old."

The Absorption Center was euphemistically named the Ulpan. The Ulpan, a Hebrew word for a language learning center, was what most residents referred to when asked for their address. It was, in truth, a brilliant concept. The underlying assumption was that new immigrants would have far greater staying power if they had a working knowledge of Hebrew. Total immersion in language studies, it was contended, was the proven method of providing immigrants with the language skills necessary to facilitate assimilation. Additionally, the Center, a cultural melting pot, very much like Israel in general, was a mish mash of immigrants from over one hundred countries around the world.

The Israeli government and diaspora world Jewry, went to great expense to assist in the absorption and assimilation of Jewish immigrants. We, the new arrivals, were required to make a nominal monthly contribution toward our room and board. Our Ulpan was designated as a point of assimilation for about two hundred professionals from a wide range of origins. We were not quite sure how the professional rubric was defined or what the criteria were for being identified in that classification, but it really mattered little to us.

It didn't take us long to ferret out those couples (few had children at the Center) with whom we could identify and look upon as friends. We became very good friends with an architect from Venezuela and his wife, a dentist from Rhodesia and his South African wife, as well as couples from Turkey, Australia and Mexico. Elie Wiesel's sister, Batya, lived a few houses away from ours. John, a barrel-chested, sixty year old, retired physician from Vancouver, paraded around the grounds regularly with a bare chest and his shepherd's walking cane irrespective of the weather. It was a unique and exciting eclectic mix of interesting individuals.

The apartment assigned to us was anything but exciting, with all of the furnishings identifiable by the style Aviva and I termed "Very Early Kibbutz." The entire living area of the apartment was about three hundred fifty square feet. Our small kitchen, the perimeter walls of which I could touch simultaneously with outstretched arms, provided us with a bit of warmth in our chilly apartment. Our intimate bathroom featured a "telephone" shower, the use of which stumped us for about two weeks. As an appendage to our very cozy new dwelling, a small four foot by three foot balcony overlooked a field of sagebrush and weeds. I never felt at ease standing on that rickety balcony.

As our first month slipped by, and the weather turned cooler, we were assigned a "Friedman Deluxe," kerosene heater for our drafty apartment. Aviva and I called it our central heating, as long as we placed the space heater in the center of the room. We made it homey and, with Aviva's nice design touch, the apartment actually assumed a bit of charm. We were quite comfortable, and soon began entertaining friends in it. This was to be our home for six months and we were determined to make it as attractive as we could.

We studied the Hebrew language from nine a.m. until the lunch break at one o'clock, six days of the week. It was a grueling schedule which required keeping a bottle of aspirin handy at all times, as we had persistent headaches. It was more difficult than we thought to get accustomed to total immersion language acquisition, but it worked. I came to Israel with a basic understanding of biblical Hebrew, I could read very elementary Hebrew sentences and so, I was assigned to an advanced class, which was an excellent experience but very challenging. Aviva, who had no knowledge of the language prior to arriving in Israel, was an excellent example of the successful combination of total immersion and a dedicated and willing student. She finished the six months speaking Hebrew at a very good level.

We looked forward to our unremarkable meals in the communal dining room, as it was there where we socialized with friends in-the-making. The quality and diversity of the menu was of minimal importance to us. Developing relationships in the Center was both easy and difficult at the same time. There were numerous couples that struck us as being quite interesting; language differences often created almost insurmountable barriers. Conversely, with those couples with whom we shared a common language, the need to socialize and reinforce our commitment to this difficult immigration process, seemed to bring us together more easily.

The six months on the absorption center generated a unique blending of so many emotions and conflicting observations. Aviva's thoughts about our assimilation process were insightful. "We have a protected, almost cocoon-like opportunity to experience Israeli society from afar, but don't you think that it has prolonged our being exposed to all of its challenges directly?" We were able to share our hopes and trepidations with fellow immigrants about living in Israel. "Aviva," I would continually ask, "how often can we be besieged with their complaints about the rudeness and inefficiencies of Israelis? It really is demoralizing."

Many of those observations were temporarily put aside when the massive, first wave of Russian immigrants arrived in Israel. Over one hundred of the new immigrants were placed at our Center. They arrived penniless, hungry, and clearly victims of The Soviet Union's persecution and, ultimately, exile of Russian Jews.

Those who spoke English, would give thanks to being safe and not persecuted in Israel, while they simultaneously cried, speaking of their Motherland, Russia. Oddly enough, this generated a deep yearning for our Motherland, America. It was heart-wrenching to see the Russians, arriving in about our third month at the Center. I delicately approached one ruddy faced Russian, who appeared to be in his fifties: "Sir, there really is no need to fill your pockets with rolls here in the dining hall. There will be more rolls here tomorrow." My well-intentioned advice was met with a blank, unbelieving stare.

The following waves of Russian immigrants, long after our stay on the Ulpan became a fading memory, were comprised of greater numbers of scientists and other professionals. The new immigrants at our Center, had been in Russian prisons, exiled or had been placed in the wide range of sub-human institutions that Russia seemed to have designed for Jews and dissidents. The sorry state of so many of these new arrivals, created for us a stark and vivid reminder of the need for Israel as a Jewish homeland, offering a welcoming embrace, not just to us, but to those who had no viable future in their land of origin.

Encouraging the new Russian arrival standing on our buffet lunch line, was linked in my mind to my parents narrow escape from the Nazi onslaught. Sharing thoughts with those Russians, who had even an elementary command of English, about the conflicting emotions of desperately missing their beloved homeland, while attempting to digest their newfound freedom, brought back memories of my mother's yearning for the Vienna of her youth.

On a quiet Sunday morning in October, now the beginning of our second month in Israel, I decided to trust our modest second floor terrace and sit outside and enjoy the autumn breeze blowing off the Mediterranean. Both Aviva and I had no classes that day as it was the holiday of Sukkoth. High above us, there were three delta winged, Mirage fighter planes twisting and diving like frolicking birds. Their presence was always felt on the Ulpan, as there was an air force training facility nearby. The previous week, a camouflaged Mirage thundered over our Ulpan repeatedly at an altitude of no more than five hundred feet. It was chilling. We joked that the pilot must have been sent to us by the Israeli government to bolster our flagging spirits.

Somehow, it was these quiet periods that gave rise to an almost overwhelming sense of ennui. Perhaps it was the restful periods that paradoxically made me restive. The hectic, six day a week schedule of intensive language and cultural immersion, gave one little chance for introspection. We were always busy with our homework, thinking about where we would live upon leaving the Center, and what kind of employment we would secure. It was the down time that brought into bold relief that, aside from our cousins, we really didn't know anyone in the country. Our dear cousin Zvi was still in America studying at MIT. Melinda's wave goodbye at the airport haunted me, and the quietude afforded me the unwelcome opportunity to more closely examine the challenges ahead of us. This morning was serenely quiet, people were sleeping late, or taking advantage of the ten day holiday period by visiting relatives or friends.

The country seemed to have come to a virtual standstill. Many stores were closed, public transportation systems, spotty at best, ceased to operate and business offices that were open, closed at twelve-thirty, daily. We found the holiday hiatus incredibly annoying, in particular for those of us with no car, who needed to get some business transactions completed. With no public transportation available, the only alternatives were prohibitively expensive taxis or hitchhiking. What was quite a revelation to us was the virtual omnipotence of the religious political parties in Israel. We struggled to understand this, as the vast majority of Israelis are secular, yet there is a pervasive acquiescence to the orthodox elements. Perhaps, of the plethora of cultural upheavals that we encountered, this issue of orthodox domination, was most confounding.

Aviva and I continually reinforced one another, as our enthusiasm for our intercontinental venture waxed and waned. Social get-togethers with other couples often centered on reasons for one's immigration to Israel. Mariano and Daniella, our Venezuelan friends, shared a bit of why they emigrated from Caracas. "We always feared revolution, there is no middle-class. You are either very rich or very poor." Rhona and Morris, of Rhodesia and South Africa, would observe: "We were also fearful of revolution and the repugnant apartheid regime that we lived with." For many couples with whom we socialized, the fear of revolution or anti-Semitism was wrapped in Zionistic hopes and dreams. I often felt how our rejoinders were very different. We were not fleeing revolution or anti-Semitism and we were not ardent Zionists. When asked about our emigration from America, we would respond, "We came to Israel to live in a society that we felt we could, eventually identify with. Although we are not fleeing from our native land, the way that it seems you are, we are determined to help build the country of Israel."

What I had not included in my naiveté about building a country, was confronting the extraordinary inefficiencies and inconveniences, and trying to cope with them, let alone trying to effect some change. For the most part, it was the émigrés from Western Europe and the USA who were driven to distraction by the Levantine bureaucracy, and the lack of concern for detail and courtesy. Appointments were made and broken with regularity: several of our new friends drove to neighboring cities for job interviews, only to find the party they were scheduled to meet with was on vacation.

Purchasing an item such as furniture, an automobile or any electronic equipment could take months and, more times than not, the paperwork would be lost in the process. And all was defended by that familiar mantra: "we are just a young country." Despite all of the growing pains of this fledgling country and its bureaucracies, which we believed were designed by some sadistic Caliph of the Byzantine Empire, we found that we were falling in love with Israel.

We were able to make a clear distinction between the clerks of an unfathomable and murky bureaucracy, with whom we of necessity, came in regular contact, and the average Israeli whom we found helpful and charming. Americans, it seemed, had the most difficulty in adjusting…and forgiving. Perhaps it was a bit easier for us because we had been prepared, to the extent that it was possible to prepare, not to expect "Scarsdale in the Middle-East."

Many of our American colleagues on the Ulpan had moved to Israel for religious reasons. Feeling comfortable wearing a kippa, having unbridled access to the Western Wall and Jerusalem and living in complete Jewish freedom, were predominant reasons Americans shared for their immigration to Israel. Many had been steeped in Zionism from childhood. What most irritated us was the continual kvetching and complaining, mostly from the American contingent. Perhaps fewer complaints were heard from our growing base of friends from European or South American countries, because they had experienced similar governmental bureaucracies. Their countries' civil servants were also apathetic at best and malicious at worst. America's systems were more refined and often did not require personal appearances.

We found ourselves minimizing contact with American couples. It was hard enough coping with our own apprehension and disappointment, we did not need to have our social get-togethers reinforce those feelings. As we became more friendly with couples of other countries, we were told repeatedly that we did not look like Americans and more importantly, they observed, we did not act like Americans. This was somewhat confusing to us, as our homeland generated in us feelings of pride and accomplishment. Aviva and I often commented to one another, how lucky we were to be born in America. Conversely, we also felt a bit relieved about our not falling under the umbrella of complaining American immigrants.

Our observations of the goals of many American Ulpan residents, were that, in addition to their stated aspirations of religious openness, a number of them had come to start businesses and acquire wealth. Too often when speaking of Israelis, they did so with a condescending tone. Our American counterparts also seemed to be having the greatest difficulty learning the Hebrew language. So many Americans speak only one language and so, they exert a subtle pressure on anyone wanting to communicate with them, that it must be done in English. The reluctance to make the effort to speak other languages, in this case Hebrew, certainly does not endear Americans to the rest of the world.

The six month indoctrination period afforded us a unique opportunity for introspection. Our days of study and the planning of how we were to fit into a new society, resembled a suspended animation, a departure from the incessant drive to tend to the immediate necessities of life.

How we interrelated with couples from societies so different from the one that we had recently come from, was one issue we wrestled with, but that was superseded by issues far more important. We had come from a society that was open and, for the most part, accepting of its Jewish citizens. The ingathering of Jews, from so many countries on the Ulpan, so many with heart-wrenching stories of anti-Semitism and persecution, was a daily reminder for us of the indispensability of Israel as a Jewish homeland.

The world seemed quite comfortable having Jews in vulnerable, minority societal positions. In particular, it seemed, that European countries were continually flirting with resurgent anti-Semitism. I thought of my parents and sister Josephine secretly following my father's serpentine escape route to Casablanca and evading the Vichy government's eager assistance to the Nazi regime to thwart such escapes. America was my parents' address for salvation. I was beginning to understand, for how many others in the world, Israel was that saving address.

Our long and unstructured afternoons were not always laden with heavy thoughts; they also gave us an opportunity to hit the books and socialize with those who either had no car, like us, or who enjoyed the quiet afternoons, as we did. One of those lazy afternoons left an indelible impression on us and temporarily shattered the notion of internal Israeli security.

We had just entered our fourth month in Israel. The winter wind was whistling, rattling our loose fitting windows. The Bank Hapoalim calendar, hanging on our kitchen wall, was rustling in the breeze, despite our closed windows valiantly fighting off the cold, Mediterranean chill. Our "Friedman Deluxe" was doing all that it could to keep our apartment at a livable temperature. We were preparing dinner in our apartment when a halting, almost apologetic, knock on our door penetrated the howl of the mischievous wind.

Morris Goldberg, our downstairs neighbor, stood in our doorway with his blue sweatshirt's hood drawn up, covering his thinning brown hair. Morris had a perennially gentle and inquisitive smile on his face and was easy to talk to. He, his lovely wife Flora and their two college age sons, had arrived from Mexico City on the same day, and virtually the same time, that we were registering at the front desk of the Ulpan upon our arrival. They spoke English very well, flavored with a charming, Mexican lilt. Aviva and I connected with them immediately and often shared a table in our communal dining room. We were intrigued by Flora's firebrand personality and her iconoclastic approach to Israeli politics.

Morris wasn't at our apartment at six thirty in the evening to socialize with us. He inquired if we had seen Flora as she was three hours later than expected from her walk on the nearby beach. It had been dark for nearly one and a half hours and no one had heard from her. I told Morris that I had seen Flora that morning and that she had complained of an ear ache resulting, she maintained, from her beautician's appointment.

"Well," Morris sighed, "it's not like her to be late so, I am officially worried. I'll be in our apartment if you hear anything," his voice always seemed to trail off at the conclusion of a sentence. "Morris, I will contact you as soon as I hear anything. I am certain that all is OK with Flora."

"Big shot," I thought as I shut the door behind Morris, berating myself for phony and baseless assurances. If Aviva were to be five minutes late for an appointment with me, I always assumed the worst, everything from under-the-radar tsunamis to extra-terrestrial body snatchers.

Morris' knock at our door and his query about Flora soon was overtaken by our bumping into one another and laughing as we tried to negotiate preparing a meal in our tiny kitchen area. We jokingly designated various corners of our modest apartment: the chef's corner in our kitchen, the dining room, the library and the living room. Actually, all of these areas were the same spaces with interchangeable names. The joviality was short-lived, as we asked one another what could have caused Flora's unusual lateness.

"It's hard to believe that any ill could have befallen Flora," Aviva offered hopefully. Our meal assumed an unusually somber tone and we were silent for extended periods. Our attempt to convince one another that no harm could come to Flora was halted by a firm rap on our door. It was Morris again, this time with five of the men of nearby apartments. It was now pitch black outside with a stiff wind blowing a chilly mist into our apartment. I barely noticed, as my heart beat faster.

"Come with us, Harry," Morris blurted out, leaving little doubt as to what my answer would be. "We will search the coast line, perhaps she has injured herself and cannot get back home," he stated in a wishful tone. Suddenly, an injury seemed to be an optimistic resolution to this developing situation.

For the next three or four hours many men from the Ulpan methodically combed the shore. Car headlights crisscrossed the areas in front of and behind us. The many flashlight beams seemed to be making geometric designs in the moonless darkness. I hoped that I would find some trace of our good friend Flora, while I simultaneously dreaded it. After hours of searching, we agreed that we would return home and resume the search in an hour.

We arranged to meet in front of the administration center, and at 3 am, as I neared the building, I noticed a group of residents standing in front of the center. Even from a distance, the group had a pall cast over it. Trackers from the police had discovered Flora's lifeless body beaten, strangled and partially buried in a nearby sand dune.

The early morning scene was grim and surrealistic. Morris and his sons were in a state of disbelief and shock and asked the authorities the same questions repeatedly. Two days later, many Ulpan residents attended Flora's funeral in the nearby town of Herzliya. The police apprehended the perpetrator, who was not a terrorist in the 'traditional' sense, but an escaped inmate from a psychiatric institution's violent patient ward.

Aviva and I, while shaken by Flora's murder, were determined to move ahead with our assimilation into Israeli society. Simultaneously, I determined not to let Aviva out of my sight, at least for the foreseeable future. The impending pressure to successfully become a part of Israeli society and the unreality of our current life, provided a buffer and distraction that helped us to overcome, even so devastating an occurrence as Flora's brutal murder.

We were aware that the final two months on the absorption center were critical. Our language skills had been nicely developed in our first four months, but now we were focused on employment and housing. I purchased a car, a Volkswagen Beetle, which was to arrive from Germany in the last two weeks of our six month stay on the Ulpan. The Jewish Agency arranged to have an employment recruiter visit the Ulpan twice weekly, assisting all of us in the search for employment. The recruiter would set up employment interviews and requested feedback on their results.

Social work positions were abundant as the country had innumerable social problems, as it continued to offer its "Law of Return" policy to Jews world-wide. In addition to the influx of many thousands of Russian Jews, the great majority of recent Jewish immigrants had been settled in Israel from Arab countries where they were marginalized at best, or worse, suffered severe deprivation and persecution. The prevailing joke asked, when the immigration from Switzerland could be expected.

Aviva connected with the prestigious Batsheva Dance Company, Israel's premiere modern ballet company, and was to join them shortly thereafter. I was offered a very promising position with the Tel Aviv Municipality. We were on our way to securing a four bedroom apartment in Southern Tel Aviv. While employment, at a good professional level, was a critical element in the survival rate of new immigrants, obtaining our newly constructed apartment was perhaps the single greatest harbinger of a positive, post-Ulpan assimilation. The Jewish Agency had offered us several apartment options for purchase.

We decided on the Southern Tel Aviv apartment due to its significant size, new construction and its location, which was not far from where my future office would be. We had only to apply for a mortgage, which was a rarity for the average Israeli purchasing an apartment, for whom bank loans were virtually unobtainable. The Jewish Agency offered this arrangement as an additional perk for new immigrants, so as to encourage immigration, especially from developed countries.

The Israeli banking industry inspired fear and dread in most immigrants, only a click below Palestinian terrorism. The banking systems seemed preternatural, arcane and submerged in a sea of molasses. Clerks in this unfortunate system were friendly enough, but were universally equipped with an abundance of colored, official stamps that must have once had value to a sadistic bureaucrat and were affixed to all legal documents, lest they be rendered invalid.

It was with this fear and trembling that Aviva and I entered the main branch of Israel's largest bank, Bank Leumi. We arrived at about ten in the morning and had to wait about fifteen minutes while the banking world went into a uniform, suspended animation, better known as the mid-morning tea break. We sat patiently in the waiting area of the small, mortgage department of the bank. A very pleasant clerk took our names, she was evidently a refugee from the tea break world, and handed me some forms to review prior to our interview. All the forms were in a legalese Hebrew; I could barely understand ten percent of the content. What I did comprehend, puzzled me.

"What I cannot fathom," I confided in Aviva, "is why, in the modern state of Israel, the Jewish homeland, we need to have two Arab witnesses for our mortgage. Perhaps it is a throwback to the Ottoman Empire, that had such influence on the region. It might also," I suggested, "be a sign of the egalitarianism pushed for in Israel; perhaps it is a signal of greater Arab empowerment generated after the humiliation that the Arab world experienced after the Six Day War."

My scant and suspect knowledge of geopolitical dynamics was soon exhausted. When the seemingly endless tea break came to an end, we were invited into the department manager's very modest office. After some brief, introductory remarks she began to review the documents, which I informed her we did not understand. I did, however, have a procedural question.

"Why would we be required to have two Arab witnesses for this mortgage?" I inquired. "We are new to this country and have not had a chance to meet any Arabs."

She looked puzzled, until I pointed to one of the few paragraphs that I believed I understood. She burst into laughter and, in an attempt to control herself, informed me, "The Hebrew word for guarantor is "areyvim" while the Hebrew word for Arabs is "aravim." She felt compelled to share my error in Hebrew translation with her colleagues, many of whom may still be laughing to this day. For some time thereafter, Aviva felt obliged to verify my interpretations through a third party.

We soon received notification that our new immigrant mortgage had been approved. Bank related incidents featured prominently in our years in Israel. Perhaps the most intriguing narrative involving a bank occurred about three weeks before the end of our stay on the Ulpan.

We were pleased that my textual blunder in the mortgage department had no negative consequences, as our mortgage was approved, and we were to move into our new apartment in a few weeks. Our car had not yet arrived from Germany and so, we were dependent on our ability to secure a hitchhiked ride for a while longer. Hitchhiking was an accepted mode of transportation for a significant segment of the population-including soldiers with military gear.

We were headed in to Tel Aviv to visit a furniture showroom. We waited no longer than five minutes on the access road to the main highway linking Netanya and Tel Aviv, when a shiny, black Peugeot pulled up and the driver beckoned to us to get in. At that time in Israel's history, it was not unusual for a lone driver, male or female, to offer a hitchhiker a ride. The driver, Ella Yeffet, was an attractive middle-aged woman who spoke English impeccably. She was bubbly, effusive, articulate, inquisitive and a resident of Tel Aviv, although she was born in Germany.

We answered the string of usual questions: "Why were we in Israel?" "How did we like it?" etc., etc. Toward the end of our twenty mile journey Ella asked: "What are you doing for your seder, Passover is only three weeks away?" We had no plans, we said, and had given it no thought. "Well, that settles it," she commented, warmly and spontaneously, "You will come to my house for the seder." As we arrived at our destination, Ella pulled over to a curb, wrote out her name and address, and insisted: "You must appear on Passover eve at 6:30 p.m. No later." We thanked her warmly and made our way into the furniture district in North Tel Aviv.

Several days before Passover, and only days away from moving from the Ulpan into our new apartment, we decided that we would take Ella up on her offer. Our car had arrived from Germany, but I was still reluctant to drive in the labyrinthian streets of Tel Aviv. We decided to take a taxi on Passover eve to the address that Ella had scrawled on a piece of note paper.

I tried to brace Aviva, and myself, for disappointment: "This address may turn out to be a junk yard or massage parlor." We were prepared for anything. As we approached North Tel Aviv, we entered a lovely, seriously upscale neighborhood with beautiful, detached homes, unusual in size and design for Israel. The taxi pulled up to the front of an elegant home in the center of this upscale neighborhood.

"Here we are, nice house," our driver offered, as we nervously left the cab and made our way up the inclined walkway to the house.

"Be ready for anything," I muttered, more to myself than to Aviva, as I rang the door bell. To our pleasant surprise, Ella answered the door with a big smile.

"I am so happy that you came as our guests," she said with a disarming and charming sincerity. I handed her the bouquet of flowers that we had thankfully, remembered to bring.

Ella ushered us into her spacious living room, with furniture reconfigured to accommodate a beautiful seder arrangement. She introduced us to her guests, an extraordinary "who's who" of Israeli society: her cousin, Abba Eban, then Israel's Foreign Minister, and his wife Susan, Pinchas Sapir, Minister of Finance and Yehoshua Rabinovitz, Mayor of Tel Aviv. Ella's husband, Ernst, we soon learned, was the Chairman of Israel's largest international bank, Bank Leumi. Ella was the Chairperson of a large women's auxiliary organization.

Ella beckoned to Aviva to sit next to Susan Eban and I found a space next to Abba Eban. To my utter amazement, I found myself discussing the virtues of training troops for Idi Amin's Uganda with Israel's Foreign Minister. My Israeli cousin Ari, had been involved, as a member of the armed forces of Israel, in the training of Ugandan troops. Amin was also preparing to visit Israel in the following year.

The seder service, conducted by Ernst, was thankfully, short and participatory. The meal served soon thereafter, was sumptuous. Ella cheerfully passed around a large platter of Moroccan chicken submerged in a sweet, redolent sauce with apricots, prunes and dates among the steaming fruits that I recognized. What a dramatic departure from our Ulpan meals which, after six months, had worn out their initial welcome.

The taxi ride back to our Ulpan was marked with our frenetic discussions and our sheer disbelief at the evening we had spent with such an entourage of unique characters. Meeting with people holding such high public office who were so prominent in the public arena was a unique experience for us. It seems that the size of the country made public figures much more accessible to the ordinary citizen. "It must be difficult," Aviva surmised, "to hold public office in Israel, where there is so little room to hide and so little personal privacy." Our taxi approached our Ulpan's administration building. The reality of the challenges ahead of us in the upcoming weeks suddenly tempered our euphoria, as we arrived at what was to be our home for only a few more days.

Chapter Sixteen

LIFE IN ISRAEL was like riding on a perennial roller coaster. The zigs and zags of our daily routine wrought emotional highs, that came when we were conversing with Israelis in Hebrew and basking in the illusion of assimilation. We hit our doldrums, upon encountering the archaic systems and the riotous confluence of refugees from over one hundred countries. There were times when the seven thousand miles that separated us from our prior existence seemed like a measurement in light years.

The move into our new apartment was surprisingly uneventful and well-organized. The four bedroom apartment was spacious and airy with three balconies. The fourth floor walk up didn't bother us, but our moving men probably held different viewpoints. By the beginning of our third week in our new apartment I was ready to begin my work at the Municipal Building. I took the public bus to my office and generally left the car for Aviva, as she navigated Tel Aviv's dance world.

Our apartment was in Southern Tel Aviv, bordering the slum neighborhoods of Kfar Shalem and Shchunat Hatikvah. Both of these downtrodden areas were misnomers of the highest order: Kfar Shalem, meaning village of unity, a name antithetical to the reality of its fragmentation. Shchunat Hatikvah's meaning was even more far-fetched, with the wildly inappropriate interpretation of neighborhood of hope. Both areas were notorious in Israel for crime rings and violence.

What impacted us more viscerally was the city's garbage dump, which was about three miles away. We got to know the wind patterns and when to close all windows to fend off the intolerable stench. None of this caused us excessive grief or concern, as we focused more on meeting our neighbors, mostly new immigrants from western countries. Our apartment was now our new home.

My position was a work in progress. The City's Director of Social Services, Batya Mintal, was my direct supervisor. She was well-intentioned, intelligent, very Germanic and appeared to me to be a political appointee, in a position beyond her professional expertise. She declared unilaterally, within days of my arrival, that I was now the director of community organization for Southern Tel Aviv.

My Master's Degree from Columbia University, was hailed as a significant upgrade to the Department of Social Services, even though my greatest accomplishment to that point was befriending the tea cart lady. I decided early in my new career, that I would request a change of location for my office: away from the officious and insulated, eleven story Municipal Building, to the target area of our services. Batya responded favorably. All that she needed to do was to locate an appropriate site for my office in Shchunat Hatikvah. I assured her that I would not need a guard and the office need not be air-conditioned. Three weeks later, I made my way to my new office.

The six day work week, which included Sunday, never developed into one of my favorite aspects of the Israeli workplace. Sunday, as I headed toward my new digs in Hatikvah, it was already very hot and still, even though it was only seven thirty in the morning. My first day also found me trying to navigate the one mile walk from my house through precious, shaded areas. I learned quickly, that the middle eastern *Chamseen*, or dry, hot desert wind, is a force to be reckoned with. The walk to my office was anything but pleasant: alleyways that smelled of urine, garbage strewn in those same places. Shchunat Hatikvah was a serious slum, not unlike areas in New York that I had worked in. From all appearances, my new home base suffered from a similar lack of services.

Arriving at the store-front office site with a sense of challenge and excitement, I turned the door key in a rusted latch. Begrudgingly, a creaking door swung open to welcome me to the 450 square foot space. Not surprisingly, it was dark and musty, with its most distinguishing characteristic, a windowed partition separating the work space from a tiny sink. Adjacent to the grimy sink, was a minuscule toilet that would challenge Clark Kent's ability to transform himself into Superman. Two formica-topped desks covered the cracked stone tiles that lined the left side of my new office. Two bulletin boards hung askew, with newsprint tacked to them, noting events long past. I switched on the lights to find that, thankfully, one of the eight fluorescent bulbs was working.

Despite the outside heat of the *Chamseen*, I felt chilled. Had I done the right thing? Had I exhibited my customary "ready, fire, aim" approach to planning? Was my short stint at the Municipal Building really enough time to make such a radical change to my work environment? Would I miss the tea lady's clanging cart at nine thirty? Was the intolerably, slow and removed pace in my comfortable Municipal environment really so unbearable? Despite the questions that I mulled over, I never seriously doubted that this was where I needed to be. I set out to explore my new surroundings.

Exiting my new office, an abandoned neighborhood restaurant, I followed a narrow alleyway that snaked about forty feet to the main street in Hatikvah. The haze, that often accompanies a *Chamseen*, had lifted, and the morning sun shone brightly. I continued to the right on the main street. Less than one hundred yards from my office, Hatikvah's main shuk, or open-air market, was already a bee hive of activity.

Walking through the market it struck me that the pendulum of time had halted its arcing dance. The market was a teeming, bustling, sweltering confluence of a dizzying array of North African Israelis. It seemed that, at once, one could be removed from the daily travail of a "ghetto" life, while at the very same time, be swept unconsciously into the tactile, cacophonous and relentless ambience of the shuk. The attraction for the area's youths, seemed to be the very chaos of the environment. Young people lounged about waiting to either cause trouble, maybe to pass the time away, or to earn a few coins by moving vegetable laden crates for the vendors barking the quality and price of their goods.

Hunched-over elderly shoppers, weaved their way fearlessly, through the maze of stalls, carrying shopping baskets that were too heavy for their time-wearied frames. Mothers called out to their toddlers to return the fruit that they had taken from an array of vendors tracking all movements within five meters of their stands. Street sewers were backed up, contributing to the acrid odors of discarded and spoiled produce behind each vendor's stall. The shuk was an eternal junction of people from disparate North African countries exhibiting timeless acts of bargaining, negotiating, complaining, relating, which no doubt, was a collective inheritance acquired over centuries. I felt invigorated, saddened, energized and, oddly, convinced that I was in the right place professionally. I turned back through the shuk and bought a bag of clementines.

It didn't take too long to transform that inhospitable work space into a respectable looking office. Two weeks into my solo performance, I was fortunate enough to hire Ella, a tough, twenty-five year old, wisecracking Israeli, who had great respect for the client population. The word was out in the community, that representatives of the Social Services Department were now located in their neighborhood. We became inundated with requests for welfare benefits, medical assistance and other means of financial assistance. We made it clear that those benefits were the domain of the Municipality and not any part of the services we were able to provide.

Most folks didn't get it, but Sarah and Klara weren't most folks. They had been energetically exploring ways to empower Hatikvah residents, and we became their vehicle for making it a reality. Both Sarah and Klara were virtually daily visitors at our office and, in turn, we visited their homes. They were firebrands and major contributors to any successes that we achieved.

Within a few months we laid the groundwork for a community day care center; a neighborhood library comprised of books that we had donated from many sources; and a Hatikvah newspaper that featured articles written by Sarah and Klara, community residents as well as local politicians. A community planning committee was established and met every other week. I was very pleased with our progress, but not so pleased with my monthly supervisory session with Batya.

I had not met with Batya for about two months having been too busy to visit the Municipal Building. I was continually trying to keep up with Sarah and Klara and their unbounded commitment to community improvement projects, and had lost contact with Batya. I entered her office, received a warm greeting from her, and sat at her conference table. It was hard to read her expressions as she had a perennial smile and was extraordinarily even-tempered. But, she wasn't happy today.

"Harry," she began, and I knew, when a conversation begins with your name, it's not good. "I have the distinct impression that you don't like to work hard, is this an American characteristic?" I was shocked.

"What makes you say that?"

"You wanted an office in Hatikvah, we got it; you wanted an assistant, you now have Ella, what have we gotten in return?" Batya stated as peremptorily as her personality would allow.

When I shared with Batya what we had accomplished for the first time in Hatikvah, in just a few months, the tone and nature of the conversation changed radically. She was going to include this progress in her written report to the Mayor, with whom she acknowledged, I had shared a Passover seder. I had learned a great lesson that stayed with me for years: keep your supervisor informed and current about all your professional activities. I had evidently subscribed to only two of a Chassidic tripartite classifications of man: He who thinks about an action; He who says he will perform an action; and, He who actually performs that action. I learned that the "saying" category has merit as well.

We retained the strong friendships that we had forged on the Ulpan with our South African friends, Rhona and Morris and the Venezuelan family, with whom we became very close, Daniella and Mariano. We visited our Ulpan friends quite frequently. Most visits were to our friend's homes in the northern sectors of Tel Aviv and beyond. While we generally paid it scant attention, it was more prestigious to live in those sections of town than where we lived, which probably accounted for our traveling northward for social contact rather than the reverse.

The months passed quickly and our Hatikvah, alleyway office became a hub of community activity. Even the bone-chilling cold of the damp, coastal winter, fended off minimally by a small, three coiled, Japanese space heater, was bearable, given the emotional heat generated by our results in the previously forgotten Hatikvah Quarter.

Our best results, however, were produced in the summer of 1972, when Aviva informed me that she was pregnant. We were both ecstatic, but, the next months were not easy for Aviva. Her pregnancy was marked by a prolonged sensitivity to odors, light, noise and movement. We never went anywhere without a supply of paper bags. Our apartment was generally about as brightly lit as the Bat Cave and our meals had to be prepared with minimal cooking odors. I felt a sense of powerlessness to help Aviva and knew that, given her strong constitution, and a disinclination to complain, she must have been suffering. Perhaps, the discomfort was compounded by our sense of isolation from family, in particular from Zita.

Aviva's dancing soon took a back seat to her pregnancy, probably contributing to an even greater sense of disconnectedness. It took me some time to understand the impact wrought on a dancer's psyche and physical well-being by remaining sedentary. As a result of her prolonged feeling of nausea due to the pregnancy, Aviva was like a race horse being limited to an occasional trot.

It was about the fifth month of Aviva's pregnancy that two unrelated events unfolded. The public relations department of The Jewish Agency contacted us and asked if they could fashion an article focused on us, as an example of a couple that had successfully integrated into Israeli society. We were flattered and agreed. Photographers came to my Hatikvah office and a journalist interviewed me extensively. There was a repeat performance at our apartment for Aviva.

Unfortunately, the first time we had an opportunity to read the lengthy article describing our splendid assimilation, with many pictures of us at home and my office, was when we were living on 97th street and Amsterdam Avenue in Manhattan.

The return journey to the States took an unusual and circuitous path. Soon after our interviews with The Jewish Agency reporters, I received a letter from Columbia University School of Social Work. I opened a personal letter from the Dean, in which he informed me, that the School had identified nominees for its Doctoral Program. Columbia was prepared to offer select candidates, a four year full fellowship, which included all tuition-related expenses and a modest annual stipend. Interested candidates were asked to complete a questionnaire identifying the academic function they would be prepared to perform, should they be selected to receive the fellowship.

The academic areas identified were, among others: research assistant, teaching assistant, statistician, field experimentation and analyses. I answered negatively on all queries, my stated reason being, that I wished to complete my doctorate as soon as possible, so that I may return to Israel. I collaborated with Aviva on my responses and we both surmised, that this would be the last that we would hear from Columbia. It wasn't.

One month after returning my response to Columbia, I received a letter congratulating me on being one of the selected candidates to receive a full National Institute of Health fellowship for four years. To this day, I am unclear how this happened: Were there surplus funds that National Institute of Health (NIH) had to dispose of? Was this meant for another Harry Stern, as occurred some years back in Naples? Was it divine intervention? I was a good student in the Master's program, but not that good!

That proverbial die was cast. We would leave Israel just long enough for me to complete my doctoral degree and then return as soon as possible. We made plans to leave Israel in June of 1973, with our yet-to-be-born infant.

Throughout her pregnancy, Aviva had been cared for by Dr. Jacks, a wonderful, Australian ob/gyn. Dr. Jacks was warm with a wry sense of humor. He was regarded as among Israel's finest physicians, a reputation that was well-deserved. He inspired confidence in both of us. Aviva was to give birth in Asuta

Hospital, one of the few private hospitals in Israel. We were aware that our child was to be born as a breech delivery, but we did not want to know its sex in advance. As Aviva was twelve days past her due date, Dr. Jacks informed me in the hospital waiting room, that Aviva would undergo a Caesarian delivery. After what seemed to me an eternity, Dr. Jacks met me in the waiting room, and informed me that Aviva was fine and that we had a lovely, beautiful, healthy daughter.

Several days later, we were on our way home to our apartment. We were well-prepared for all of the immediate necessities of a newborn infant, except for the violent sandstorm that unexpectedly hit Tel Aviv. We were in our apartment with our new born Lora no longer that two hours, when the mid- day sky turned dark. The wind swirled with a vengeance, howling with a unique gusto. Tel Aviv was experiencing its first sandstorm in years.

Windblown sand was forced beneath and alongside our firmly closed windows; white sand was forced under the closed doors of our terraces, a testament to the intensity of the wind gusts. I secured our bedroom windows with wet towels but noticed some sand already on our new daughter's crib sheet. Ten minutes of frantically blockading doors and windows seemed to prevent dune formation in our bedroom. The storm ended as abruptly as it began. The sun reappeared and I peered out of our bedroom window to see the streets white with sand, reminiscent of a New England snowstorm. Aviva and I looked at one another and wondered if this tumultuous welcome home for our newborn infant Lora, presaged a personality trait for our new daughter.

The birth of our beautiful daughter and the joy that I felt made leaving for work every morning a soap opera scenario: a reluctance to say goodbye to both of my "women." I felt great about my work and the development of so many community initiatives, but I had lesser feelings for my supervisee Eli. His unrelenting intensity was unnerving.

Eli was from Bombay (now Mumbai), India. His family had been active in the small, but influential, Jewish community in India. He and his family had emigrated to Israel five years earlier and had settled in Southern Tel Aviv, not very far from our apartment. Eli was twenty-three, about six foot tall, nice looking with an aquiline nose highlighting a slim face, that glowed with a deep, olive complexion. His dark, brown eyes appeared magical and penetrating. Those piercing eyes were bordered by thick, bushy, black eyebrows and long, beautifully arched eyelashes.

He was a serious, fourth year social work major at Tel Aviv University who had selected me, sight unseen, as the supervisor for his twice weekly field work requirement. He had a great interest in applying social work theory to practice. Unfortunately, I felt that the theoretical underpinnings for the field were apocryphal at best and bullshit at its worst. Eli was an intense student, who had difficulty being an intense student, at our cramped and busy office.

Our Hatikvah office was a vortex of activity with community residents popping in unannounced to share an idea or complaint. Providing Eli with the quiet, focused and thoughtful supervision that he wanted and deserved, was virtually impossible in our close quarters. Interruptions to our one hour supervisory sessions were disconcerting to him.

Throwing caution to the wind, I asked Eli if we could conduct the upcoming supervisory session at my apartment, where we could focus uninterruptedly on his social work practice issues.

Knowing that we had just had a baby, Eli asked, "Might it not be an imposition on Aviva and your private lives?" About the only thing I loved about Eli was his clipped, British accent. "Eli, I appreciate your concern, but it will pose no problem, and will allow us to deal with some professional issues that our office environment has made impossible." I should have known.

At about two fifteen of that next day, fifteen minutes before my meeting with Eli, Aviva informed me that she was going to the store and would return shortly. We reviewed all of the steps required should our sleeping, twenty day old, daughter wake up. I had a nagging worry about her leaving at this time, although I was happy that she was getting out of the house, having been homebound for almost two weeks. She knew of my determination to satisfy Eli's academic requirements and understood how his rigidity was unsettling to me. I insisted that she leave, but I implored her not stay away too long.

"Don't be so uptight, Lora's sleeping, this is her long sleep time."

Somehow, I wasn't comforted by those observations as she left. I set out some orange drink, two glasses and a few cookies on a small platter. The doorbell rang about ten minutes after Aviva's departure, and Eli appeared with his Tel Aviv University notebook in hand, ready to take notes of our meeting.

There was minimal small talk with Eli, which was fine with me, as my internal metronome was ticking away, waiting for baby Lora to awaken. Five minutes into our review of Eli's agenda, I heard Lora stir and then cry. I caught a slight raising of Eli's thick, bushy eyebrows out of the corner of my eye.

"Eli," I said unapologetically, "I'll be right back." But, baby Lora was still crying, and so, I gently picked up her warm body, snuggled her, and walked back to the living room. She had stopped crying, now that I was holding her, but I felt a warm, wet sensation as her cloth diaper (no Pampers) had been peed through. I bade Eli to continue, while I changed her diaper on the couch. Diaper assembly concluded, I excused myself for a quick moment while I returned Lora to her crib. The quiet and our focused conversation continued for about five minutes as we chatted, while I slipped on a clean tee shirt.

Lora cried out again, and I was a bit more apologetic. I carried her out to witness our living room supervisory session when she promptly had a loose, newborn, bowel movement which managed to elude most corners of my poorly arranged diaper. A good deal of the movement now adorned my new tee shirt. "Eli, hang in there, I will clean and change her and be right back." I slipped on my third shirt of this ten minute meeting.

Eli stood up and warmly and respectfully said, "I see that this may not be such a good idea, let's find another time to meet." Mortified, I agreed. I gently returned Lora to her crib, but she wasn't happy. With her crying as a backdrop, I escorted Eli to the front door. As I opened the door, a large, unfamiliar, brown dog ran into my apartment, barking away, while a stranger stood at the door entrance holding a motionless woman in both arms.

"Who are you, and what's wrong with that woman" I asked beseechingly.

The dog's high pitched barking was intensifying and persistent, while Lora was crying more forcefully. The man answered: "I have no idea who she is. She fainted on the staircase as I was walking behind her to make a grocery delivery." Without waiting for an invitation, he stepped into my apartment still holding the woman, who was now beginning to stir.

"Eli, please go into our kitchen and get her a glass of water," I beckoned to my now dumbfounded guest.

He returned seconds later to say that he had turned on the faucet and that no water streamed out. I raced to our terrace, which overlooked the main street, to see worker's trucks and men with jackhammers, breaking up the concrete in front of our house. I yelled down to them to ask what was wrong, only to discover that they were working on a water main breakage. The water would be turned on in about an hour.

I am not sure that Marx brothers script writers could have replicated this scene: Lora crying, the now conscious woman asking for water, the dog barking, the delivery man asking if he could continue his delivery route, no water and Eli. I thanked Eli for his help and patience and said that he could leave.

The faint victim was now quite herself and Eli was eager to depart. As he opened the front door, we heard workers calling to one another as they were carrying a large, American style sofa up the four floors to my neighbor's apartment. The sofa had become wedged in the narrow space between the wall and the bannister. They could not work it loose. Eli, now desperate to escape, asked if he could climb over the sofa, balance against the wall and reach the lower floor to continue his flight to safety and sanity. They agreed. Eli never returned to our Hatikvah office.

Chapter Seventeen

WE LEFT ISRAEL in June of 1973, our lovely two month old daughter in tow. Moving back to New York City thankfully lacked the anxiety of flying eastward, to Israel, three years earlier. Our friends, Eric and Hagar, had a small apartment on 88th street, just off Riverside Drive, that they offered to us until we got settled in our own apartment. The apartment was nicely situated, only a few blocks from shops on Broadway, while bordering Riverside Drive Park. They were, coincidentally, spending the summer in Israel and so, were able to make this generous offer.

I had resigned my Municipality position with mixed feelings: we had nourished a sense of pride in Hatikvah's leadership. On the other hand, I was very excited about my entry into the doctoral program and being close to family once again. Within a few weeks, we rented an apartment on Amsterdam Avenue and 97th street, only a block north of 96th street, Manhattan's equivalent of the DMZ, which separated middle class neighborhoods from south Spanish Harlem.

The brief hiatus between our departure from Israel and our move to our 97th street apartment, with a six week stint in the Moss's apartment, passed quickly and pleasantly. Perhaps reuniting with our families and sharing with them our precious new package, Lora, cushioned the reabsorption. That period also provided me with an opportunity to assess our past three years in Israel. We were definitely "hooked." Returning to Israel after my degree was a certainty and an inevitability for us. What was it that so impacted us in Israel and prevailed over the warmth and delight of reunification with our families and friends?

My mother, during our visit to their new apartment, looked at both Aviva and me and asked with unusual calm and intensity: "Why are you planning to leave us again? Haven't you gotten it out of your systems yet?" The theme of abandonment was generally the leit motif that informed so much of our interaction with her.

"Mom, we both love Israel, with all of its imperfections. You certainly must have had a sense of the vibrancy of the country and the quality of life we enjoyed when you visited us."

"I did see that," she granted, "but, it is so hard without the three of you here."

In truth, I was no more able to answer my internal (and family) questions coherently than when we first left for Israel. The country was cacophony personified, financially incomprehensible, with bureaucratic systems that seemed to have been malevolently designed to stymie one's quality of life. I was generally appalled by the growing political power of the myopic, orthodox political parties and felt an alarming portent of discord with the post-Six Day War, West Bank settlers. We lived in a constant state of bank overdrafts and witnessed a spiraling inflation that was, at times, in excess of one hundred percent annually. War and terrorist violence was rarely sub dermal, in fact, the war drums were beating as we'd left Israel.

The notion of helping Israel in any way that we could was always on our horizon. The friendships that we had developed seemed deeper and more personal, perhaps because the assimilation pressure cooker had peeled away some of the defenses and impersonality that characterized our New York friendships.

Except when visiting our South African friends, many of whom had amassed pre-emigration fortunes in the very uneven playing field of apartheid, we were taken by a more modest and temperate need for possessions, that seemed to personify Israelis and most immigrants we befriended. It never occurred to us that we would not return to Israel, despite an increasing awareness that our lack of funds led us to face the reality that our permanent stay in Israel was a work in progress.

In Israel, one of the jokes one hears about the country, went like this: "If Moses wandered through the desert for forty years, leading the Israelites to the Promised Land, couldn't he have wandered for forty one years and ended up in Switzerland?" What is it, about this rocky, desert terrain in the midst of outrageous violence, with hundreds of millions of its neighbors pledging its destruction, that has made it into a bastion of progress, progressiveness and military power? How is it that, in a few short years, the castoffs from so many European countries, the victims of genocide and centuries of pogroms and persecution, would rival and soon surpass the military and technological might of virtually all of the countries that had so blithely expelled them?

Robert Ardrey's cultural anthropological trilogy, written in the 1960s and 1970s, offers an interesting viewpoint. "The Territorial Imperative," the middle study, was a lucid examination of the natural inclination of humans and other living beings, to be territorial, to own real estate of their own. Study after study cited by Ardrey, depicted the amplification of power assigned to the residents of a territory, and the acceptance of that power by territorial invaders, often larger and stronger. It occurred to me, that Israel was a prime example of that thesis. It was too glib and facile simply to say: "A Yiddishe Kopf," although there was certainly some truth to that. For the first time in several millennia, Jews had a homeland; all the rest of us had been visitors in a mostly unwelcome diaspora.

As inhospitable as the landscape was, that greeted the late nineteenth and early twentieth century pioneers of Palestine, as fraught with danger as the real estate was, that welcomed the hundreds of thousands of Eastern European immigrants fleeing the pogroms of Russia, Ukraine and Poland, as foreboding as the restrictive British Mandate was toward the masses of Jews victimized in so many ways by the Holocaust, and despite the impending, post-independence war with its Arab neighbors looming, for Jews, it was home.

In the Middle-East, I had learned that the idiom, "Home is where the heart is," is only part of the equation. Home is also where the air force, tank divisions and sophisticated combat units are. We Jews in the diaspora feel rather comfortable in our disparate environments, but, the Jews of New Jersey do not have an air force and the Jews of Connecticut have no tank brigades.

And so, if Ardrey's territorial thesis has any merit, we are all Jewish Gastarbeiters, dependent on the political and economic winds and whims of our host society.

Israel's Six Day War achievements left me, and most of Israel, with an aura of invincibility. My sense of Israel as an unrivaled, regional power lasted until about six thirty in the evening, Tuesday, October ninth, 1973. I was sitting in the front row of my Columbia Teacher's College classroom, coming to grips with the statistics formulae on the blackboard at the front of the classroom. I had been enjoying advanced statistics, now in its fourth session since the beginning of my doctoral program.

Several days earlier, the Yom Kippur attack on Israel initially, by Egypt, Syria, Jordan and then Iraq, had caught Israel by surprise and was weighing heavily on my ability to focus on anything else. The attackers were achieving significant early stage success and causing substantial casualties. Israel was taking an early pounding and America was holding back the resupplying of Israel necessary after several days of multi-front battles.

Thankfully, within a few days, Kissinger and Nixon ceased their power play with the Meier government, and the arms supplies flowed to Israel helping to turn the tide of the war. I was able to refocus on my studies. It was only when we returned to Israel three and a half years later that we had a better understanding of the profound impact that the war and the costs to Israel in human, economic and psychological terms had wrought.

I had to focus on my classes and dissertation in earnest. As usual, I paid little attention to the administrative strictures that the doctoral program imposed upon the eleven students in my first year class. Full time employment was not allowed in the first year; commencing with one's dissertation in year one was also seriously frowned upon. The ten thousand dollar annual stipend, over and above my full fellowship which covered all tuition expenses, was not enough to sustain a family in New York City.

Frowning upon commencing one's dissertation in the first year of studies, was based on the School's desire to have students focus on theory and practice in the classroom setting. That restriction conflicted with my desire to return to Israel as soon as possible, as it would draw out the dissertation process unnecessarily. Columbia, and many Ivy League schools, had a plethora of students who had ABD degrees: "All But the Dissertation," with some degrees taking up to ten years to complete. I was determined not become a member of that very popular club.

My initial fears about the oscillating life style of full-time employment and full-time doctoral work soon diminished. Handling the academic requirements seemed to be working out fine. I simply could not divulge that I sought full-time employment to any of my classmates or instructors. My course work was going well, I was homing in on my dissertation subject, I had the faculty advisor one only dreams of, and my employment search was going fine. The stars seemed to be aligned just right. In fairly short order, I lined up a statistician, key punch operator (1975!) and, some months later, after the first year embargo was lifted on dissertation formulation, arranged to have the Chairperson's secretary type the various drafts and final copy of my dissertation.

My attention was now directed at how to pay for these services. More good fortune came my way, as I was faced with securing the verboten first year employment. My good friend Eric's father was the CFO of a large, not-for-profit agency providing work training and employment opportunities for former drug abusers and criminal offender. This contact helped expedite an interview for a planning position which went well, and resulted in a job offer. I arranged my class schedule so that, to the extent possible, there was an accommodation with my work requirements.

My classmates at Columbia were an eclectic and interesting group. Frances, was a minister from Nigeria, with whom I had endless discussions about his government's persecution and genocide of the Ebo. Karen, was an American transplant, having lived in American, Samoa, Pago Pago for years. Myrna, was bright, American, divorced and dangerous. I liked talking with her, but only for short periods of time and in public. Shane, was a Catholic priest, very intelligent and quite gay. Shane was as dangerous as Myrna.

The professors were, for the most part, the who's who of the social policy field: Alfred Kahn, Richard Cloward, Francis Piven, George Brager. I had great respect for the faculty and, for obvious reasons, dreaded having them on my dissertation defense committee. For the most part, I found the classes to be only moderately challenging and so, felt free to dedicate myself toward dissertation completion. As it ultimately turned out, I believe that I was the only one in my class to complete the dissertation in 1977, defend it, and be awarded a doctorate.

Having a wealth of experience circumventing, what I considered unreasonable administrative constrictions, I planned a reprise. Midway through the second month of my first year of studies, I began formulating the thesis for my dissertation. A stroke of luck brought a positive response to a critical faculty request. Professor George Brager agreed to be my dissertation advisor. George, he requested I address him by his first name, was a highly respected social policy theorist. He was down-to-Earth and unpretentious, despite having authored a myriad of seminal articles and books that were regarded as staples of the profession. George had a robust sense of humor, which camouflaged his uncanny strategic sophistication, and his great skill at navigating the serpentine canals of pretentious academia.

George, a Jew who was sympathetic to Zionistic ideals, understood and identified with my desire to complete my dissertation as quickly as possible, and return to Israel. A consummate politician, George ensured that I touch base with the professors who were either influential in my subject area, or were certain to be on my dissertation defense committee. Perhaps his most helpful and directive advice, came a few weeks before the scheduled date of my defense.

"You know this stuff," he advised me, referring to my three and a half years of sweat as stuff, "so sit in your defense meeting and mostly keep your mouth shut. You will have a group of heavyweights on your committee. They are intent upon impressing one another. Don't intrude on that process, answer only when asked a direct question." This advice would be helpful to me in the future.

Two important tracks to my life were now on course in my first year, with dissertation defense still only a murky notion on my horizon. I now worked with Aviva to set up our new apartment and prepare it for our active daughter, now about seven months old. Her tight, blond curls and rapidly maturing motor skills made her even more adorable and challenging. As our seventeenth story apartment had only one bedroom, it was becoming urgent that Lora have her own designated room.

My friend Norman, with whom I had lost contact while in Israel, reemerged on my friendship radar screen at just the right time. He was amazingly handy for a Jewish man, perhaps enhanced by his conversion to Greek Orthodoxy. Norman had married a Greek woman, whose family insisted on his conversion; now, Norman Irving Schwartz was an acceptable Norman Black. He offered to help me build a sliding door, which closed off the breakfast nook, creating a small room for Lora. In Norman's case, my helping him meant, for the most part, holding the tools for him. The Israel hiatus in our friendship, had allowed me the space to be more aware of Norman's increasingly imperious demeanor, and his general restlessness, it appeared, with life itself. Aviva was generally uneasy in his presence.

More in line with my interior design skills, was the "cloffice," a unique blending of a coat closet with my work space. The twenty five foot square coat closet, just off the front door of our apartment, served as my quiet space. I fashioned a small desk, using crates and a wood panel, ran a wire for a small rotating fan, and made peace with the sixty watt, incandescent bulb dangling overhead, serving as my lighting. Lora was getting increasingly rambunctious and inquisitive which made working in my "cloffice" more challenging, and so, I occasionally used Melinda's Mount Sinai medical school I.D., and camped out in that school's nearby library.

Perhaps more intrusive was the "Bappo and Jocko" challenge. The schoolyard, seventeen stories below our apartment windows, proved to be an oasis for pot smokers and bongo drum serenaders, until late hours of the night. We settled on the names Bappo and Jocko for the players for some reason that we both never really understood, possibly because it had some onomatopoeic association.

My new employment brought me in contact with a clientele for whom pot smoking was an entry level, social expectation. I was now officially a program planner for Wildcat Service Corporation. The name, initially, seemed ludicrous, until I understood the association. Just as a wildcat oil strike may yield unanticipated positive results, so too, giving the Wildcat Service clients an opportunity to succeed, might produce positive results. I felt at ease with these young men and women, many of whom had spent a good part of their young adult lives in prison. In addition to a life of crime, many clients had years of heroin or cocaine abuse histories.

In truth, the men and women served by Wildcat were not clients, but rather were employees. They received a salary while simultaneously benefitting from job training and, ultimately, employment in the private or public sector. My direct, daily contact with those served was minimal, as I spent the first year and a half of my three and a half year's with Wildcat, in a corporate office. When I did come in close contact with work crews, I felt energized and enjoyed my conversations with them.

While I was working at breakneck speed at Columbia, Lora was growing up. Aviva was braving the New York winters, taking our little one for long walks on Broadway. At about two years of age, Lora started attending a preschool in a church on 91st street. Lora fell in love with her teacher, Annie; the feeling was quite mutual. It was great being in fairly close proximity with my parents, Melinda and Josephine, and Zita, Carol and

Richard. We had missed family very much for the three years in Israel. Aviva rekindled her dance life with classes at nearby Broadway studios. She discovered a new dimension of creative energy, beginning classes, and working in an apprenticeship in ceramics at an Upper West Side studio.

After one and a half years of working in Wildcat's planning department, the directorship of the agency's clerical and administrative training center was offered to me. The center, a joint venture of the IBM Corporation, The New York City Board of Education and The Ford Foundation, trained several hundred clients in office and administrative skills and sought to secure full time employment in the private sector for those successfully completing training. The skill acquisition came quite easily to most clients. What was infinitely more difficult was accepting office decorum, and overcoming a pervasive, ingrained sense of failure. I was flabbergasted at the rapidity and ease of skill development of our constituents. Their battles with a negative self-image and very low expectations for success, resonated with me for many reasons.

Halfway through my third year at Columbia, I informed my advisor, that I would soon be prepared to submit my thesis for review and would be ready to defend it at some point thereafter. I didn't really mean it, as I was nervous about the defense process, despite George's sage advice. We had so much riding on successfully completing the degree and returning to Israel. I knew that Columbia was stodgy and conservative, and made one sweat for their prestigious degree. I started the sweating process weeks in advance of the defense meeting. The pressure to successfully complete the degree process was significantly increased by a visitor I received several weeks before the date of my defense.

Yonah Rosenfeld, the Dean of the Baerwald School of Social Work of Hebrew University in Jerusalem, arranged to interview me for a faculty position, which I would assume upon our return to Israel. I was not certain how he located me or knew of me at all, but I welcomed the interview and jokingly informed Aviva that the Mossad had been tracking my progress. Yonah was pleasant, bright, steely-eyed and straightforward. He spoke English fluently, albeit with a trace of a German accent, familiar to me as a prerequisite for a top level position in Israel. It occurred to me that I should be practicing the German of my youth.

Virtually every person in a decision-making position in Israel seemed to us of German extraction. Germans it appeared, perhaps equaled by those of Polish origin, were the ruling elite of Israel. Evidently, I answered his questions about social policy theory at an acceptable level and so, prior to leaving our meeting he offered me a position commencing that autumn, dependent upon the successful completion of my doctoral degree.

"Can you teach in Hebrew?"

"Yes," I answered, even though I wasn't clear yet if I could teach in English.

The University, he informed me, would pick up all expenses for our relocation to Israel. It appeared that the re-entry into Israel was set, all I had to do was successfully defend my dissertation.

Aviva and I prepared to leave our New York home again, part with our families and friends, terminate my employment at Wildcat and prepare Lora, now over four years old, for entry into a world that would be very strange to her. I was busy preparing for a dissertation defense that I could now successfully accomplish in my sleep. The day of my defense arrived at warp speed, and I soon found myself seated in a conference room with the committee that held my fate in their hands. All went surprisingly well, I carefully followed George Brager's formula of keeping my mouth shut and answering only direct questions with unaccustomed brevity. I was soon Dr. Stern and ready to move on.

However, moving on, when it applies to Israel, is never linear and usually turns out to be a unique soap opera. Despite all of the assurances by Dean Rosenfeld that our move was to be fully paid for by the university, no funds had yet materialized. The international moving company was booked, our apartment was set to be vacated, all of the goodbyes completed and yet, three days before the scheduled move and flight, the Dean's office said they were "working on it." The uncertainty about the funds and the leverage that I would lose by fronting the funds, which we barely could assemble, was disconcerting. I knew that the University had scheduled three classes for me to teach and that they would be hard pressed to find a replacement at that late date.

In desperation, I called an American colleague and friend, also an immigrant in Israel, Dorothy Becker. She was on the National Board of The Joint Distribution Committee (JDC) and very influential in Israel. One hour after my call to Dorothy, the Dean's office called and said all was settled and that the funds would be waiting for me upon my arrival in Israel. I never asked Dorothy how she worked her magic, I just thanked her for the result.

Moving to Israel a second time proved to be much less challenging than our initial saga seven years earlier. We owned an apartment in Tel Aviv, I had a position at Hebrew University waiting for me, Aviva and I were now proficient in Hebrew and we had many friends in Israel awaiting our return. My parents were in good health and prepared to visit us in Israel. Melinda too, would soon visit us, but had voiced some concern about the perception of Israel mistreating its Palestinian neighbors.

Mostly, however, little Lora ensured, that the focus of our attention and energy was aimed at her. Our concern for her cultural upheaval upon return to Israel mitigated our own self-absorption. We had, during our recent three and a half years in New York, become even closer to Carol and Richard and were going to miss them very much. Through their incredible generosity, we were able to visit them annually at their Sanibel Island, Florida condominium. Every year they sent us airplane tickets and had a rented car waiting for us upon our arrival. Lora's sassy, self-assured charm had helped draw all of our family's love and attention. We were sure that she would be a magnet attracting visits to us in Israel.

Chapter Eighteen

Back in Israel again, life returned to abnormal quickly. Our Tel Aviv apartment had been rented out for well over a year. Fortunately, our cousins Igal and Niza, were in the States for the summer and offered their suburban Tel Aviv home to us. My Volkswagen Beetle, that we had left with them to use while we were in America, was waiting for us at their home. Unfortunately, what was also waiting for us, were seemingly implacable problems with the tenant in our apartment.

As my university position was to begin in one month, we had to resolve selling our apartment, and securing living arrangements in Jerusalem. The trip from Tel Aviv to Jerusalem was sixty miles each way, and was not a viable daily commute. My faculty position required one evening class, committee meetings and additional responsibilities. Our tenant refused to move. It soon became clear to us, that he had a criminal background, which our rental agent had failed to uncover.

Removing this tenant, his pregnant wife and infant child, proved to be a dark cloud that temporarily enshrouded our joyous return to Israel. Vacating our apartment of our reluctant tenants was only one of the challenges we faced. When we first visited Israel as tourists in 1969, we were besieged with requests to immigrate to Israel. Shopkeepers, shuk merchants, all strangers to us, were quasi recruiters, a veritable armada of Israeli chamber of commerce marketers. It seemed that the Yom Kippur War, with Israel's early losses and hard fought victory, had cast an invisible pall over the nation. The question that so many now asked us was: "Why did you return to Israel? What is wrong with going to California?"

It seemed that almost every family had suffered grievous losses or were connected to others who had been profoundly affected by the war. Shortly after we succeeded in renting an apartment in Jerusalem, we arranged for a plumber to install our washing machine, on our rear terrace in Jerusalem. He emotionally described the bravery of Israeli fighter pilots roaring over his infantry unit in the Sinai, and encountering scores of missiles from Russian SAM 2 and 3 anti-aircraft batteries. Everyone had harrowing war stories that seemed embedded in the national psyche.

The degree and nature of the mood change saddened us, but we focused on the myriad of tasks ahead of us. I had not yet learned to navigate the treacherous economic shoals of Israeli economics. The country's annual inflation rate was still in excess of thirty five percent, and prices for goods and services changed on a daily, if not hourly, basis. We were soon to be significantly affected by governmental actions, positively and then negatively.

The Jewish Agency, had offered us our four bedroom apartment with a mortgage of forty thousand Lirot, which was then Israel's national currency. Our monthly payments were also in Lirot. The mortgage was not linked to the American dollar, or any international currency index and so, with the rate of inflation and Israel's consistent currency devaluation, The Jewish Agency forgave our entire mortgage. The administrative and postage expenses, they maintained, that were required to manage our loan, exceeded the value of the mortgage. We were selfishly ecstatic.

The future appeared reasonably bright, as I envisioned the purchase of an apartment in Jerusalem with the unencumbered proceeds. I tried to have our Tel Aviv apartment vacated by enlisting the Municipality to shut off the water supply to the apartment. The tenant, in response, hooked up a connection to a neighbor's water pipes. I arranged with the power company to disconnect the electricity. When several days passed and the lights were still on, I asked the district's manager what was wrong. He informed me that the technician refused to disconnect the electricity as the criminal's pregnant wife implored him not to.

"How could he do that to a pregnant woman?" he admonished me. I was feeling increasingly desperate as I saw that Municipal agencies would be of no help. It was at the nadir of those feelings that an acquaintance informed me that a friend of his, a police officer, was looking to purchase an apartment. The deal was perfect. The officer, a burly veteran, said he had no problem in vacating the criminal and his family. The finances were quickly arranged, paperwork signed and the sale was concluded…in three days.

The funds from the sale soon became worth a fraction of their value. In the time that the sale was consummated, and we were free to search for an apartment in Jerusalem, Israel suffered a disastrous economic devaluation. Only a few years later, Israel implemented a currency change from the Lira to the Shekel. The proceeds that we had derived from our sale had, overnight, been degraded by about fifty percent. We no longer had the means to purchase an apartment.

Our joint determination to make it in Israel was put to a test. We decided to rent an apartment in Jerusalem. The rental market was limited, however, we found a lovely apartment in Kiryat Shmuel, a beautiful section of Jerusalem, very near the more exclusive neighborhood of Rehavia. The two bedroom, fourth floor walkup, was modest in size. We were pleased at its spacious kitchen and the beautiful, twenty foot long terrace off both the living room and main bedroom. Lora's bedroom had a small terrace connected to it as well.

In retrospect, it seems virtually inconceivable that we made the financial aspects of this arrangement work. Our rent was three hundred dollars per month, paying in dollars was prevalent; my salary at the university, amounted to about four hundred dollars per month. Supplementing my salary with dollars drawn monthly from our savings, and the proceeds remaining from the sale of our apartment, was now a prerequisite to managing our monthly expenses. We understood, with some bitterness, the prevailing immigrants' joke: "How does one make a small fortune in Israel? Come with a large one!" We had no large or small fortune, but what we had, was rapidly diminishing.

Our landlords were German ascendants to Israel's aristocracy. Mr. Doron, pleasant and fiftyish, was the CEO of a holding company of several large and luxurious Israeli hotels. His son, Gal, was efficient, courteous and very helpful. Gal, was indignant when we informed him that we were on a three year wait list to receive a telephone. Many residents of Jerusalem had been waiting for years to receive a telephone for their homes. He counseled me to use, with great excess, my title as Dr. Stern, which lent a sense of urgency to the request for a phone, and played into the general sycophantic nature of Israel's public servants.

It worked. Within the unheard of time frame of three months, Dr. Stern, and his family, had a telephone. We also had its whopping monthly bill to accompany other outrageously high utility bills. It was not uncommon to receive a utility bill on the first of the month and then ten days later to get the monthly increase in the rate. Utility rates were a diabolical force rising on a monthly basis.

Among the costliest of these bills, was the price of oil. While we had adjusted to the lofty price of gasoline, the high cost of heating oil was a unique challenge. Our Jerusalem apartment flooring was constructed entirely of attractive stone tiles. For the most part, housing in Israel was built with the country's blazingly hot summers in mind. Stone tiles remained relatively cool during that period, offering some relief. For nine months of the year, this interior design plan was helpful, while for three months it was misery.

Jerusalem, very hot in the interminable summer, experienced dramatic climate shifts in the winter months. It snowed on rare occasions and was damp, chilly and blustery from December through February. The building's central heating was regulated, and controlled, by a "house committee." The finger could be pointed at them, for the policy of turning on the heat from six a.m. until eight a.m., with no sign of boiler life again until six p.m. The return to boiler dormancy at eight thirty in the evening, left apartments bone-chilling. Severity of weather had no discernible impact on this policy. The committee met monthly to discuss a variety of issues. There were only eight apartments in the building and so, all the tenants were well-acquainted with one another.

My first committee meeting fell on a November evening, with a cold rain falling noisily, outside Mrs. Argamon's second floor apartment. Yaacov Lorch, the other apartment dweller on our fourth floor, sat across from me. Yaacov's brother served as a prominent, Israeli Knesset member. The atmosphere was quite pleasant, with our second floor septuagenarian, Mr. Dernburg, providing some humorous remarks in Hebrew, which could easily have been mistaken for German. The placid tone of the conversation changed somewhat, when I asked if we could alter the policy on apartment heating.

"Our apartment is quite cold," I offered, not meekly, but certainly not with gusto.

The following three or four minutes were opportunities for all of my fellow tenants to offer me suggestions, all well-intentioned, on how to assist Aviva to get more comfortable in the cold months. They unilaterally assumed that I was presenting a recommendation that affected only Aviva.

"Perhaps she could wear a sweater?"

"She already wears two," I answered.

"Extra woolen socks?"

"Also two pairs, and sheepskin slippers," I responded. Finally, Mrs. Argamon, ended the discussion of agenda item number four: "Harry, so, who told you to live on the top floor, where the heat is always weakest?" Check-mate! We moved on to item number five on the evening's agenda.

Aviva and I were able to shrug our shoulders, laugh a bit, share our bewilderment at the myriad of societal issues that we confronted daily, and measure them against the many extraordinary virtues of Israel, in general, and Jerusalem in particular. Just walking through our neighborhood, breathing in the intoxicating, ever-present pine-caressed breezes, we felt a unique connectedness to the country, our history and, even our Jewishness (which was not under duress).

Among the primary goals in our first two weeks in Jerusalem was enrolling Lora, now four years old, in a nearby preschool. Lora, a very articulate, active and assertive youngster (who would have guessed it?) was in for a bit of a challenge. Despite Israel being her birthplace, she was about eight weeks old when we left the country for almost four years. She would now be thrust, having no knowledge of Hebrew, into a preschool class of Israelis, who spoke only Hebrew. Within a period of a few weeks, Lora had her entire class sitting on the carpeted classroom floor, attentively listening to her stories to them in English. Within three months, Lora was speaking Hebrew like an Israeli native, and apologizing for her parent's poor Hebrew accents to her friends visiting our apartment. The irony of the similarity to my excuses for my parent's Viennese accents didn't escape me.

Thankfully, our evolving Hebrew accent was not an issue with our friends, many of whom lived in Tel Aviv. Virtually every Saturday found Aviva, Lora and I making our weekly pilgrimage to the coast. While we loved Jerusalem for its beauty, history, bustling Old City and the profound sense of Jewishness that pervaded our very being, it was the stultifying Shabbat silence to which we never quite adjusted. The influence and power of the very conservative, religious establishment was never more pronounced than on Saturday in Jerusalem.

I often felt the need to flee the languorous Jerusalem Shabbat. The pervasive and unrelenting heat of the summer made strolling in public parks, or traditionally vibrant avenues, a virtual impossibility. So, almost every Saturday, we revved up our indefatigable white Volkswagen Beetle, and made for the Tel Aviv area, some sixty miles away.

The first moments of each of our Shabbat sojourns made me feel uncomfortable. There were very few cars on the Jerusalem roads, as orthodox communities often blocked off their neighborhoods, to prevent cars from entering. Driving on the Sabbath was near the top of the very long list of 'the strictly forbidden' for observant Jews. Our car was continuously exposed to the ad hoc, orthodox, tenant surveillance committee. Our Volkswagen was parked, fully exposed, for all of our Shabbat critics to see, in an above-ground designated space. Cranking the ignition, shattered the oppressive Shabbat silence with its air-cooled engine sputter. Undaunted, we nonetheless headed to the beach, or to the homes of our more liberal Tel Aviv friends.

It was on a mild, Saturday evening in November, 1977, that Anwar Sadat, Egypt's President, decided to fly over the home of our friends, the Moss's. We had just finished having dinner in their apartment in Kfar Saba, a bedroom community north of Tel Aviv, when Israeli television news announced that the invited airliner, carrying Egypt's President, Anwar Sadat, had entered Israel's airspace. One of the few benefits of living in the flight path to Tel Aviv's international airport, was the clear viewing of the plane's gradual descent on this historic visit. We stood on the Moss's rear balcony and watched, as Sadat's airliner descended toward the airport, its Egyptian flag on display on its fuselage. It was flanked by three Israeli, fighter planes, with equally visible flag of Israel markings. There was no doubt that we were witnessing a unique, historic occasion.

Unfortunately, we witnessed unique and historic occasions too many times over the next few weeks. Sadat, together with Israel's Prime Minister, Menachem Begin, had been planning this extraordinary visit aimed at opening negotiations toward a lasting peace between the two enemy nations. It seemed unreal that these talks would take place only four years after the bitter, Yom Kippur War.

Many of the planned negotiations were held in Jerusalem; several at the Jerusalem Theatre, not far from our home. On numerous occasions, my ride through our neighborhood and down past the Valley of the Cross, Israel's Knesset and the Israel Museum, toward Hebrew University's Givat Ram Campus, was held up for up to one hour. Sadat's caravan, and the connected secret service details, on their way to yet another negotiating session, required extensive security precautions.

This tiny country in general, and Jerusalem's compressed geography in particular, exposed one simultaneously, to a pervasive anxiety and a staccato exhilaration. We did get to see Sadat once as he entered the Jerusalem Theatre for yet another meeting with Israeli leadership. He was tall, handsome, distinguished and rarely seen in public without his meerschaum pipe. He looked like an olive-skinned, university professor. Both Sadat and Begin, at the invitation of President Carter, visited Camp David in August of

1978 and signed the accords, named after that location in mid-September of that year.

Those momentous pacts brought a lasting, if cool, peace between the two nations and simultaneously sealed Sadat's fate. While officiating at a 1981 celebration heralding Egyptian achievements during the Yom Kippur War, Muslim Brotherhood extremists, virulently opposed to peace with Israel, assassinated him and several other officials in attendance. The date of the murder, not coincidentally, was October sixth, the day that Egypt invaded Israel, eight years earlier. Sadat, while a hero to many on the international stage, was a bitter enemy to Egypt's underground, terror network.

For many of us living in Israel, however, Sadat's 1977 daring visit was a ray of hope. Not long after his arrival and the inconvenient road closures due to his caravan negotiating the streets of Jerusalem, I had a straight shot to my workplace at the University. I was teaching three courses in my first year.

At the outset of each course I gave students a choice as to whether I would conduct classes in Hebrew or English. Hebrew was always the unanimous choice. It was very difficult and frustrating for me but, ultimately, it helped me immeasurably to improve my spoken Hebrew. Year two found me teaching three classes and heading up the School of Social Work's continuing education program. These two positions helped me to minimize my monthly bank overdraft, but, only somewhat.

Teaching at Hebrew University was both rewarding and challenging. The school's academic standing was very high, and so, much was expected of the faculty. My lack of fluency in Hebrew, often put me on the defensive. I believe that it was mostly my own insecurity, as most faculty members were quite pleasant and understanding. Except Monica.

Monica, was the Germanic queen who sat on the Director of the Master's Program throne. Her heavily, German-accented Hebrew was hard to understand, and her imperious demeanor often left me flummoxed. She touched many raw nerves that I didn't know I had. As secure as I had become, about my academic achievements, and my ability to function in many challenging environments, something about wicked Monica unnerved me.

I struggled to understand what it was about this Wagnerian demon that so affected me. Her heavy, German accent made me uncomfortable, perhaps rekindling my deep, well-imbedded dislike for Germans. But, so many of those in leadership positions in Israel were of German descent. Her intense gaze and smirk when talking to me, made me feel, that she had uncovered my anxiety about teaching (my first classes), as well as my difficulties in describing complex concepts in Hebrew. I spoke Hebrew with her in all situations. I insisted on discussing all professional issues with her in Hebrew, despite her apparent fluency in English.

Monica appeared to me to be unstable in many ways. She was famous for her spontaneous rants about the inadequacies of all faculty in her department. She did little to help me maintain the precarious balance of my new professional assignments. I persevered, but often felt inadequate with her. Unmarried and In her late fifties, Monica's life was the University, a territory that she seemed determined to guard as her inherited and solely owned domain. I avoided her whenever possible.

However, I loved the students. They were audacious, challenging, intelligent, although often a bit too personal. The professional line drawn between faculty and student in an American university, was only hazily discernible in Israel. At the outset of each semester the choice was given to my students: they may call me Harry or Doctor Stern, it was up to them.

I was feeling increasingly confident in the classroom, and found myself relaxing more during my classes. I gradually realized how tense and rigid I had been in my first teaching experience. Many of the students of my three different classes would visit me during office hours for clarification of assignments or to discuss the central themes of term papers that I had assigned the class. I felt so much more comfortable and competent in these one-on-one meetings with students.

One student appeared with increasing regularity. My initial reaction was one of surprise. The questions asked in my office were often rather fuzzy and repetitive. Sarah, a post Israeli army student, about twenty five years old, was in my social policy class held twice weekly. She seemed intelligent and often asked penetrating questions, that appeared incongruous with the inanity of her inquiries in my office. Sarah insisted on calling me "Doctor" Stern on her visits to my office, emphasizing the doctor, while looking at me coyly. "Doctor Stern, could we review what Professor Schorr means when he talks about The Nonculture of Poverty?" "Certainly Sarah, but you seem to have had a good of understanding of that concept in this morning's class, only two hours ago."

Often, as she asked me her questions, she would lean forward, more than a bit. She made no effort to rearrange her sagging, loose-fitting and low-cut blouse. She was too attentive not to notice that I was involuntarily mesmerized by her arched, pale pink and brazenly inviting breasts. I had noticed in class, that Sarah was too well-endowed not to wear a bra. But, here she was, in my office, exposing what I had only conceptualized in every one of my Social Policy classes that she attended.

I couldn't believe how dense I was: she was coming on to me. Notwithstanding that Sarah was very attractive, my reaction upon my slow-baked realization, was: escape. I contained my urge to flee from my own office, maintained my cool, and managed to stammer: "Sarah, I think that you have a firm grasp of the concepts we have been discussing." I tried very hard not to think of the firm grasp that might have been her preferred choice. I politely signaled the end of our meeting and opened my office door to bid her goodbye, visualizing that this door would remain wide open for all future meetings.

As she left my office, she turned and asked, "Doctor Stern, when can we review the concept of welfare rights? I am a little fuzzy about it." That same drawn out "Doctor Stern." She didn't wait for my response. I was assailed by a mix of emotional responses. On the one hand, I was flattered by the apparent come on from an extremely, attractive young woman. On the other, much more dominant hand, was the guilt at my fantasies which, thankfully, remained just that.

This, however, was not the last to be heard from Sarah. The term papers that I had assigned were soon due. Students were required to hand in their written copy of their papers for my review prior to their class presentation. The unwritten rule, passed on like a nation's folklore, was that students were not required to type their papers, but, rather, all work could be submitted as a legible, handwritten document. Perhaps there was a written ruling in some remote archive. I surmised that this arcane policy may have been a dictate of a past, well-intentioned socialistic administration.

And so, two weeks before the semester's conclusion, I was the proud possessor of twenty term papers, each at least ten pages long, in cursive Hebrew which was barely intelligible to me. I was certain that the students believed that there was no way that I would read the papers, and might assign grades based on the weight of the document or the uniqueness of its title. Those who thought so were wrong. I spent evenings, a full weekend, and personal time between classes, with my dictionary close by, to painstakingly read every page…every word.

Something struck me as strange as I combed through the pages. Four of the papers seemed vaguely similar. Upon closer scrutiny, the similarity became less vague. In these four term papers, identical paragraphs appeared, placed at different points of the document. I enlisted help from our friend Marga, an Israeli, who was as fluent in English as I was. She was an accomplished interpreter for Israeli films. She confirmed my observations: these four papers were, in actuality one paper, arranged differentially across the ten pages. It was clear, that these students had assumed that I would not read their papers, and if I did, would not identify their group plagiarism. One of those students was Sarah, whose visits to my office were, more than likely, a careful plan of diversion and cooptation.

While disappointed about that part of my fantasy, I was incensed about the plan to try to fool me. I believe that the students were shocked when I invited the four schemers into my office. I offered no introduction: "As of this moment the four of you have failed my course. As you are aware, two course failures will result in your being asked to leave the school." I asked for no discussion and presented no proof. They all sat in silence. "I offer you an opportunity to achieve a maximum "C" plus grade, if each of you will write an original, ten page paper and submit it within a week from today." I did not need to convince them that the papers would be carefully read. Without entertaining one word from the students, I stood and ushered them out of my office. Nothing of this nature occurred again during my years at the university. Sarah never visited my office again.

To my dismay, I found university life somewhat boring. The languid pace, the committee meetings, and the workload of three courses per semester didn't quite suit my more action-oriented persona. When my friend and colleague, Armand Lauffer, asked me if I would be interested in directing the School's continuing education program, I jumped at the opportunity. This additional responsibility would add a half position to my workload, and I welcomed it.

Armand, a respected theoretician in the field of social work, had been the founder of the con. ed. program at the school, but he was leaving the country on sabbatical. He had already recommended to the Dean that I take on the responsibility. Not long thereafter, I was officially offered the position and gladly accepted. The additional income brought us up to only a modest monthly deficit.

Not long after assuming this new role, Landcrafts emerged as our new entrepreneurial venture. Landcrafts was Aviva's and my brainchild, combining our love for Israel and for the arts. It featured a workshop approach over a three or five day period. The in-depth approach allowed for intensive immersion, led by a leading Israeli craftsperson. The end goal was the acquisition of the rudiments of an Israeli craft, while learning about the history and evolution of that craft in Israel.

The workshops were conducted by leading Israeli crafts persons and included: Bedouin weaving, Mosaics, Middle-Eastern cuisine, Jewelry design and fifteen additional crafts. Participants were generally tourists, although a number of Israelis participated. The venue for each workshop, was one of five hotels under the Israel Resort Hotel holding company, of which our landlord was the CEO.

Participants came to us through word-of-mouth or from Israeli travel agencies. Each participant would conclude the workshop with an article that they had designed and created. An acid test of this evolving concept, came when my parents visited us in Jerusalem. My mother, admittedly not very nimble with her hands, entered a three day workshop on jewelry design. My father had always been helpful in the kitchen, but rarely exhibited an inclination to experiment in the preparation of new dishes. We enrolled him in a three day, session on Middle-Eastern cuisine, conducted by the culinary critic for The Jerusalem Post. Both parents produced astonishing results, loved the experience and provided us with the incentive to continue.

The budding company gathered momentum when the Jerusalem Post featured a full page article on our new concept. Before long, the company featured workshops for over one hundred participants per session in Dead Sea area hotels. The company was growing, was well-received by hoteliers and travel agents, and even secured an endorsement from the Ministry of Tourism. A number of people, none of them named Aviva and Harry, derived a profit from the Landcrafts concept.

Within a year, we had decided that we would interest others to take over the company as it was both a financial drain on us in its embryonic period, and was too great a distraction from my university work.

David Macarov, an American transplant, was a full professor at the School of Social Work. His diminutive stature and affable personality masked an inquisitive and probing nature. We shared a common theoretical and practice-based interest in the employment arena, and how personality traits, impact one's probability of success. We discussed jointly writing a book on this subject. One afternoon, during a free hour, I was sitting in David's office when his daughter Varda, a veritable clone of her father, visited him.

After exchanging some preliminary Jewish geography notes, she asked where we were living. I gave her what Melinda always referred to as my "scenic route" response, most notably, that we were renting an apartment. Rental of one's residence in Israel too often connotes an ephemeral attachment to the country: the renter had not, it appeared, put down permanent stakes.

Varda gave me a brief introduction to a nascent project. "My husband and I, along with several other American transplants, are in the process of developing a housing concept. We have identified a tract of land in Ramot, a developing town just outside of the Jerusalem city limits. We are in the midst of forming a central, administrative committee that would oversee the design of the new community. This committee will develop governing by-laws and a method for attracting families who might be interested in this exciting venture." Varda continued enthusiastically, "the parcel of land should accommodate about one hundred and twenty five homes." She asked if I would be interested in joining their core organizing committee. I agreed, in theory, and indicated that I would give my final approval after conferring with Aviva.

Aviva liked the idea and we moved forward with our involvement. I attended meetings with a central committee comprised of bright, energetic individuals all of whom looked upon this project as an opportunity to obtain, what was rapidly becoming unobtainable in Israel: an affordable home. The committee decided to play an active role in the design process, with the belief that we would minimize expenditures by becoming our own project managers. My contribution to the by-laws was a series of restrictions aimed at avoiding speculators. The most restrictive of these articles was the requirement to complete a started construction project before being offered an opportunity to sell one's stake. Little did I know that my contribution to the by-laws, would virtually unravel our own investment in the project and our ability to continue to live in Israel.

We secured the services of an architectural firm. Three distinct building plans were designed for the project. The attached homes ranged from about sixteen hundred and fifty square feet to about two thousand square feet, sizable by Israeli standards. The initial prices were estimated at from forty thousand dollars to sixty thousand dollars. Aviva and I believed that, given the remainder of our funds, and the possibility of a modest mortgage, we might just be able to squeeze out the necessary funds.

Project development was moving ahead rapidly. Unfortunately, Israel's inflation, especially in the construction industry, was moving ahead even more rapidly. Within a few months of our initial estimates, construction costs were pegged at a fifty percent increase from our original projections. We were faced with the stark reality that we were significantly short of funding for our new home. We had already sunk virtually all of our available funds into the "House in Israel" project, our newly adopted name. We were not able to withdraw those funds, as they were now irrevocably dedicated to the completed construction of our projected home. Actually, we had no intention of withdrawing funds, even if we were allowed to.

In early 1980, Howard, knowing that we were in a financial conundrum, informed me of a unique opportunity. Howard, and a group of business consultants, had secured several promising contracts with New York based companies. If I were to consult with these consultants on a short-term basis, I could earn one thousand dollars per day of consulting. A quick, but by no means complicated mathematical computation, would reveal that each day's earnings in New York, was about twenty five percent of my annual university salary in Jerusalem. Benefitting from the myriad of holidays on the Jewish calendar, each one causing a virtual societal standstill and a university shutdown, Aviva and I agreed that, consulting in the States for a ten day period would not affect my university position and offered us a chance to fund our housing project.

We often joked, that it was impossible to book the services of, for example, a plumber, because it was either just before a holiday, the actual holiday itself, or a catch up period just after the holiday- and just before the upcoming holiday. However, my holiday-speckled school calendar provided me with the flexibility to accept Howard's offer. With the school's spring break on the horizon, I booked a flight to New York, planning to stay for a period of ten days.

Leaving Aviva and six year old Lora was immensely difficult for me. I was concerned about Aviva's managing without me and completing the chores that we shared. I was not really surprised to learn that, in my absence, Aviva fared very well and even went camping in the Sinai desert with Yaacov and Shlomit. I realized, begrudgingly, that she functioned better independently, than I did.

Chapter Nineteen

I WORKED HARD TO contribute to the group's consulting process. The groundwork had been laid for a future visit and expansion of the consultation effort. Upon leaving the States, my compensation, for the ten day period, amounted to two year's salary at Hebrew University. I was ecstatic to return to Israel and Aviva and Lora. Virtually all of the consulting earnings went immediately to cover our burgeoning construction shortfall. I was beginning to feel like Sisyphus, as my substantial contribution covered only the inflationary shortfall of construction costs. And so, the die was cast for another trip to the States.

Thankfully, the Shopwell Supermarket chain consulting project, was progressing successfully. I believe that about the time that we planned my second trip, both Aviva and I realized, that we were not going to be able to right our economic ship and build our home in Israel with my back-and-forth international consulting. We were committed to our lives in Israel, understood that apartment rental was not a long term solution, and that my overseas sojourns would become too disruptive.

We remained optimistic, as I planned my next trip to JFK only three weeks later. That trip was to prove even more emotionally challenging than the first departure, as I would miss Lora's seventh birthday party. Aviva assured me that she would be fine, and reminded me why I was undertaking these stressful journeys. Lora added her hugs and understanding…which I doubted were fully sincere, as I had always played a significant role in her birthday parties.

Three weeks later, I again arrived at JFK and, shortly thereafter, met with Howard and Zita, with whom I would live, for the next week and a half. The consulting work had expanded significantly, and I was back at our main contract, Shopwell Supermarkets, the next morning. I was now driving Sandy's car with out-of-state license plates.

Sandy, the third partner in our consulting project, was an extremely competent professional, who thankfully, also had an extra, unused car. The work days flew by, while the evenings and nights crawled along at a maddening and sluggardly pace. Once again, my nine day consulting effort produced another significant sum. I was soon on my return trip home to Israel.

Upon my return to Israel, Aviva and I analyzed our financial situation, as it was now inexorably linked to our "House in Israel" venture. We painfully decided that we would leave Israel, hopefully, for no more than two or three years. We would save as much as we could from my earnings, and return to live in our newly built home in Ramot.

We arranged to have our furniture stored in a warehouse on our friend's, Yizik and Nurit Noi's, Moshav, a communal project with privatized ownership, south of Tel Aviv. We sold them our trusty Volkswagen Beetle, which to this day, I believe is indestructible. The prospect of moving again was far from ideal for Lora. She had made a magnificent adjustment upon our return to Israel, spoke Hebrew fluently, and had a cadre of inseparable friends. She was completely Israeli. The return to the States would require yet another accommodation on her part. Our decision to return was painful, and especially difficult for our seven year old Lora.

I was leaving the University on good terms and with substantial notice. The Dean had invited me to rejoin the University upon our return to Israel. I fervently hoped, that when that day arrived, I would find that my nemesis, Monica, would be put out to pasture or would have been abducted by an alien space ship.

Leaving our very good friends Eric and Hagar, Yaacov and Shlomit, the Goldbergs, the Cohens, and the Strausses was very hard for us. Life in Israel encouraged socializing. We were constantly visiting friends, having dinners together, and spending weekends as overnight guests in Tel Aviv. We had grown much closer to our cousins Zvi and Sima, and Igal and Niza, who had returned from the States. We also had increasingly warm and personal contact with Ari and Yehudit, with whom we were to become much closer.

We had unpleasant recollections associated with a visit we had made to the States as a family in 1979. We stayed with Zita and Howard at their home in Teaneck, New Jersey. Aviva and I went for an early morning stroll. Teaneck, a typical suburban town, with neat and manicured lawns and tidy, small front porches, looked deserted. No one out walking, no mothers or fathers pushing strollers, no sign of life, except for the occasional Mexican gardener. Every few minutes, a garage door would open and a car would make its silent way to Route Four, heading toward the George Washington Bridge and a downtown, Manhattan office.

The lubricated garage doors closed effortlessly behind the emerging vehicle, at the command of a mobile remote control. It was deafeningly silent and stultifying. No contact, no social exchange. Our streets, in Jerusalem teemed with children, every morning we would hear parents reminding their school-bound children to behave or finish their lunches. Was this what we were returning to? The trappings of well-being, the isolation of a suburban, insulated community life?

We departed from Israel with a few suitcases of clothing and the diametrically opposed feelings of both leaving home and going home. The enveloping warmth of Israel, the ubiquitous communal feeling of belonging, the social get-togethers that seemed to render irrelevant any age distinction, would soon be behind us. Much to my amazement, I would miss raising a glass of mediocre, local merlot at a neighbor's party, answering such questions as: "what's your net salary at the university?" or "how much is your monthly mortgage payment?"

We were returning, for however long a period, to the rigid social and demographic isolation of life in America. We would now, first hand, encounter the suburban ennui, as the thought of spending the next few years in New York City with Lora, who had become accustomed to the less restrained lifestyle of Israel, seemed even more daunting.

Both Aviva and I held on to our unflinching belief that we would return to Israel within a few years, after I had earned enough money to fund our ever-increasing construction costs.

We would soon have the home of our dreams in Jerusalem, and be reunited with our Israeli friends and family. There was something about Israel that added an indescribable additional dimension of belonging. Despite our return to our birthplace, and the immediate proximity of our loved ones, I felt a resounding emptiness and sense of failure.

Prior to our leaving Israel, friends had recommended that we consider moving to a town in northern New Jersey where they knew of a number of Israeli families who were transplants and had been there for several years. Fair Lawn, New Jersey was about twelve miles from the George Washington Bridge, and, should one decide to leave home for the commute to New York at three a.m., access to the city was quite direct and easy. Every half hour increment after that, added fifteen minutes to one's ride.

We arrived in June, and in short order, rented a modest four bedroom home, in Fair Lawn. To our pleasant surprise, a lovely Israeli family lived two houses away. The Riemer family, living in Fair Lawn for three years, had three young daughters, close in age to Lora, whom she befriended almost immediately.

We took the leap of purchasing that house one year after our initial rental. We were emboldened to make the purchase, as I continued the lucrative consulting work that I began in our last months in Jerusalem. On a daily basis, I would brave the New York bound traffic on Route Four, headed to the South Bronx headquarters of Shopwell, a privately held supermarket chain, which was owned and operated by family fiat.

Much of our consultation was aimed at the ruling troika: Marty, the Chairman; Glenn, Marty's favored son, who, at thirty-five years of age, held operational control of the company's seventy two stores; and Jay, Marty's thirty-eight year old son, responsible for all of the management, finances, and administration of the company. The family dynamics toward me were uncomplicated: Jay loved me, Glenn was suspicious of me, and was en route to disliking me, and Marty was amused by me. Howard, Sandy and I had a good understanding of the personality foibles of each member of the ruling triad, and had forged powerful relations with the second tier of managers, who really ran the company.

When Jay invited me to lunch at Maxwell's Plum, an upper East-Side restaurant, that I was not yet able to afford, two months into our return to the States, I was uncertain what his agenda was. His family was famous for its mercurial decision-making. The luncheon could have been a fare-thee-well sandwich, or something less sinister….anything was possible.

When we were seated at our nicely appointed booth, I was impressed with its soft and supple leather. The Maître D' and the servers were painfully obsequious and deferentially addressed Jay by his family name. This was not the first time Jay visited this restaurant. With his friendly demeanor, and disarmingly, charming smile, Jay was the kind of guy you would like to have a drink with during some noisy happy hour. He generally spoke so slowly, that it could have been mistaken for careful and thoughtful consideration. However, he often seemed distracted; Howard and I had assessed that his attention span was, at best, of a three minute duration. Today seemed no different; he appeared preoccupied, and somewhat ill at ease. We had been seated no longer than five minutes when he got to the point: "Harry, we would be honored if you accepted the position of vice president of human resources for Shopwell."

I stayed calm and kept my gaze directly on him, which seemed to make him even more uncomfortable. Frankly, I was shocked. Jay obviously thought that he was hiring me out of a successful consulting firm, and that he needed to convince me to take his surprising offer. "We have, in our sixty year history," he continued, "never hired a vice president from outside the company. You would be the first, should you accept." The salary he quoted was at the top executive level of the company and matched that of vice presidents who had been with the company for years.

Long after accepting the offer, my vice presidency as an "outsider," my salary level, and all of the public accolades of my addition to the company, provided for ample dissension and grist for the rumor mill at Shopwell. I knew, at this time however, that it was important for Jay, et al, to believe that they had "hooked a big fish" and so, I declined to give him a direct answer pending some discussion with my partners (who in this case was Aviva). The next day, I informed Jay that I accepted the offer and would be prepared to start soon.

Meanwhile, back in Fair Lawn, our new house was virtually devoid of furniture. With all of our belongings in a Moshav warehouse in Israel, we borrowed lawn furniture from Zita, which served as our living room decor. We bought a bed for Lora and had a simple platform bed made for our bedroom. We had no television, much to Lora's chagrin, and cobbled together a table and some chairs as our dining room "set." A cot that Zita loaned us served as our living room couch. Aviva and I laughed when I accepted the position at Shopwell, as we thought how amusing it would be, to invite members of the company's administration for cocktails at our exquisitely minimalist home.

It was not that we couldn't afford to modestly furnish our new home, it was simply a conundrum for us. On the one hand, we did not want Lora to feel that she was living in a perennial state of Nomadic dislocation and deprivation. On the other hand, we were planning to return to Israel and did not want a total replication of what we already had purchased in Israel. On the largest third hand, we were sending virtually all of my earnings, save the barest essentials, to fund the construction of our dream house in Israel.

1981 brought extraordinary happiness to our lives. It was also a time when the stark realization that our dream of a home in Israel had become unrealistic, and worse, unobtainable. April of that year brought the joy of the birth of our son Ilan. After twenty-five hours of unrelenting labor, Aviva gave birth to our beautiful son. Both Melinda, and her husband Lon, were pediatricians in The Albert Einstein Hospital in the Bronx, where Aviva gave birth. Melinda was Chief Resident, which allowed for some personal contact and diversion for Aviva during her labor. Melinda was a source of comfort, professionalism and humor. My parents were ecstatic that we would be living only a few miles from them, and that they would be a part of Ilan's growing up. They adored Lora, and now could shower their grandparent affection on our second child as well.

Our contact with the core committee of our "Home in Israel" project, however, continued to produce increasingly demoralizing news. Construction costs for our proposed home were now approaching one hundred sixty thousand dollars, close to three times our original estimates. There seemed to be no end in sight to the spiraling costs of construction. We had to make a decision. We had already sunk ninety thousand dollars into the project and had no idea where the remaining funds would come from, or what the final costs would be.

The fluidity of the Israeli economy was mind-boggling, being seven thousand miles away from our project was intensely frustrating. Our new infant's arrival would add to our cost of living in New Jersey, straining our already meager remaining resources. We decided that we would seek to extricate ourselves from the project. We would try to circumvent the clause in our Israeli by-laws: that no sale should be approved and no invested funds returned until the unit's construction was completed.

Our decision was not a welcome one in Israel. The core management group had added new members in our absence, with whom we had no personal relationship. Our request was denied and the burden to complete our exponentially more expensive project was placed squarely upon us. Upon receiving our unwelcome news, I contacted an Israeli attorney, with whom I had completed a variety of contractual arrangements before leaving for the States.

I asked that he attempt to find an investor who was willing to allocate the remainder of the required funds, complete the construction and try to sell the home at a profit. The contract, I informed the attorney, must stipulate clearly, that we receive the first ninety thousand dollars that we had invested. It should also outline a plan for distributing the remaining funds between us and the investor. Within two weeks, I had a copy of the contract mailed to me. The internet was not yet developed and snail mail, telegrams or telephonic contact were our sole means of communication. I called him and approved of the language of the contract and his moving ahead to find an investor. We remained naively hopeful.

Baby Ilan brought much joy into our lives. He had a pleasant disposition, slept well and was incredibly adorable. My parents could not get enough of him, Lora was already a wonderful big sister and Aviva loved being the mother of an infant. I believe that her even temperament and calm demeanor rubbed off on our children, at least for a while.

I cannot say that I encountered too many people with similar demeanors and temperaments at Shopwell. I was now surrounded by a sea of Italian and Irish veterans who, from my first day on the job, saw me as an aberration, anomalous to the "up-from-the-ranks" culture. My peers would sarcastically refer to me as "the good doctor" or "Doctor Stern."

Fortunately, I had connected with, and was virtually "adopted" by, the operational kingpin of the four thousand employee company. Guido Parisi was the Director of Operations, and had been with the company many years. He was soft spoken, highly intelligent and respected and revered by all. His word carried a great deal of clout with the owners and all management levels. I rode his coattails for my three years with the company. I never questioned the origin of this unbridled respect for Guido, there was no need.

Guido liked me and respected my judgment and opinions about areas of weakness that I perceived in the company's operations. Several times a month, Guido would come to my unglamorous office and invite me to visit a company store. I jumped at the opportunity, as it usually produced an unusual luncheon experience, as well as an opportunity to get to know him better. Guido was funny, inquisitive and from a world with which I had little experience. We both had new company cars, but it was always his car we left with. His black Oldsmobile ninety-eight, would silently glide out of the company's guarded, South Bronx parking lot. We would head toward, either The Major Deegan or Cross Bronx Expressway, slowly making our way past the gauntlet of prostitutes, each beckoning to us with one lewd gesture or another.

"Want to stop for a blow job?" Guido joked.

"Is that how you get action when one reaches sixty years old?"

"You should only be so lucky as to one day have the action that this guy had."

We took a slight detour past the busy and raunchy South Bronx Hunt's Point produce market, and made our way up to, either the Taconic or Saw Mill River Parkways, and the exit in or near Tarrytown. This area of Westchester County, was home to numerous, family run Italian restaurants, each with an apocryphal story of its own. We pulled into the parking lot of Rienzi's Ristorante and, as we always did, found our way to the most secluded spot at the rear of the lot.

Guido would slowly emerge from his black chariot, scan the lot, slowly and carefully, as we entered the restaurant through the rear kitchen door. After a while, I stopped wondering why he always carried his attaché case to this non-business luncheon. Same visual scenario inside the restaurant each time: mahogany wood paneling throughout the dining area, with autographed Frank Sinatra or Joe DiMaggio photographs bearing personal salutations, strategically hung near each of the fifteen or so, tables. Somehow magically, perhaps through some silent predetermination, we made our way to a reserved table at the rear of the restaurant.

We always sat in a dark corner, far from any external windows, that made it difficult even for my, still youthful eyes, to read a menu. Guido always faced the front of the restaurant. But, there was no need for a menu. In each restaurant, the owner, or the chef himself, would politely inform Guido, and his Jewish sidekick, what they recommended for our lunch. Voices were never above a hushed, decibel-deprived, level and rarely did anyone smile. I loved it, and felt that I was living a scene that had been edited out of "Godfather II."

"Mr. Parisi, today, the veal is especially fresh and well-prepared."

"How is Pietro preparing it today?"

"Milanese...but, whatever you desire. We have any style of home-made pasta for your pleasure."

"Sounds fine to me, you know how I like my bucatini, al dente, yes?"

"Of course, Mr. Parisi."

And then the after thought, me. With an air of restrained indifference, the proprietor glanced my way: "I'll have exactly what Mr. Parisi is having."

Perhaps an even more formidable challenge came from an unsuspected source. Our Israeli attorney had informed us that he had identified a reputable investor who had reviewed our contract and agreed to its terms. The attorney requested our permission to move ahead with this arrangement and we agreed. This was a difficult time for us. We loved Israel deeply, wanted to bring our children up in an Israeli society, but, it was becoming increasingly unrealistic. Aviva and I were saddened at the prospect of losing our dream house in Israel, but relieved that we would soon have the ninety thousand dollars that we had invested in our jettisoned project.

Aviva was again pregnant and was due to deliver in July of the following year. We were thrilled, although Aviva's disclosure was accompanied by the physical discomforts that seemed to be her destiny with the pregnancies. The bad news, that regularly seemed to accompany our good news, sent shock waves through our systems, although we were determined to fight it.

Our Israeli attorney notified us, only weeks after executing the investor contract, that the home that we had begun building was recently completed. The investor, who had been brought in to conclude the required construction, had very little trouble selling it. The problem was, that he was disregarding the covenants of the contract, and was willing, our attorney informed us, to consider giving us twenty thousand dollars.

His rationale was criminally and deceptively simple: he is there and we are not; he did the work selling the house, and the money was coming to him. Our attorney, seemed powerless to act and, for all we knew, was in collaboration with the investor. I felt hamstrung being seven thousand miles from this fraudulent act. The money that we had invested in the construction was virtually every penny that we had.

I called our good friend Morris in Israel, whose sister-in-law, Janine, was an attorney in Chaim Herzog's law firm. Herzog was soon to become the President of the State of Israel. Janine agreed that abrogation of our contract was illegal, and recommended that Oded, a young, bright up and coming attorney, represent us in attempting to overturn this criminal act. Oded agreed to argue on our behalf for a nominal fee. I had explained to Janine, that all of our funds were now in the hands of this devious "investor."

What ensued was about a year and a half of intercontinental correspondence. Oded had filed legal briefs to the Regional Court on our behalf. I reviewed, as best I could, all of the verbiage in these legal documents before the final submission; my knowledge of legal terms and concepts in Hebrew was minimal. I wished fervently that Guido could accompany me to Israel, I would need his atypical approach to conflict resolution. I continued to respond to Oded, whom I had never met, as completely and quickly as I could, although privately, I had given up all hope of any positive resolution.

In the middle of this emotional vortex, Ayal, our second son, was born and made our spirits soar.

The wonderful appearance, after Aviva's twenty-five hour labor, of infant Ayal, brought light, hope and joy into our lives. He was a beautiful infant with a lively temperament, delicate skin and a unique and wonderful cuteness. We once again were called upon to be creative in rearranging our living room lawn furniture, and our family-donated kitchen and dining room "sets" to accommodate our new arrival.

Toward the late autumn of 1983, with Ayal now about four months old, our Israeli attorney Oded, called us and said that he had been granted a court date at the Regional Court House in Tel Aviv, and that I was required to attend and testify. The following Thursday I was on an El Al overnight flight to Tel Aviv. I took a cab from the airport and arrived at Oded's Tel Aviv office in a surprise rainstorm.

Oded welcomed me at the door. He was about six foot tall with a wiry build, nice looking with a shock of sandy colored hair that needed some trimming. He wore a sport jacket with no tie and brown slacks that cried for significant pressing. I was also not exactly ready for the cover of "Esquire," as I had just gotten off a twelve hour overnight flight which yielded about two hours of sleep in a contorted position. I too, had a wrinkled shirt and pants and a jet lag induced headache. I greeted him enthusiastically: "Oded, I want to thank you for all of your dedicated work helping us. When must we would appear in court?" His apologetic answer was: "in twenty five minutes."

Oded explained, as he slipped on a well-worn, tan trench coat, "The court will shut down for Shabbat at three o'clock, or in about four hours from now. Who knows when the next court date could be set?"

Thankfully, we were able to hail a cab just outside of his office. The ten minute ride to the courthouse was devoid of niceties and mutual introductions. Oded was highly intelligent and exuded optimism. He focused on the points I was to make and the arguments that the investor's attorney would forcefully present. I was trying hard to dispel my sleep-deprived haze, and struggled to follow Oded's logic. None of this was new to me, as we had communicated via a mail exchange for several months.

We entered the courthouse which looked like any typical Israeli public building. Off-white stone tiles greeted us upon entering, an occasional maintenance worker's mop and pail left unattended in the hallways, no art work adorning the corridor walls and a pervasive dankness. It all seemed very familiar to me. I had never thought it strange while living in Israel, to find the walls of public facilities speckled with printed posters announcing someone's demise. How out of place it now looked. How sinister.

Oded guided me into the main courtroom where we were asked to register and present identification. We took our seats at a rickety and pock-marked table facing the vacant judge's elevated chair and desk, on the left side of the courtroom. I was able to get my first look at our investor, who was sitting opposite us next to his attorney. Both the investor and his attorney were wearing yarmulkes. The investor appeared to be in his forties, a bit paunchy and sporting a closely-cropped, red beard. As I scanned the courtroom, I observed that the bailiff was wearing a yarmulke, as was the male scribe already recording data on what appeared to be a transcribing device. "Oded, have you noticed that you and I are among the only men present not wearing a head cover?" "First thing I noticed," he answered.

As the judge entered the courtroom, from a chamber door behind his chair, we all rose. To my chagrin, he too was wearing a Yarmulke, while sporting a darker version of the investor's groomed beard. After some preliminary opening remarks, the bailiff summoned me to the witness dock. What ensued was about two hours of cross examination by the investor's attorney, countering remarks by Oded, and comments of mine which may or may not have helped my cause. All of the dialogue was in Hebrew, much of it in legal terms, that I struggled to understand.

To my surprise, the judge appeared quite sympathetic to our position. The judge concluded the hearing, with remarks that I neither understood nor cared about, as all rational thought had exited my saturated brain, about one hour into the hearing. Upon the conclusion of my court appearance, I asked Oded: "So, how did I do?"

"You weren't Clarence Darrow, but it went well," he answered. "We should receive the judge's ruling in about one month."

Two days later, I was back at my desk in the South Bronx. My relationship with Guido had deepened, with the same intensity, that my interaction with Glen, Jay's mercurial, hot-tempered, imperious, and clandestinely gay, brother, had declined. Glen, nominally the Chief Operating Officer of the company, but really the bratty son of the company chairman, called the shots. He demanded obsequiousness, which was not a strong suit of mine.

Glen sanctioned, and probably encouraged, ongoing attempts to undermine my achievements at Shopwell. Despite three years of substantial success in the human resource and training arenas, and perhaps, because of the public accolades, I knew that my days at Shopwell were numbered. Luckily, my office had been on the pathway to the owners' offices. I had an unobstructed view of the constant parade of persons of questionable character, and dubious legal standing, as they passed by my office to Glen's hideaway. Few of those on that parade route, would have been considered among America's most upstanding citizens.

My relationship with Guido and my many intimate conversations with him regarding company operations, served me well. My strong bond with him and the quiet, but clear, control that he exerted over all management levels, except the ruling class sons, had become increasingly important to me over my three year tenure. Both, observing the cast of characters visiting management regularly, and a number of unusual business practices that I was aware of, buttressed my position for the upcoming and expected event. Aviva and I had for some time been searching for a way that I might extricate myself from the company, without exposing our family to short term economic problems. Jay, inadvertently, provided me with an escape route.

Not long after my return from Israel, which featured my less than memorable court appearance, Jay's attractive assistant,

Louise, demurely invited me to Jay's office. Louise was hot, and not exactly demure. We had a joking and pleasant relationship. I accompanied her for the seventy five foot stroll to Jay's office, entertained by her sexy, slow gait. We entered his office and Louise, without being asked, shut the door behind us. When Jay began a serious conversation, his upper lip would quiver, several beads of perspiration would rapidly position themselves just below each flared nostril, and his initial sentence or two, would characteristically be of a tremolo quality.

"Harry," he warbled (starting with my name again), for a moment, I felt like his boss, "this is probably the most difficult conversation I have ever had. I have to ask you to resign your position. There is just too much animosity coming from Glen and it is wearing me down." My initial thought was, thank God for Glen. I knew that every vacation that I took, every absence from my office, provided those veterans of the company, Andy, Bobby, Alan, an opportunity to formulate a very creative array of scenarios, to "overthrow the palace resident"...me.

This conversation with Jay was a golden opportunity. I had learned, over the years, that "he who speaks first in a business deal, loses." I feigned surprise and deep disappointment, but refrained from a more elaborate response. "You have contributed so much to the professionalism of our company, in such a short time. The training programs you initiated have been very helpful to the company, that's what makes this talk so difficult." Jay continued, "I would ask that you publicly indicate that this decision was yours alone. Perhaps, you could say, that you are returning to consulting, after a successful stint with us." My family, the company's owners," Jay continued, "would be embarrassed, as they had made such public proclamations about hiring you, and highlighted your achievements, in the recent annual report." I agreed, that I would do so, "Jay, I would never want to hurt or embarrass anyone in the company that has been so good to me." This was what Jay was waiting to hear.

"Harry, we are prepared to give you six month's salary and sell you the new car that we just assigned to you last month, for a very nominal sum. Additionally," he continued, "you may use a company office for that six month period." The conversation went on longer than it should have, and when I left his office, I was in a state of euphoric shock. Six month's salary after only three years, a luxurious, one month old, Oldsmobile Ninety Eight for a modest sum; much more than I could have imagined. And so, my brief stint as a supermarket mogul came to a quiet and productive conclusion. I was convinced that this magnanimity was to buy my ignorance.

Two glorious months passed: a full executive salary, a brand new, virtually free, luxury automobile and no castle intrigue. The tranquility came to an abrupt end upon receiving a bulky envelope that had been stuffed into our Fair Lawn mailbox. The parcel, from Oded in Israel, contained about twenty five pages of the Regional, Tel Aviv court transcripts, with each section highlighting the judge's opinion. Each of the eight or ten sections seemed benign enough, with the judge commenting on the validity of the points made during my testimony. The conclusion, however, was anything but benign. The judge's summation stated numerous times, that Stern made a valid point here and there, but, he ruled exclusively in favor of the investor.

As I read the essentials of the document to Aviva, I explained that this meant that we had, in essence, lost our ninety thousand dollars invested in the project, and that perhaps, we would receive a few begrudging dollars at some distant future point. We were crestfallen, but tried to put it into perspective, the clarity of which, I could not yet conceive of.

We tried very hard not to let it sour our love for Israel, as the whole courtroom ambience reeked of a religious cabal. We had been very focused on our return to Israel, a dynamic that influenced all of our thoughts. The names that we chose for both of our American born sons, were Israeli, in anticipation of our return to Israel. Our vision of our future had always revolved around the return to Jerusalem, and our newly constructed home.

Our funk was only mildly lifted two days after receiving our bad news. Oded, our attorney, called us on a Sunday afternoon. "I apologize, not for the negative result of the judgment, we presented the facts and made valid arguments, but rather, for what is clearly a "travesty of justice." With your permission, I must pursue this decision all the way to the Israeli Supreme Court." He indicated, that this was now a personal and professional matter for him, and he would accept no compensation from us. "Thanks Oded, for all of your effort and determination. You have our approval." To say that we had no hope of a positive outcome, would be a significant understatement. Something far more important was on our immediate horizon.

Early on the morning of March twentieth, we received a distraught call from my father, informing us that my mother had suffered a cardiac arrest, and was in a hospital near their home. She had been resuscitated, was in a coma, but still living. The next month and a half were spent in a constant vigil, waiting for signs of awakening that never came. Melinda and Lon were constantly by her bedside as well. I worried a great deal about my father, who seemed so bereft and suddenly so immensely vulnerable. My mother, so vibrant, vivacious, so devil-may-care, such a lover of life, so irreverent, succumbed to the ravages of her cardiac failure, and died on May first, 1984.

My mother, who had always maintained that she had powers of alchemy, managed the dates of her demise consistent with those magical beliefs. The date of her cardiac arrest, was the day that her dear brother Karl passed away, six years earlier, while visiting the States from England for our wedding. The day that she passed away, May first, was May Day in Europe, a workers' holiday, that she always held in very high regard.

Our focus was now on supporting my father. It was very difficult for me as I wanted to care for him, but knew that the next few months were very important for him to regain his equilibrium and maintain a sense of independence. He and my mother were "two peas in a pod," although much of that "pod" time, was spent in what seemed to be petty wrangling. My father was very proud and self-sufficient. I had to restrain myself from damaging that independence by over protecting him. Zvi, whose mother's death had preceded his father's as well, counseled us to support my father's desire to stay in the apartment he had shared with my mother.

With the birth of Ayal and the virtual vigil that we were observing at my mother's bedside, I had not kept track of how rapidly the six month severance compensation passed. We now faced a triangular conundrum: our six month paid "vacation" was soon ending, we had no cash reserve, and I was increasingly drawn to the Jewish communal field. Finding employment in another city or state would mean leaving my father at a difficult time.

Both my father and mother adored all three of our children. Unfortunately, my mother's untimely death, came only months after Ayal's birth. Her love had, for years, been focused on Lora, and for almost three of those years on Ilan as well. My father loved being with Ilan; they often played building and fireman games. Leaving town for new employment, should that become necessary, would be very difficult.

While Lora presented a challenge to us with her pre-teen willful behavior, testiness and constant flaunting of authority (mostly, our authority: from where could this have come?) Ilan, posed a different and, for me, more challenging scenario. Ilan's childhood asthma was likened to a runaway locomotive by a Fair Lawn pediatrician. Any preliminary sign of a cold might precipitate an asthmatic response, which might rapidly accelerate into labored and raucous breathing. These reactions necessitated hospitalization, three times prior to Ilan's second birthday.

It was painful to feel so inadequate while addressing Ilan's acute symptoms. Thankfully, Melinda introduced us to Mark, a medical colleague, specializing in pediatric pulmonary diseases. Mark helped relieve us of the mystique and our irrational fears surrounding asthma, while prescribing an aggressive treatment plan. He also assured us that Ilan would outgrow the infantile asthma and would be virtually free of symptoms by his teen years.

I was offered employment with the Jewish Federation in Washington, D.C. The position coincided with my search for ways to contribute to the Jewish community. My father was very stoic and supportive, and encouraged me to take the job. He would, he maintained, be able to visit us by train on a regular basis. We agreed, in Aviva's Aunt Carol's words, " to put food on the table," by moving to Washington.

Leaving the New York area had now become exponentially more difficult. Aviva had established an affiliation with a New York sculpture gallery, Lora was now approaching her teen years and had to, once again, say goodbye to close friends a few houses away, we had grown comfortable with Ilan's physician and the treatment plan for his asthma, and we now had two year old, Ayal as an active toddler. I would incessantly grapple with my guilt about leaving my father and, once again, we would be parting from Melinda and her husband Lon and their two lovely children, Jared and Mara.

The job would not wait. The head of the Federation needed the important fundraising position filled as soon as possible. Not wanting this opportunity to dissolve, we agreed to move quickly.

We would list the house for sale. I would begin work in Washington. With Lora still in school until the end of June, our house only recently placed on the market by a local real estate agent, and our bank account having reached subterranean levels, I began my new career path in an unorthodox manner.

I left our Fair lawn home at four a.m. on Mondays and returned home on Thursday evenings, just about bed time for our three children. Their bedtime was always a precious time for me. I would lie on the floor of the bedroom, shared by Ilan and Ayal, and offer them three totally absurd options for a story. They would argue over such selections as: "the grasshopper with no shoes," or "the horse that played the piano." I had to make up a story with that central theme- and try to stay awake, while lying on the carpeted floor. I missed that terribly, while away from home.

The four and a half hour drive would bring me to the Federation's Chevy Chase parking lot in time for our nine a.m. Monday staff meetings. My nights were spent sleeping at a local Holiday Inn. This arrangement continued for thirteen weeks. Aviva became a single mom, and I was engrossed in my new career during the day, and spent the late evenings having conversations with Aviva's hologram.

I worked hard to establish myself as an asset to the Federation, and was made to feel welcome and valued by the agency's staff. During that thirteen week period, I managed to find a house that I believed suited our family needs, and was in a good school district. Through the magic of Federation major donors, I managed to secure a bridge loan, as our Fair lawn home was not yet sold, and, even more surprisingly, qualified for a mortgage at a reasonable interest rate.

The house that we purchased was on a nice parcel of land, but the interior was nothing short of revolting. A depressed, alcoholic bachelor had owned the home, and had neglected any semblance of maintenance. I was very happy that Aviva had not seen it in that state and I never mentioned it when I told her that I had found a home that suited us just fine. I resolved not to tell her, that I had a crew of six maintenance specialists, work for four days scrubbing, sanitizing, painting and repairing the home so that when she first saw it, she was quite pleased.

The thirteen weeks thankfully, passed quickly and productively. Lora finished school with good grades, Ilan's asthma had gone underground temporarily, Ayal was a cooperative, fun-filled and undemanding child. We sold our Fair Lawn home for twenty thousand dollars more than our purchase price. We were on our way to Washington, D.C., once again leaving family and friends behind- only this time at a distance of only two hundred fifty miles.

Two days after the full family arrival in Washington, we were faced with the dreaded unpacking that came with every move. We were all involved in these pleasantries, when Lora loudly announced the arrival of our dear relatives, Carol and Richard. They arrived as a total surprise, to help us in the earliest stages of arranging our new household. This was to become a most pleasant ritual, wherever we moved, Carol and Richard were there to help us in our transition. They were such a wonderful help, such great friends, and a great relief from the tension of yet another move.

Ilan and Ayal were enrolled in a not-inexpensive preschool at a local synagogue, while Lora entered a junior high school that was competitive and snobby. Our backyard was made to appear even larger, by a power company easement that extended for several hundred feet behind our house. The yard allowed for serious football and baseball catches with the boys and a substantial vegetable garden.

I found my work at the Federation challenging and exciting. I had never worked as a fundraiser and, to my surprise, had few problems raising funds for Jewish causes. I found that I had very little difficulty establishing rapport with major donors, many of whom were scions of mega wealthy families and the aristocracy of Washington's Jewish community.

Richard Rubin was one of the significant contributors, surprisingly earthy and unrefined, with whom I established a nice professional relationship. Richard would be the Chairperson of the first fundraising event that I would manage in my new position. The Inaugural Division: Federation had endless giving categories, was reserved for the elite contributors with an entry level, minimum annual gift of fifty thousand dollars. I was generally amused by all of the various giving level monikers, but the Inaugural Division was where the power brokers of the community resided.

The Inaugural Division dinner was the annual campaign kickoff, and often was an accurate barometer for the success level of that year's fundraising effort. Richard and I first met in my new office. He was a burly, grey topped, six foot tall, hard driving, straight talking, fifty something year old. "OK, here is what I would like for our Inaugural event. As the Chair of that event, I have opted for it in an exclusive setting. Before your arrival, I decided on the newly renovated Willard Hotel, it's only a stone's throw from the White House." He had already arranged for the guest speaker, Charles Bronfman, Chair of the Seagram's Corporation. "I would like for you to make arrangements for a meeting at The Willard." We would decide on a date with their catering and event department. As he rose abruptly from the chair in my new office, he smiled, a wry smile with his right lip curled upward, "Oh, and thank you, it will be nice working with you." Tough, but, will be good to work with, I thought.

I arranged an appointment with the Catering Manager's assistant who informed me that Mr. Klaus Schweinfurt would see us two days hence. The name left me with an uneasy presentiment, which I repressed. I informed Richard about our meeting, and he said that he and his wife would pick Aviva and I up at our home, and that we could have dinner together after making our event arrangements.

Wednesday afternoon, at precisely five p.m., a shiny, black, stretch limo pulled up in front of our modest, Potomac home. Richard's chauffeur hastened to open the door to this cavernous, rolling village. As we got in, Richard was already pouring us a drink from the well-appointed bar separating us from his driver. This was my first experience in a non-rented limo, and I was amused at the novelty of riding in a limo that someone actually owned. The twenty minute ride downtown was pleasant: Richard's wife was surprisingly demure and engaging. Richard's gruff, but approachable, quality made for easy and unaffected conversation.

He seemed not to have a drop of aristocratic blue blood, but rather, I assumed, had become successful as a hard-nosed, from "the back streets," businessman. We arrived at the hotel's circular driveway and, after opening the doors for his patrons and their guests, the chauffeur was asked to wait for us. Richard whispered to him, that the meeting shouldn't be too long.

The hotel was exquisite. Richard seemed to boast, as he informed us that renovations and upgrades had been completed only a few months earlier. There were twinkling, crystal chandeliers everywhere, rich, intricately designed, Persian carpeting partially bedecked the cream and black inlaid, marble floor tiles. Busy staff were scurrying in all directions. The front desk clerk indicated that they were expecting us and had a bellman, in a wrinkle free uniform, show us to the catering office. Aviva and Richard's wife were to wait in the beautifully appointed lobby.

We were ushered in to Mr. Schweinfurt's office by his attractive Asian assistant. "Good evening Mr. Rubin and Mr. Stern, please have a seat," Mr. Schweinfurt greeted us with a thick,

German accent. He was about six foot tall, probably in his fifties and had a Germanic, full head of blonde hair and piercing, blue eyes. The office was large and somber with dark brown, possibly walnut, paneling and a deep, purple, plush carpet.

"Mr. Schweinfurt, thank you for receiving us on such short notice," Richard began.

"Please call me Klaus, and I am happy to be meeting with you," Klaus answered with rehearsed politeness.

Richard continued by outlining the planned event, the number of anticipated attendees, and a date that he was recommending. Klaus, referred to his open event log: "Mr. Rubin, I am so sorry, but that particular date is unavailable as we have booked a very large wedding on that day."

"OK," Richard answered politely, "what about October sixteenth?" That date was one week later than we had planned.

"Oh, Mr. Rubin," Klaus moaned, "we have two events on that day, I am so sorry."

Placid was not a description that came to mind in describing Richard's reaction to not getting his way, but this proved to be the exception.

"Oh well, Klaus," Richard continued, calmly and quietly, "I know how busy the hotel is this time of year. How about October twenty-third?"

Klaus carefully studied his event log, and with indignation, aimed at his overflowing event calendar, apologetically responded, "I am so sorry Mr. Rubin, it just doesn't seem to be working."

With each response to Richard, I thought I detected more-and-more of Klaus's Germanic accent. Maybe it was just my imagination.

Richard never batted an eyelash and continued in a steady and unhurried tone, "I understand Klaus, but I wonder if you could do me a favor?"

"Certainly, Mr. Rubin, what is it?" Klaus seemed so eager to please.

"Would you kindly dial this telephone number for me, and hand me the phone?" Richard asked in a restrained, but pleasant fashion. He called out the number, as Klaus started dialing. As Richard dictated the final digit, Klaus gently hung up the phone.

"Mr. Rubin," he offered politely, "isn't that the number of our General Manager's office?"

"Yes, it is Klaus, I just want to tell him, that the President of the bank that furnished all of the funds to refurbish this hotel, is sitting in your office and cannot get an event planned for his organization." I thought I saw Klaus click his heels, it could have been my imagination, as he consulted his log and turned to his assistant.

"Amy, would it not be possible to shift existing events to accommodate Mr. Rubin?" Thankfully, I was merely a fly on the wall. Instantaneously, she responded, "Yes, Mr. Schweinfurt, it is possible and I will make all of the necessary arrangements." The tenor of the conversation was frighteningly consistent. No apologies and no recriminations. No voices raised, no flaring nostrils.

"Mr. Rubin, we will use all new china and cutlery so as to ensure Kashrut," Klaus added gratuitously.

"Very nice of you," Richard concluded, "Mr. Stern will coordinate all details with you at a later date." Richard rose from his chair, wished the two of them good day, and ushered me out first. No smiles, no handshakes. As we left the office area

Richard looked at me, with the slightest trace of a smile, and simply said: "Fucking Nazi."

Washington power plays were often of a similar nature. Voices were generally calm and understated; anger and consternation were generally repressed at the time, but often generated a lethal aftermath. The major donors had little to prove when it came to their social position and affluence. It seemed that everyone understood the hierarchical structure of the community, with its two main ingredients: wealth and political influence. I needed to remind myself on a regular basis, that, irrespective of the apparent fluidity of my relationship with those pillars of the community, I was not one of them. As a Jewish communal professional, I was regarded as a means to an end, organizing events and raising money for causes that may prove important to them. I felt like a communal butler. I was however, learning a great deal about Jewish organizations, and the ongoing fundraising required to sustain them. On many levels, it was a relief to be far afield from my gun-totting colleagues in the supermarket industry.

My father visited us regularly. He would take Amtrak to Union Station, where I would meet him.

He would stay with us for a long weekend, although we often badgered him to stay longer. The kids loved having him around, and he was marvelous with them. Each time that he arrived to stay with us, I wanted to push for his living with us, but I restrained myself, knowing that it would mean leaving his friends, and all that he was familiar with in New York. Additionally, I soon came to see Washington as a transitory location for us, a stepping stone into the field that I found increasingly compelling. It was clear, that significant advancement would require yet another relocation.

We decided to take a midweek break from cooking, and planned to go to an early dinner at Hamburger Hamlet. That neighborhood restaurant had become a favorite quick dinner joint for us. Our most notable recent visits highlighted watching their oversized television, as the ball trickled through Bill Buckner's legs, enabling the Mets to win the World Series, and for Ayal throwing up his dinner on our table. Putting that last event behind us, we prepared our rambunctious Lora, now thirteen, and wild and wooly; Ilan, at five, a pesky big brother to Ayal, now three, and learning to fend for himself when Ilan picked on him. As we prepared to leave, the phone rang. It was Oded, our long-forgotten attorney in Israel. My first thought was, did we owe him any money?

"We won," he sounded elated. It was about a year since I last spoke with him, and was unsure what he referred to.

"What did we win?" I asked. He seemed surprised by my nonchalance.

"The Israeli Supreme Court overturned the regional court's travesty of justice by a vote of three to zero. All of your funds," he continued gleefully, "will be returned to you, and all prior legal and transportation costs that you incurred, will be awarded to you. The court has put a lien on the investor's home, to ensure payment in full is coming to you. So, all I need, is your Riggs Bank international transfer account number, and within ten days you will have your funds."

"Oded, this is not a joke, I hope," I managed to mutter.

"No, not a joke, I want no fees from you but, it is late here, and I can now sleep easy."

I thanked him profusely. The funds came ten days later, over ninety thousand dollars, just as he had said. I sent him ten thousand of those dollars, despite his commendable and sincere protestations of a no fee representation. Our hamburgers tasted glorious one half hour later.

I shared the good news with my father when we next spoke. He was very happy for us. His advice had always been so sound and reasonable. In fact, the entire family, had for years, sought his wise counsel on so many disparate issues. He always seemed to have a cogent answer.

That visit was the last time I saw him. About two weeks later, Lon called us early on a Sunday morning, to tell us my father had a heart attack and had died en route to the hospital. I felt crushed. Only a tick over two years, and both of my dear parents were gone. It seemed so ironic, that the older I got, and the more I was involved in raising my family, the closer I felt to both of my parents. I felt cut adrift in a surging tide, but was anchored by my family: Aviva and three great kids.

Just as my father adored Aviva, so too, did she love him. It was hard not to love my parents: my mother's zany, loving, larger than life, id speaks first personality, and my father's intelligence, humor, and warmth. Unfortunately, both of my parents had borne out a popular belief: that many spouses tend to follow their partner's demise, often within a two to three year period. It's as if the living partner gives up his or her desire to continue living alone.

I had blown it. For years I had wrestled with the idea of chronicling my father's extraordinary early years. He had a photographic memory, and would describe for Aviva and me scenes of their escape, through an unwelcoming Europe, during World War Two. I resisted asking for the opportunity to create a document for posterity, because of the reluctance I had to even intimating to him, that I believed there would be a time when he would no longer be with us. How infantile of me, how unrealistic it was for me, to avoid the subject of one's demise. How I wished that I now had a clearer picture, of the cultured and intellectual cocoon that my mother thrived in during her youth in Vienna. How I yearned, for the humor with which my father shared his family's smuggling enterprises, greatly facilitated by the five passports that he always kept nearby. Now, it was too late. Perhaps this loss, this lacuna in my family awareness, has motivated me to complete this work.

Working in a Jewish agency at a time of personal crisis, proved to be an unanticipated comfort. I felt their real compassion when I informed my colleagues of the loss of my father. I didn't have to explain why I had to abruptly leave to attend the hastily organized funeral. There was no need to describe the meaning of sitting shiva, and why I would be away from my position for almost a week and a half. Surrounded by Jews at a deeply distressful time, brought me a level of comfort, even consolation. Strangely, I felt somewhat reconnected to Israel. Perhaps, in retrospect, this period solidified my resolve to pursue a leadership role in the Jewish communal field.

That opportunity came several months shy of my second year in Washington. I received a call from Bessie Pine, senior management recruiter, of the Jewish Welfare Board, the national umbrella organization for Jewish Community Centers. That organization would undergo a name change a few years later. Would I be prepared to interview for the position of CEO of the JCCs of San Diego, Bessie inquired? Quite coincidentally, Melinda had just returned from a vacation in California and had rapturously described the beauty of La Jolla, where the center was located.

Two weeks later, I was on a plane to San Diego for my interview. The position was offered to me before I prepared for my return to Washington two days later. I accepted. I was grateful for the rapidity of the interview committee's decision, and mortified at the prospect of again moving my peripatetic family. Leaving Washington would be easy for Aviva, Lora and me and quite unimportant to the boys. None of us really cared much for Washington's rigid social stratification, and we had few friends and no meaningful community connection. Leaving my colleagues at the Jewish Federation was different. I had connected personally with many of them and felt very much at home in that environment.

One week before our departure for San Diego, the staff and Board members held a farewell party for me. While I had only been employed at the agency for two years, I had made many friends and performed beyond the agency's expectations. I worked hard to submerge the deep ambivalence that I felt about leaving them.

All too often, employment opportunities supersede the deepening of extended family and friendship roots. To this day, I wonder whether the more cosmopolitan exposure of new and interesting locales our family moved into with regularity, outweigh the predictability and continuity of life in the community of one's origin. I wrestle with the uncertainty of the impact of our virtual nomadic existence on Lora, Ilan, and Ayal.

It seemed that our lives were replete with goodbyes. A few presents were exchanged. My gift to the staff was my windshield ice scraper, with a note indicating that I would no longer have need for it in Southern California. I answered several questions about my future position. One Board member asked:

"Aren't you afraid of the possibility of California earthquakes? San Francisco just sustained quite a significant temblor." I answered, "I grew up in New York City, in an area surrounded by violent gangs, I have lived in Israel, surrounded by hateful countries and now, I have lived in Washington, surrounded by Republicans: what was there left to be scared of?" My mostly Republican major donors in attendance, smiled perfunctorily. One week later, the moving van arrived at our Potomac home.

Chapter Twenty

THERE WAS SOMETHING about San Diego that evoked a feeling of having moved to a remote corner of the world. Perhaps it was that the east coast, other than our forays to Israel, was for me the center of the universe. San Diego's three hour time change never sat well with me. Sunday's professional football games began at the ungodly hour of ten a.m. It was relatively easy to adjust to diurnal and nocturnal zig zags, but more difficult now living far away from Melinda, Lon, and their children.

We purchased a house in Del Mar Heights, about twenty minutes north of my JCC. Lora was enrolled in a high school, the campus of which, resembled an ivy league university. Ilan attended a Jewish Day School, and Ayal was my next door neighbor in the JCC's preschool. Aviva, shortly after our arrival, converted one section of our three car garage into a working ceramics studio. Our new home was only three years old, quite modest in size, and had a lovely backyard that we used frequently. An eclipsed view of the glimmering Pacific Ocean from our bedroom windows, mesmerized us.

The sun shone daily with a monotonous regularity, and the weather was mostly sublime. I was reminded of my studies of ancient Greek literature and philosophy, and a theory of how the predictably fair weather, affected their maritime trade and their philosophy theories.

My highly anticipated inaugural experience as a CEO found me lodged in a series of connected trailers, with my eighty square foot office just across the narrow hallway from Ayal's preschool classroom. This was not exactly the setting from where I anticipated wielding my royal scepter. I accommodated to it quickly, and soon concluded that there was an indirect benefit to my humble lodging. I was determined to minimize the great divide, between my position as CEO, and all other staff members. It came easily, as it was my natural approach to management.

One typically, perfect San Diego day, I received a phone call from Melinda. She and Lon had completed their two year, post-residency obligation as physicians at a New Mexico Navajo reservation. They enjoyed it and found it rewarding. They had spent the following two years in hospitals in the New York area, and now had a choice before them. The decision that required immediate attention concerned their next home base.

"We have two strong options that we are considering: one is a partnership in a private practice in Connecticut, the second, and I know that you will be surprised, is San Diego."

While I was beside myself with joy at the prospect of having Melinda and her family live in the same town, I cautioned her that the decision should be made on what was best for them.

"Melinda, this is a crazy career path I'm on: if I want to continue to advance to larger and better paying JCCs, it inevitably involves moving to a new community." Within a few months Melinda, Lon, Jared and Mara were living about two blocks away from us, in Del Mar Heights.

Directing an organization with three distinct locations and about sixty professional staff proved exciting. I called upon my entrepreneurial drive to expand programming, while my less developed and less favored, cost containment skills, often proved to be a yin and yang approach to management. For the first time in my work career, I came across inherited operational deficits and had to continually balance the agency's financial status with the need for expanded services.

The professional staff was woefully underpaid and burgeoning operating costs stressed the budget. At a board of director's budget review meeting, one young, successful entrepreneur put it succinctly: "A not-for-profit agency is a rotten business," he declared, "if it were a good business, we would all be in it." I was determined to make that "rotten business" work.

To accomplish this, however, I would have to employ- to a great degree- the fundraising skills that I had honed in Washington. It didn't take me long to learn that the effectiveness of my position would be judged, in large part, on my success as a cultivator of donors with significant wealth. I would, of course, give them the opportunity to part with some of that wealth, in order to help sustain the JCC. Into my life came Larry Lawrence, reputed to be the largest individual contributor to California's Democratic party.

Larry was a tough, Chicago bred, up via one's bootstraps, multi-millionaire- not unlike my Washington chairman, Richard

Rubin. Larry had only passing interest in Jewish affairs and his main interest in the JCC appeared to be his friendship with my Associate Director, Marcia. Larry was the owner of one of San Diego's hotels, The Del Coronado, a landmark, luxurious enclave on the tip of a San Diego peninsula. Marcia facilitated a meeting with Larry, and we hit it off very nicely.

Larry was about sixty years old, his athletic build made guessing his age difficult. He sported a full head of brown hair, which he unattractively combed across his head, in a rendezvous with his neatly trimmed, slightly elongated, sideburns. He appeared fit, never without a tan and surprisingly agile for his age. He spoke freely of his cancer, and was thankful that it had been in remission for several years. I would visit Larry periodically and looked forward to having a luncheon of giant prawns on his office veranda, with appropriately attentive servers, and a backdrop of the shimmering Pacific Ocean and its white, sand beach.

Over the course of my first year, I visited Larry with another wealthy, JCC donor, Lee, who had asked that I set up a joint meeting with Larry. Lee was about sixty or sixty-five. Despite being an outspoken advocate of his rigorous fitness regime, he appeared considerably older than Larry. I would sit quietly during our luncheon meeting, with an occasional snicker, as they impressed one another with real or imagined sexual exploits.

"I was always intimidated with these women in their thirties, you know, trying to keep up with them. Until, I discovered vitamin E. I take mega doses, who knows if it really helps," Larry would laugh. "Frankly, I don't give a shit, if it's physical or psychological, but I'm an improved man with that stuff." Lee would just smile and trade exploits, that may or may not have been figments of a vivid imagination, or of a long gone reality.

Larry was very helpful to me in the course of my four year tenure at the JCC, as helpful as he was destructive in our final, three months in San Diego. The JCC benefitted from Larry's largesse, receiving a million dollar gift toward construction and about three hundred fifty thousand dollars for the operating fund. Larry's support brought community influence, board acquiescence and docility, increasing attractiveness in securing additional donors, and not least, a boost to my reputation.

Thankfully, it was my second meeting, not our initial get together, when he introduced me to his pearl handled, thirty eight caliber, Glock. Although he had requested the meeting, Larry appeared harried and short-tempered, as I was ushered into his office by his knockout secretary. As I entered, he motioned for me to sit on a chair near his desk, as he opened his upper right drawer, and drew out this sparkling, pistol and placed it in front of him on his paperless desk. He looked at me and smiled, "I do this every so often when workers piss me off, just to remind them who is boss." I wanted to ask him if this was a reminder to me, but thought better of it. The remainder of the meeting was jovial enough.

Numerous San Diego newspaper articles had been written of Larry's military exploits during the Second World War. The articles waxed effusive about his actions, while aboard the Merchant Marine ship, "Horace Bushnell," which was torpedoed by the Germans. Larry, the article described in some detail, had rescued a number of wounded sailors, despite having sustained some minor injuries himself. He was hailed as a true war hero.

Our lives in Del Mar Heights were considerably more placid with no torpedoes yet on the horizon. All three of our children developed a very nice circle of friends, the weather was consistently pleasant, our house was lovely, Melinda and the family lived only a few blocks away, and I was making some significant inroads in new program development. I had managed the agency's operating budget to a standoff for about three years. So, why was I so bored?

There seemed to be little opportunity to grow this JCC. I began to feel that the consistency of the weather, the cozy home in a cozy neighborhood, and a sense of professional claustrophobia at my agency, overwhelmed me with a pervasive restlessness and feeling of stagnation. I needed more challenge, more diversity.

Lora had completely recovered from her serious car accident and was approaching her senior year in high school. Soon, her choice of college would inevitably contribute to a family structure change, irrespective of what college she decided on, or qualified for. Ilan, now ten years old, and Ayal eight, were involved in the many sports programs offered in the area. They seemed happy, and had growing circles of friends. However, here we were again, facing a next step in our Bedouin-like planning. I informed the national organization of JCCs, that I was soon to be in the market for a growth opportunity. I soon discovered the risk of being honest and forthright about one's career path choices.

Once Aviva and I faced the realization that the tranquility and placidness of suburban San Diego drove us both to distraction, we aimed for June of 1991 as our target date to leave San Diego. All three kids would be finished with the school year, and most importantly, Lora would be through with high school. I dreaded sharing the news of our plans with Melinda, but we knew, that she would understand and even support our decision, however, reluctantly.

My associate director, Marcia, in whom I confided my intentions, assured me that Larry would be livid. "He doesn't respond well to abandonment, and he will see your move as just that," Marcia warned. "Larry owns people," she continued, "this is compounded by the fact that he has been out in the community supporting the JCC and by extension, you, and has given the Center a sizable sum of money. Hold on to your hat," she counseled.

With my proverbial hat in hand, I arranged to visit Larry accompanied by Ken, The board of director's President. Ken was a bright, young attorney who was guileless as both a board member and community player. We arrived at the Del Coronado just before mid day and were ushered in to Larry's office by his assistant. He must have had a premonition as to why we were visiting together and he appeared irritated. I began by informing Larry of my intentions, how much I loved the San Diego JCC, and valued his support and friendship. Larry, with a short wave of his hand, dismissed all that I had said, and with a well-practiced calm, asked me when I was planning to leave. I informed him that I was planning to leave in June, thereby giving the agency a three month notice.

"Well, I think you should leave now, maybe tomorrow," his voice was now plainly bellicose. "I am planning to leave our agency with an orderly transition to new leadership." I needed to put my house on the market and quite plainly, I was not ready to leave just yet. Larry countered, "I will buy your house, at list price, and will place somebody in your position. You need not worry about transition. Just leave as soon as possible." Ken, my co-visitor, sat next to me aghast and muffled.

Larry was a supreme power broker. Forbes Magazine, in 1991, had identified Larry as one of the four hundred richest men in America, with an estimated wealth of three hundred fifty million dollars. When Larry spoke in San Diego, most of the community listened, very attentively. When Larry was angry, the dangers of the San Andreas Fault paled in comparison. I responded, to Ken's shock: "Larry, I will leave in June, and not before, the agency is too important to me." I hoped that my gulp was not apparent.

I never took well to being bullied. Perhaps my rejection of authority as a teenager and a young adult had morphed into a protective veneer that shielded me from feeling humbled or intimidated by the Larry's of the world. Certainly, my mind quickly calibrated the negative impact of a salary-less period ahead, but, all feelings of vulnerability and my future precarious position, took a temporary back seat to my resolve not to be intimidated.

We left Larry's office as quickly and gracefully as possible. Larry did what he could to make my life miserable for the next three months. He was reasonably successful. He convinced the board that it needed to have the financial oversight of his hired troubleshooter. "One never knows what an outgoing CEO might do to 'cook the books'," he dictated to the board. He did what he could to cast doubt on my accomplishments, and that I was a traitor leaving before whatever personal goal *de jeuer* he had in mind.

To the board's credit, it paid little mind to the aspersions, but played along with his dictates. Larry insisted that the board stop paying my salary from the day that I gave it notice, informing them that he would no longer give them donations, should they refuse his dictum. To my dismay, the board acquiesced, necessitating that I withdraw our still meager accumulated pension funds, to sustain us until my next position. Marcia had understated his venomous response.

I continued working until my announced June departure date despite receiving no salary. Legally confronting this political and financial powerhouse was not a realistic path for me. I would not, however, give in to Larry's maniacal shift in allegiance. I continued, in vain, to hope that the board would stand up for what was fair, despite the imperial decrees of the wealthy, hotelier. The agency had made great strides in my four year leadership; Larry could not erase that.

While painful and disappointing, the coda to my San Diego CEO position, was a profound learning experience. The proverbial "Golden Rule," that is, he who has the gold rules, was blatantly true. Not-for-profits are, in large part, dependent upon the largesse of major contributors. The larger the organization, in general, the more dependent it is upon the generosity of major donors. All too often, that philanthropic gift comes with a myriad of stipulations and strings attached: naming opportunities, political influence, community prominence, board of directors persuasion and so many additional dynamics.

Boards of directors are in a cross-fire when the CEO and a major donor are at odds with one another. More often than not, those who have acquired great wealth were not shining examples of personal consideration for others or their viewpoints. They were the by-products of a business world worthy of a Darwinian theme of survival of the least meek. Larry was a classic example of the world of "take no prisoners," he owned me, in his eyes, and the JCC board as well. Defy him at your peril, was his unspoken community credo.

For three years after leaving San Diego for a new, and far more satisfying position, the "Larry" news got worse. Melinda continued to update me on the increasing political clout of Larry Lawrence in California. It only got worse, until it got better.

When Melinda sent me an article that she had clipped from The San Diego newspaper, I was crestfallen. Larry, of the pearl-handled thirty eight, of the vicious response to my announcement of a planned and orderly succession of leadership, of the bullying the board to withhold my salary and of doing all that he could to make our lives uncomfortable, had been named Ambassador to Switzerland by then, President Clinton.

What a cruel twist of fate, but I had an increased appreciation of what money could buy. It did, however, get worse, before it got better. Larry passed away in 1996, as a result of the return of the cancer that had been in remission during my tenure at the San Diego JCC. He was accorded the highest military honor by the U.S. government, and was interred in Arlington National Cemetery, at the request of Richard Holbrooke, assistant Secretary of State.

This appeared to be a reprise of Oded's "travesty of justice" at another time in my life. Burial in that cemetery was reserved for heroes and those who had served our country with courage, nobility and grace. That was not, in my opinion, Larry. And then, there was cosmic intervention. It was a personal *'Deus ex Machina'* not unlike the elated call from our Israeli attorney, Oded, some years earlier.

Melinda sent us a three page, local newspaper article about the latest Larry revelations. His military history had been a fabrication. There was no record of his having achieved the rank of "Seaman, First Class" nor was there any indication that he had been aboard the "Horace Bushnell" when it was torpedoed by the Germans. He had been enrolled, it was thought, as a student in a community college in Chicago. He was to be disinterred from the cemetery reserved for America's war heroes. His remains would be privately reinterred in a San Diego cemetery.

However, now and for the remainder of our stay in San Diego, prior to all of the later revelations, Larry remained on our radar screen and continued to affect an erosion of my hard won relationship with my board.

The national office of JCCs in New York, thankfully, assigned minimal importance to the Larry imbroglio. There appeared to be many excellent employment options. In addition to the positions presented to me by that office, a colleague contacted me and asked that I interview for an executive position with the Jewish Federation of Dallas, Texas. Aviva and I did go to Dallas and I was offered the position. Both of us agreed, that we would rather live in The Outer Seychelles than in Dallas. It appeared that the greatest elevation of that monotonous terrain, was at the apex of the shopping mall's speed bump. The environment appeared as bland and flat as the people interviewing me.

Even before the phone call from Atlanta, Georgia, we put our house up for sale. When Gerald Cohen, a community leader, and Marilyn, a professional member of the Jewish Federation of Atlanta, called me early one sunny June morning, I was ill-prepared. Atlanta was not mentioned as one of the possible options for me, and I had great difficulty understanding

Gerald's lyrical southern accent. I struggled to picture where Atlanta was, on my hastily conceived mental map.

Initially, I found it hard to take our conversation seriously. However, it didn't take me too long to understand that Gerald was brilliant. In the course of our forty-five minute conversation, he gently and politely, pointed out inconsistencies in my answers and, on several occasions, repeated verbatim, points that I had made in earlier parts of our call. He was very impressive. I felt humbled, after my initial, flippant responses to his thoughtful questions. We agreed on an interview time and date in Atlanta.

We were soon to be living in the one area that Aviva and I had agreed we would never consider, the deep south. Growing up in New York City, we were under the impression that life, as we knew it, ended at Fort Lee, New Jersey, just across the George Washington Bridge. We had already violated that sacrosanct New York myopia, by living in Fair Lawn and Washington, D.C. But the deep south, that was a different story.

Melinda, even more politically progressive than Aviva and I, wondered how we would fare in a region that, it seemed, was still fighting the Civil War. We all understood, that remaining in the Jewish community agency field was no longer feasible in San Diego. I had, however, discovered that this arena was where I could make a significant contribution and achieve my greatest personal satisfaction. It was clear to all of us, that money had not been, and would never be a primary motivating factor for me. Having functioned in the Jewish communal arena, I was convinced that this was the field in which I would make my greatest contribution.

It appeared that I had left the corporate world far behind and was increasingly devoted to developing and advancing Jewish causes and programming. Perhaps, on some level, my parent's family credo of: "someone always has less than we do," continued in so many ways to influence my uncompromising drive to assist persons in need. Financial gain and accumulation of possessions held little import for them, or for me.

Another difficult departure from Melinda, Lon, Mara and Jared was on our immediate horizon. It was only a few years later that Melinda would inform us that she had discovered that she had advanced breast cancer.

For now, however, they had a lovely home, and seemed firmly ensconced in San Diego. We prepared to leave, to our new destination. In mid July, we embarked on our cross-country sojourn once again.

Chapter Twenty-One

THE LAST TIME we arrived anywhere of import on July fourteenth, Bastille Day, was during our first year of marriage. The summer vacation that Aviva and I had planned upon completion of the first year of my masters degree program, would end in Paris after our Israel and England visits. Since we had almost no money left, despite our extraordinarily inexpensive Pan Am student flight to Israel, we agreed that we would rough it in cheap hotels. What we did not take into account, was how ludicrous it was to roll into Paris on Bastille Day, with no hotel reservation. We managed to find a decrepit Left Bank flophouse, just above a noisy café, down an obscure, litter-filled alleyway, with a window that could only be opened when we made room for it, by moving our bed. Aviva spent the night in tears.

This July fourteenth arrival in Atlanta, while not as unceremonious as our Paris jaunt, was not without its challenges. We arrived in a sweltering heat wave and watched our belongings unloaded from a cross country moving van, into a rented, three bedroom apartment. It was ninety-eight degrees with matching humidity. Aviva and I looked at one another and our eyes read, that human beings cannot exist here. We had come from the most glorious weather combination anywhere, with cool ocean breezes and very low humidity any time of year. As if to add insult to injury, the apartment complex that was to be our home for about three months, was named: "Mount Vernon Plantation." Aviva laughingly noted, "How far we have come in our lives, to now be plantation dwellers."

Those issues aside, the chips fell just right for us. Lora had toyed with the idea of applying to San Diego or San Francisco universities, but had been very impressed with the classes and social life offered at University of Georgia. The university's campus was very attractive and was located in Athens, Georgia, only about sixty miles away from Atlanta. She had been accepted there, and was to begin classes in September. Ilan, now ten and Ayal eight, were enrolled in The Epstein School, a Jewish Day School of a very nice standard. I believe that for the boys, our new home was a bit of an adventure and for Lora, the move came at an opportune time as a college freshman.

Aviva and I knew that we now had to make a push to find a permanent home, and provide some stability for Lora and the boys. We purchased a house with an open design that was in line with our newly acquired California aesthetic. Suburban Atlanta architecture was uninspiring, as it seemed enamored with antebellum traditionalism. We were, however, impressed with the modest price tag of real estate in Atlanta. The house that we purchased was well over double the square footage of our San Diego home at a considerably lower price.

By the time we moved into our new home I had been on the job for about two months. The prior CEO had been eased out of his position, despite from what I could see, was a commendable performance. It was clear to me that all of the existing staff was jittery and was waiting to see what my initial organizational moves would be. Too often, newly appointed execs feel compelled to implement immediate changes, thereby displaying to the board of directors how decisive one is. I resisted this call to action, and took my time to assess all aspects of the agency. Overcoming the agency's accumulated six million dollar deficit would require existing staff to help me negotiate the labyrinths of this almost six million dollar annual operating budget.

I met individually with key staff members, about thirty professionals, in meetings lasting about an hour. Each session had a very simple premise: tell me what you do, and how it contributes to the well-being of the agency. I was prepared to answer questions about my personal life, my employment background and, to the extent that I had any clear vision, where I hoped to lead the agency.

I was impressed with the tenacity of the staff during hard financial times, as well as their desire to see things change. There was an appreciation, it seemed, of the value that the JCC could have to the Atlanta Jewish community. There was a pervasive feeling, however, that the agency was under siege. Indeed, I often had the distinct feeling that JCC staff had been living in war-torn Beirut, denigrated by so many in the organized Jewish community, and under continuous bombardment from the Jewish Federation. Two staff members stood out during my preliminary meetings, with very different results.

The agency's CFO, Phillip, was a puzzle. I was completely underwhelmed by his verbal presentation about his value to the agency and his vision of it moving forward. Conversely, I was blown away by his presentation of the strengths and weaknesses of the budget. I came to know Phillip as an astute, honest, realist whose self-deprecating personality belied a deep commitment to the agency. He displayed a keen awareness of budgetary opportunities and pitfalls and a great understanding of options for the agency's future path. I valued his opinions for years to come. I was very happy that I had not yet read Gladwell's "Blink," which advocated letting your initial response guide your actions.

Phillip was the agency's budgetary guru until his retirement-just after mine. My initial instincts, however, were accurate when it came to Lionel. During the course of my first meeting with Lionel, he regarded my exploratory questions as an invasion of his privacy. He seemed to have an air of disdain for my chutzpah to ask what he, the highest paid employee in the agency, did on a daily basis. I never did discover what his job description was.

Key members of the board of directors asked that I meet with them before implementing any personnel changes. I thought that this was very sound practice and did not feel that it was "big brother" guiding my actions. From the very beginning of my Atlanta career, I wanted a sense of partnership with the board. We met on the second floor of the aged and poorly maintained eighty-five thousand square foot JCC in Midtown Atlanta. Eight members of the board sat around the chipped formica, eight foot folding table and made small talk.

It was clear to me that Harry Maziar, Chairman of ZEP Chemical Company, functioned as the dominant force in that group. Harry was highly intelligent and articulate. After some brief introductory remarks, I assured the board committee that we would balance the budget in the not too distant future. "it's a challenge, but I am certain, that with your support and partnership, we will prevail."

They looked a bit bemused. It was clear to me and to them, that it could not be done by cost cutting alone, however, personnel issues were the purpose of this brief meeting. "I want to share with you that there will be a few positions that I will remove, and I am asking for your support." Not their approval, but their support. I was convinced that they properly interpreted my comments.

Most prominent on my list of personnel reductions was Lionel. I presented my thought process and shut up. The period of awkward silence that followed the mention of Lionel's name, also featured some figurative and actual head scratching, until Harry spoke up for the group, "We support your decision and will back you, but it won't be a walk in the park." I appreciated Harry's comments and support, although I was *Tabula Rasa* to the difficulties that he knew lay on my horizon. That Friday, I informed Lionel of my decision to remove his position. He seemed surprised, and simply stood up and left my office. I soon understood why my decision was so fraught with tension.

As was the custom at the JCC, the building would close at four p.m. on Friday, in observance of Shabbat. Getting a jump on the Atlanta rush hour, allowed me to get home to our new house at about five. As we were preparing dinner the phone rang, I temporarily abandoned my helper's role and answered the phone. A gruff, unfamiliar voice asked: "is this Harry Stern?"

"Yes, who is this?"

"My name is Sy Feinberg, does that name mean anything to you?" he asked unpleasantly. One of my initial personal assignments was to compile a list of Atlanta's wealthy, prospective donors to the JCC, his name was on that list.

"Yes, I do know who you are," I replied. I knew that it couldn't be anything good as, for the most part, Shabbat was sacrosanct in the Jewish agency world, business calls were rarely made then.

"Well," he continued, "You may also know that Lionel, whom you terminated today, is a very dear friend of our family. Your actions toward him were precipitous, unwarranted, poorly thought through and showed a total lack of judgment. My goodness," he continued, "you are in Atlanta only a matter of a few weeks, you have no idea what that man can contribute to the JCC. I demand that you reconsider this rash move."

I had no intention of justifying my decision and simply said, "Mr. Feinberg, I am very sorry that you are offended, I respect your position, but will not reverse my decision," I quietly gulped.

"Well," he angrily responded, "you have made a grave mistake and a serious enemy in this community," and he hung up.

While not exactly the way that I had envisioned the start to my new position, I had once again been faced with the imperial demands of community scions. I envisioned hanging a sign around my neck that read "under new ownership." After my San Diego debacle with Larry, I understood that some of the affluent members of the community, assumed that they "owned" you as the professional guiding the agency that they supported. There were, of course, many exceptions. One glowing example of a stand out from any board member that I had encountered was Erwin Zaban.

Erwin, an immensely successful businessman, was the rare combination of great wealth, extraordinary generosity, unbounded intelligence and a deep understanding of, and respect for, community process. He had an understanding of that process, but no patience for its sometimes anemic pace. Erwin was a master politician and strategist, without getting bogged down in politics or community or agency strategic planning.

The tension and formality of my first visit with Erwin, which fell a few days short of his seventieth birthday, would have been minimized, had I then known that our relationship would continually strengthen over the next fifteen years and he would emerge as my, and our agency's, greatest supporter.

The Atlanta JCC owned and operated a summer camp on a five hundred acre site about sixty miles north of Atlanta. I believe that the "one hundred year" rainfall that pounded the camp for two days, only months before the summer camping season was to begin, had conveniently waited for my arrival in Atlanta. The dam, holding back millions of gallons of the camp's lake water, had been severely eroded and appeared ready to burst. There were numerous homes downstream threatened with inundation.

EPA had been notified by neighbors, and their inspectors had visited the site, demanding immediate restructuring of the dam and a controlled release of its waters. The dam was re-categorized to a classification C-1, whereby a breach could cause downstream loss of life. The agency was notified that it would be required to remedy the problem, or face severe financial penalties and would be barred from opening camp that season. The price tag for the dam's reconstruction was three hundred fifty thousand dollars. This news coincided with Phillip's notifying me that we would barely eke out that week's staff payroll.

At a hastily convened meeting of the board, I informed the members of the significant sum required to rebuild the dam in accordance with the stringent EPA guidelines. "We have to ensure that we do not imperil the lives of families downstream of the lake." A bellowing response greeted my presentation. Several veteran board members called for me to rent a bulldozer and have someone just move some dirt to shore up the threatened dam.

"That's the way we used to do it," some members cried out. Thankfully, several board members understood my point: we had no other responsible choice. I was pleased that I did not have to unilaterally decide and repeat my less-than-pleasant: "that's the way it is" conversation with Sy Feinberg, of several months earlier. The conflicting viewpoints prompted me to visit Erwin for his advice on moving forward with the camp project.

The polished mahogany desk appeared uncomfortably large for Erwin's slender, five foot seven frame. Five or six neatly arranged envelopes and a glistening letter opener on his desk top, were all that disturbed an otherwise barren mesa-like landscape.

One summer weekend, when my father had visited us in Washington, we ushered him up to the second floor of our house, to show him the new bed we had just purchased for Ilan, then barely four years old. Asleep in his bed, Ilan was pressed into a small corner, leaving most his new bed as vacant as Erwin's desk. My father suggested: "Why not rent out the rest of that bed?"

I suppressed a smile thinking of my father, as I sat in this office, that, together with its adjacent private dining room, I mentally computed to be forty three times the size of my San Diego office. I briefly recounted the recent board meeting controversy and stressed our need to act quickly. He laughed, "I can guess the position of each of those board members present at that meeting. Not too much creativity there." Erwin's deep, baritone voice seemed so incongruous, emanating from his slight frame.

I was in his office for advice and a strategy on steps needed to move forward. In short order, not addressing my stated goals, Erwin, nonchalantly, wrote out a check for twenty five thousand dollars and slid it across the desk toward me. He then picked up his private phone and called the chairman of a major, Atlanta foundation, who took the call immediately.

Erwin, addressed the chairman on a first name, friendly basis: "William, I need one hundred fifty thousand dollars granted to our JCC within a week. There's a serious problem at our summer camp, that I will tell you about later." He then went on to talk to him about his vacation and the chairman's family. He hung up the phone, "I expect that you will have the check within a week." Erwin's even tone, was of a man who was comfortable dealing in transactions well in excess of what had just been concluded.

I had come for advice and was leaving with one hundred seventy five thousand dollars, exactly half of our proposed construction bill. "No thank you necessary, you're doing the right thing." I left in awe of his understated influence and his personal support and generosity.

What seemed of paramount importance to Erwin, and to other successful and involved entrepreneurs, was the ability to act decisively. My temperament seemed to have evolved from, the "ready, fire, aim" approach of earlier stages, to a more thoughtful and considered method of decision making. I was unafraid to take the heat generated by my many poor decisions;

I was, however, mortified by the usual plodding "afraid to decide" modus operandi of so many of my peers.

Of course, this got me into the occasional hot water situation and earned me the titles of "cowboy" or "gunslinger" from my more conservative Federation colleagues. Executive indecisiveness drove the board captains of industry to distraction. It had become increasingly clear to me that, it was a universal truth in the not-for-profit world, that entrepreneurs generally steered clear of accepting a board position. One meeting, in an NFP, led to another meeting, with ill-defined goals and unclear outcome metrics. Decisions were often delayed for yet another meeting in the future, all under the premise of group process and full participation. It drove me crazy.

I am not sure what possessed me to participate in a Federation trip to Israel in my second year in Atlanta. Perhaps it was that all expenses were paid for by the Federation and the JCC. Federations generally sponsor at least one highly subsidized community annual trip to Israel. There are dual goals connected to the Federation's largesse: the exposure of American Jewry to Israel and, secondarily, the ever-present fundraising that is the coda to each "mission"- as they are called.

The term "mission" is unfortunate, as it reeks of paternalism and the missionary work that so many of the world's churches undertake to bring their version of organized religion and "enlightenment" to the underdeveloped world. I had steadfastly avoided these sanitized trips to Israel, which I considered more my home than Atlanta, but determined that there could be value for me in this "mission." Many community influentials were to be among the one hundred or so participants, and it would be a golden opportunity to become more closely connected to those possessors of the gold, who might, at some point, prove helpful to the JCC.

Aviva also understood the nature of this "mission" and did not want to travel seven thousand miles not to be with me. Once we were in Israel, all participants would be inextricably bound to one another, especially on tour busses that transported the visitors from one obligatory site visit to another. I had learned that, a good deal of the success in my position, lay in finding as many commonalities as possible with that crowd, and the bus rides would allow for opportunities to get to know participants.

I took advantage of the mystique that accompanied this new executive with the New York accent. Having lived in Israel and my fluency in Hebrew, which I used upon arriving in Israel, added to my reputation as being somewhat unusual. The Federation trip offered me an opportunity to develop closer ties with many of our community's key players. I think that Edna had a very different take on that closeness. On the third day of our trip, a visit to a northern development town, which was now home to recent émigrés from Russia and Ethiopia, I began to understand Edna's different take.

I was unaware that I was partially impeding those disembarking from the bus, as I was chatting with a gentleman sitting in the front row. As Edna neared the front of the bus, she passed unusually close to me and pressed slowly and fully against me as she left the bus. Instinctively, I turned around and apologized for blocking the doors. There had been, to my surprise, sufficient space for all to pass by me.

I paid it little attention until our afternoon tea break when we all sat in the stark, but air-conditioned, dining area of a local hotel. Edna, an attractive fortyish brunette, was a successful

Atlanta stock broker. On several occasions I found her seated near me, while she chatted with other participants about her recent divorce. I made small talk with all and left each time to mingle with as many influential potential donors as possible.

It was only on day four that I became acutely uneasy. Edna seemed to appear in my vicinity more often than I could attribute to coincidence. I made certain that for the remaining seven days of our trip I would stay close to group gatherings, or in an environment that was protected from all manner of assault. I was greatly relieved that the meta communication was understood. I felt an "all clear" signal had been established…perhaps in my fertile imagination alone.

The Israel that I was visiting had morphed into a less familiar entity. Despite its unfortunate geographic neighborhood, and its perennial security challenge, the Israel that we knew as residents, exuded a charming, small town ambience. There seemed now, to be a race to become America's fifty first state, and to dress the country in shiny cosmopolitan garb. Start ups were springing up like the Negev Desert's red anemones, that, released from a year's dormancy, carpet the rugged eighty square kilometers, just after a rare spring rainfall.

Advertising billboards were now everywhere and a country-wide corporate zeal seemed to have weighed heavily upon the nation's erstwhile Zionistic and socialistic ideals. Despite these less than attractive revelations, I was reminded on a daily, even hourly, basis of how much Israel meant to me and how centrally indispensable it was to the well-being of the world's Jews. The country remained a portal of freedom for Jews from around the globe; a strength and pride for the Jews of the world, despite its abundant imperfections. For me, Israel remained deeply personal.

When our bus passed near our old neighborhood in Jerusalem, I looked to see if Sarah, the flower shop owner, was in her store. Each Shabbat, she would insist that I bring home a small bouquet of fragrant carnations, as a gift for our beautiful daughter. For the duration of this three year ritual, Sarah refused to be paid for her generous bouquets. How I missed that social touch- so Jewish, in every way.

When we passed Netanya, heading north in our air-cushioned motor coach, I thought of the absorption center, where we spent the first six months of our stay in Israel. In milliseconds, I relived our arrival and our aesthetic disappointments. I felt the winter breeze, that somehow found its way through and around our poorly fit windows, and briefly relived the awful revelation of Flora's murder.

Heading further north, toward Haifa, brought back the many visits to our cousins, Zvi and Sima, living in the uppermost section of Haifa, Mount Carmel. I quietly decided, that this was the first and last organized "mission" that I would participate in, as Israel was still home for me, and not simply a vehicle for organized touring and fundraising.

Marietta, Georgia, while not New York or Israel, slowly assumed a term that was quite ephemeral for us: 'home.' During a tennis match with a Jewish community notable, he asked me if I intended to "play out the deck" in Atlanta. At fifty years old, I really had never thought in those terms, and spontaneously responded, that I liked Atlanta and also still had a number of unplayed cards in my "deck." I always abhorred talk of retirement, aging, personal resignation to a life circumstance. I believe that my mother's similar refusal and her ever-changing birth date, always later by a year or two, permeated my very being.

Nor had I considered Atlanta a desired fixed location for our family. It still was a means to an end for me. The deep south, its values, history, conservatism, history of racial bias and lack of cultural sophistication was so antithetical to the Upper West Side, liberal blood that Aviva and I had coursing through our veins. It seemed inconceivable that Atlanta would become our home for the following twenty five years (and counting).

I experienced very little anti-Semitism in Atlanta. An occasion that smacked of anti Jewish sentiment, occurred during a visit from the United Way. As a registered and highly visible community NFP, we augmented our growing operating budget through individual fundraisers, a Federation allocation of several percent of our budget and, to a far lesser extent, a modest, annual grant received from United Way.

Throughout the year, United Way would send groups of their board volunteers and staff to visit the JCC, to discuss how we were using their community funds. Additionally, these meetings were held to review statistical reports, outlining funding usage, that were submitted regularly. A good practice, in theory. The great majority of those volunteer committee members and select United Way staff were considered program auditors, but had only scant knowledge of the raison d'etre of a JCC. Despite the myriad reports continually transmitted to them, we had yet to find any "auditor" familiar with them.

Not long after my return from the Federation "mission" to Israel and my successful and persistent evasive tactics concerning Edna, we were to entertain a visit from a United Way committee. Upon their arrival, the delegation, comprised of five women and four men volunteers, and three United Way staff members, was invited into our spacious board room and offered a cold drink.

I sat at an end of the large, teak wood conference table, donated by the Cohen family, and the United Way volunteer leader sat at the other end. The traditional meeting, a bit of a "dog and pony" show, consisted of questions regarding our submitted statistical reports and, most particularly, on the number of minorities we were serving. We continually had to explain to all visiting committees that, despite being a Jewish agency, we were open to the entire community, irrespective of race, ethnicity or religion.

This visiting United Way delegation was joined by four staff members of the JCC. The woman sitting at the far end of the conference table was African-American, with a coiffure that reminded me of Angela Davis, the seasoned antagonist of many American policies of the 1970s and 80s and an accomplished and ardent anti-Zionist and anti-Semite. Before the United Way representative opened her mouth, I believed that I had her pegged. And she didn't disappoint me.

The faux Angela got right to it. She pointed to our statistical reports begrudgingly and antagonistically noted: "This agency has an 'underrepresentation' of minorities in your preschools, staff, membership and board members. How do you explain that?" My response to her was straightforward. I wanted to emphasize the content of my message, so I remained very calm. "Madam, you will earn the right to ask us those important questions, only after you return from asking The Martin Luther King Center, how many Jews they have on their staff; then inquire from The Ponce De Leon Hispanic Society, how many Jews serve on their Board, and then assess how many Jewish children received scholarships from The Catholic Charities preschools. When you have those answers, I will respond to your legitimate questions." 'Angela' got flustered and we quickly moved on to other subjects. It was one of the shorter United Way meetings we endured.

In retrospect, I ask myself why recount this seemingly unimportant incident in my fifteen plus years at the helm of the Atlanta JCC? This blip on my professional radar screen embodied many complex aspects of my persona, my approach to my profession, my feelings about a major focus of my job. The event also embodied a connecting thread of so many stages of my life. Anti-Semitism, real or merely perceived, had been a powder keg of feelings in me.

Having grown up in a home where Naziism and the Holocaust could not be mentioned, left me with a lasting frustration and vulnerability. In my youth, I had always parried the occasional anti-Semitic remark with an acerbic rejoinder, with almost no subsequent acrimony. Living in the South, with its history of unequal treatment of African-Americans, a minority presence of Jews and Catholics and, for the most part, a preponderance of those of Evangelical faith, was no surprise to me. My personal challenge was always finding the restraint, not to overreact to personal baggage that I had been internally transporting for fifty years.

Construction on the new campus, that we had been planning and raising funds for, began in 1998. Located on a fifty-two acre site in a middle class suburb of Atlanta, the new facility was to add over one hundred fifty thousand square feet to the preexisting, outdated, forty thousand square foot building. The facility would be a truly magnificent testament to the vibrancy and expansion of Atlanta's Jewish community. I was extremely proud of the design of this twenty-two million dollar hub of Jewish activity.

In that same year, an event made me infinitely prouder and happier. In May of that year Lora married Jason, a wonderful young man. Our families bonded quickly and continue to share the joys of an expanding brood of beautiful grandchildren.

Toward the end of that year we experienced a frightening blow. Melinda informed us that she had an advanced case of breast cancer. Befitting her strength of character, she seemed more concerned about the family and especially her two preteen children, Jared and Mara. Melinda and Lon informed us that they were exploring every course of treatment, every appropriate research protocol, all treatment modalities, no matter how new to the medical market. Melinda had been a trend setter and fighter all of her life, and this approach to her terrible news was so characteristic of her creative approach to medicine and her personal tenacity.

The next years of her life were filled with experimental treatment approaches and participation in cutting-edge modalities. Each new course of treatment brought glimmers of hope, and some reversal of the progression of the disease, but the cancer continued to metastasize. Her oncologist remarked to her and Lon, that she had "rewritten the text books" on fighting the disease and outliving the most optimistic medical predictions.

Melinda fought against her cancer in her typical feisty, but noble manner for better than ten years. While attempting to enter any medical or experimental protocol that seemed to hold out some hope, she invariably turned all conversation away from her battle for survival. I visited her often during that period and fought my compulsion to beg her to get better. I stayed outwardly positive, but watched helplessly, as she gradually weakened. My time with her, would enable her terrific and devoted husband Lon, to continue to work as a pediatrician at Kaiser Hospital and not worry about Melinda at home.

One visit was to the cancer treatment center, "City of Hope," where Melinda underwent blood platelet transfusions. I was happy to have my red blood cells used to help her in her battle. But, as Melinda weakened, my trips to San Diego became more frequent.

On the morning of one visit, Melinda had just finished the cream of wheat breakfast that I had prepared for her. From her early childhood, this had been a favored breakfast of hers. She leaned forward, elbows on the glass-topped dining room table, squinted a bit, in the bright San Diego morning sun, that greeted her most mornings, and said, in an uncharacteristically wistful manner, "I wonder what my bedroom looks like."

For about a month, Melinda had been sleeping in the downstairs guest room, just off the living room. She occasionally needed oxygen, and they had decided to keep all of the medical assistance paraphernalia in that room, and to give Melinda easy access to the contiguous bathroom. Negotiating any steps had become dangerous for her.

"Would you like to see it?"

"I would really love to."

"OK, we can arrange that, let's go."

She smiled, "How's this going to work?"

"Let's walk to the base of the staircase and we'll close our eyes and wish."

Once there, she stopped and looked at me while I lifted her in my arms, and slowly and carefully negotiated the twenty, carpeted and somewhat creaky steps. She was so light. My vibrant, athletic and robust sister, wrapped her arms around my neck and said, "You know, I can't do this by myself any longer." When we reached the second story, she sat on their king sized bed and sighed. Melinda breathed deeply and said, "Aha, now I remember. I was actually having some difficulty visualizing where my dresser was, and the mirror where I made myself beautiful."

"You're still beautiful." She really was.

I am not sure why I was surprised that Melinda had arranged for a book club meeting about an hour before I was scheduled to leave for the airport to return to Atlanta. She was still debating about political issues in North San Diego counties, and continued reading novels and local newspapers voraciously. As I brought my small suitcase to the front door, the book club chatter was already underway. I was mockingly introduced to four neighbors as her "big brother." As I kissed her goodbye, she whispered: "I don't want to leave you." I was so touched and saddened by those "wisps of words." I have repeated them to myself almost every day since.

My next trip to San Diego found Melinda in a private hospital room, weakened by intense stomach pains. I read from a Bob Dylan biography, which included the lyrics of many of his lesser known songs. Melinda adored him and his music. My three day visit was spent with her in her hospital room. She succumbed to the almost eleven year battle with cancer only a few weeks later.

I wondered how it would be possible to go on living a semblance of a normal life with such an irreplaceable void. My relationship with Melinda had been so deep, so close, so personal. How did my mother manage to overcome the devastating losses of her sister and cousins in the Holocaust? How was she able to cope with my antics as a youth, while she was overcoming her agoraphobic fears? I wondered why, at Melinda's San Diego funeral, I never shed a tear. I think now, that I probably feared, that I would not be able to stem the torrent once it started.

The year 2000 did not bring the millennial apocalypse that the media reveled in reporting. New Year's eve approached, as we headed inexorably toward the year 2000. Airplanes stayed in the sky, stock markets did not crash and the myriad of dire predictions thankfully, did not come to pass. That year, did however, bring the grand opening of the state-of-the-art JCC. The JCC's greatest financial benefactor, presented the opening remarks at an inaugural dedication. Through his friendship with Erwin Zaban, the donor contributed millions to the JCC. Having that family's support added substantial credibility to the importance and centrality of the agency.

A combination of external gifts from generous donors and continually developing new sources of growth and revenue, allowed the JCC to blossom. Utilizing the three criteria that the national office of Jewish Community Centers used: sizes of the Jewish population of a city, membership and operating budget, the Atlanta JCC soon became one of the four largest centers in the world. Many of the programs were uniformly successful and profitable, due in large part to my good fortune to have hired a professional staff of unlimited energy and creativity. I had the good sense to leave them, for the most part, to operate in their spheres of expertise, with minimal interference from me.

CHAPTER TWENTY-TWO

I AM A DESERT anemone, though not as pretty, nor as colorful. I emerged from a youthful, self-imposed, craggy and barren landscape, just as dormant, desert anemones greet the sun after a spring rainfall. Thankfully, I was not awarded what the iconic American novelist, Pat Conroy termed, the greatest gift that a novelist can receive: an unhappy childhood with a dysfunctional family. For almost two decades of my earliest years, I succeeded in antagonizing family, friends, teachers and just about anyone with whom I came in contact. The "rainfall" that sprung me from my dreary, desert-like self-encapsulation, came in waves. This memoir has highlighted the many crossroads that I encountered in my life and the blending of serendipity and planning that we all face.

My parents were loving, and provided above and beyond their meager resources. They instilled in us a compassion for others in need, and exemplified the obligation to share with those who had less. I cannot say that ours was a home that exuded warmth. The specter of the Holocaust cast an indelible and often imperceptible, shadow on our home. Their incessant arguing often made me sad and probably helped shape my exhausting negativism.

My relationship with Josephine, became more meaningful and important to me as we aged, and became more flexible and understanding of one another. Josephine's excellent memory has served as a check and balance for my propensity toward historical revisionism, in completing this manuscript.

I adored Melinda from her earliest years. I was in awe of her intelligence, her joyfulness, her intuition and her ability to share her feelings and, more often than not, criticize my inane behavior. Writing about her is still difficult for me, as the void she left in my life remains unfilled.

The fulcrums upon which seminal events in my life pivoted, both amuse and amaze me. Coach Eddie's non-verbal discouragement of my early military enlistment and our "mystery" visit to City College, played a significant role in my redirection. He had a unique way of encouraging my pursuit of a higher education degree…without one word of direct encouragement. Norman's entry into my banal teenage life of mediocrity and alienation, sparked my awakening to a world of art and literature that had managed to elude me for the first nineteen years of my life.

My erstwhile girlfriend Merle's insistence that, together we apply as counselors at Camp Surprise Lake, to enjoy a summer out of New York City, brought me into closer proximity than she or anyone, could have imagined, with the single most important event of my life: my Aviva encounter.

It was only one year into our marriage, when we discovered how central Israel was to us, and how its importance to us shaped, and was shaped by, the growing preciousness of our Jewish heritage. How did I survive the cloistered, and often hostile, environment of my eight year bondage in Yeshiva's primary school? How did I overcome the cavernous disdain, that I had for the rigidity and parochialism of that school, and by association, Judaism? Was this all there was to being Jewish, I wondered? It was our lives in Israel that helped me to reaffirm the centrality of Jewish values and continuity. It rendered my eight year Yeshiva "internment" obsolete.

A growing awareness of what my family, and so many others, had endured, because they were Jewish, left a trace of embryonic pride, which would one day blossom exponentially. While I was famously inarticulate about our "bolt from the blue" decision to upend our cozy New York lifestyle, for the rough and tumble, twenty-year old Israel, I am abundantly clear about it today. Playing a role in the development of the nascent, Jewish homeland became a central tenet in my life. The inability to maintain our family life in Israel, while deeply discouraging at one point in my life, came with a wide range of later rewards- not the least of which was Lora's marriage to Jason and Ilan's marriage to Marsha.

Discouraging as well, is the international intertwining of the opposition to certain Israeli policies and a global increase in anti-Semitism. It appears to be difficult for world Jewry to comprehend, that there can be legitimate disagreement with an Israeli government that appears incapable of moving toward negotiations with the enemy, without castigating the country. A government that is excessively dominated by the ultra orthodox, not known for their flexibility, only compounds the challenge. The need for a strong Jewish homeland supersedes these temporal issues. I recall with great respect and nostalgia, Herman Taube, a Holocaust survivor and poet, whom I met in Washington. At a lecture about 1980s Jewish disaffection from Israel, he asked, "do we stop going to the synagogue because we don't care for the rabbi, or do we push for changes in personnel and policies? Isn't it the same dynamic concerning Israeli governmental policies?"

My career path in the Jewish communal world, was shaped by the centrality of Jewish identity in my life and the importance of Israel in Jewish continuity. My positions at the helm of large, Jewish agencies were more than a career or a means to support my family. Jewish thought and our continuity as a people emerged as themes, as important for me today, as they were far-fetched in my young adulthood. The importance of serving persons in need and those with disabilities has, likewise, been a central theme in my personal and professional life. The petri dish in which this dedication germinated was clearly my parent's home, and their universal credo of: "someone has less than we do."

The Jewish Community Center was for me, an indispensable anchor to the continuity of Jewish life. I viewed my work as a JCC CEO over twenty years, as a platform, from which to shape the JCC, as a vehicle to solidify Jewish life and continuity in the diaspora. My emphasis was always on how to enhance the Jewish character of the JCC and how to create programming and activities that would attract and involve the Jewish community. I believe that it was my father's resourcefulness and creativity, and his unwillingness to compromise his principles, that helped shape my ability to advocate positions and principles firmly. Experience has encouraged my ability to appreciate disparate viewpoints and the art of compromise.

By 2001, Lora and Jason gave the world Rachel, the first of their three beautiful children, Ilan was about to graduate from Ohio State University, soon to move to graduate studies and eventually a PhD in physics at Tulane University. Ayal, thoughtlessly, made us empty nesters by attending The University of Kansas, on his way to his budding acting career. Aviva and I felt less than privileged and honored to be assisting their respective universities with out-of-state tuition fees.

What has shaped the arc of my life, now in its seventh decade, has been my great fortune to have a family that is comprised of extraordinary and loving individuals. Aviva, my wife of forty-eight years, my three children, Lora, Ilan, and Ayal, all uniquely gifted and more importantly, marvelous human beings. Four wonderful grandchildren, Rachel, Evan, Jake, and Aiden are more than anyone could dream of; each with their unique personalities (Aiden, at one year, is already is developing his) and charm. Jason and Marsha are such wonderful members of the family.

While living in the suburbs of San Diego, Lora, then about fifteen, remarked to me: "Dad, you have a lot of power, don't you?" My surprised response to her was to ask her to explain what she meant by power. "You can hire, fire, promote, or whatever, the many people who work for you." My answer to her, I hoped, represented my approach to managing an institution that held great importance to me. "Lora, I perceive an important part of my job, as making my co-workers feel good about their work, which, I believe, contributes to their commitment to the goals of the agency. My expectation is that my colleagues will feel as dedicated to the mission of our Jewish agency as I do. That's how I define my power."

Thinking about Lora's question helps me to reflect on my career, my family, and my unalterable dedication to Jewish continuity and by extension, Israel. Lora's fifteen year old's interpretation of power was linked to the traditional view of a CEO. The full circle that I have come, from an embattled youth, to a proud and happy parent and grandparent, includes the "power" that has come with the position of CEO. It has been that power that helped me to shape a course of a major agency's consistently Jewish agenda. The position also allowed me to create a work environment that supports the growth and fulfillment of those I worked with. These opportunities have contributed to the extraordinary satisfaction that my career has brought me.

www.ingramcontent.com/pod-product-compliance
Lightning Source LLC
Chambersburg PA
CBHW021118300426
44113CB00006B/193